# COMPLETE
# KOBOLD GUIDE
# TO GAME DESIGN

Essays by

Wolfgang Baur, Keith Baker, Monte Cook,
Ed Greenwood, Rob Heinsoo, Nicolas Logue,
Colin McComb, Michael A. Stackpole, and Willie Walsh

Edited by Janna Silverstein
Cover by Jonathan Hodgson

**Complete KOBOLD Guide to Game Design**
© 2012 Open Design LLC

Edited by Janna Silverstein
Cover art by Jonathan Hodgson
Designed by Stephen Wark

Portions of this volume previously appeared in:
**The KOBOLD Guide to Game Design, Volume 1:** *Adventures*
**The KOBOLD Guide to Game Design, Volume 2:** *How to Playtest & Publish*
**The KOBOLD Guide to Game Design, Volume 3:** *Tools & Techniques*

OPEN DESIGN LLC
P.O. Box 2811
Kirkland, WA 98083

WWW.KOBOLDQUARTERLY.COM

# Contents

*Foreword*

# A Stranger in an
# Oddly Familiar Land

I did not grow up playing roleplaying games. It was never my dream to write RPG adventures or to edit them. Dice were always six-sided. Maps appeared in history books or at the beginning of fantasy novels. Monsters appeared in horror movies. I wasn't interested in being a hero—not even a superhero. So how did I—a novel editor—end up here?

The peculiar thing about employment is that it will often take you places you never expected. I went from editing science fiction and fantasy books to editing comics- and game-related fiction to writing flavor text, in-universe reference articles, and dialog for massively multiplayer online RPGs. And somewhere along the line, working around the periphery of RPGs, I got pulled in. Not deeply, mind you, but just enough to play a campaign here or a stand-alone adventure there. I realized that I knew this territory from the novel editing I've done; at least, it was awfully familiar. Doing this work meant that I got to work and to play with some pretty extraordinary people: Monte Cook, Ed Greenwood, Michael A. Stackpole (with whom I've worked for years as a novelist rather than a designer), and Wolfgang Baur among others. These guys have all kept me on my toes in one way or another, and though I was never much of a gamer, our work together has given me a new appreciation for the art and the business of creating games.

One of the things I've learned as I've edited, first, the **Kobold Guide to Game Design, Volume III:** *Tools & Techniques*, and now this omnibus edition, is that editing and game design have certain key things in common: a need for clarity and specificity, an understanding of your market, and a deep respect for your audience. It's common wisdom in the game business that something like 10% of dedicated readers are gamers but 90% of gamers are readers. That means they're sharp, they're particular, and they know what they want. That information made working on this project a little intimidating for me. After all, I was an outsider editing a project targeted toward those who knew far more than I did and were working to break deep inside the business.

At the same time, as I read through the essays from volumes I and II, and as I reviewed and edited the new essays we acquired for this volume, I was reminded of what I learned from working on volume III: our readers—you—are in the best possible hands. The material you'll find between these covers is written by guys at the top of their game (so to speak). While this book contains nearly all of the essays that appeared in the individual volumes, the new material we've added for this volume—Mike Stackpole's essay on magic systems, Willie Walsh's on humor, and Wolf Baur's on the costs and virtues of complexity—just confirmed that understanding: you're learning from the best. If they can help *me* understand what it is they do and how they do it, you're going to find useful, practical information here that will take you to a whole new level as a gamer, writer, and designer. What's more, you're learning from people who truly love what they do. So not only will these essays provide you with a strong foundation for gaming and game design, they'll provide inspiration available almost nowhere else.

Some of the content in this book originally appeared as essays in **Kobold Quarterly** magazine or online; some of it was written specifically as part of the **Guide to Game Design** project. And, as mentioned, some of it is new to this volume. A majority of these essays—old and new—were written by Wolfgang Baur; that being the case, any essay you see without a byline, you may assume was written by him.

We've tried to fill holes where we found them in the original books. To try to maximize the value of this edition, the material has been arranged along themes and, to a lesser extent, in order of where things may occur in the design process. While each of the **Guides to Game Design** was a complete volume in and of itself, we hoped to create a synergy with this collection—to take those books and to combine them in a way that provides you with something more, something useful, powerful, something really special. I hope we've achieved that goal.

I've been privileged and delighted to work with these designers. You already know how awesome they are. With their work here, they'll prove it to you yet again.

*Janna Silverstein*
November 2011

# GAME DESIGN

*1*

# What is Design?

The most obvious question when it comes time to think about game design is not, as you might expect, "What is design?"

The question I get most often is how to design, in particular how to approach the mathematical and mechanical elements of design. Some of that is addressed elsewhere in this volume.

The second most-common questions have to do with how to go about pitching design to a publisher, how to refine and playtest a failed design, and so forth. Prior volumes of the **Kobold Guides to Game Design** have addressed the practical elements.

To my mind, the first question—defining game design—is maybe less practical but is clearly more important to understanding what it means to design well and what it means to create novelty, excite gamers, and publish a breakthrough game or setting. If the work you do on design is entirely a matter of mechanical refinement, pitching, and playtest, you can be a successful game designer. You can be even more successful if you think about the underlying nature of design. I might go so far as to say that newcomers wonder about how, but veterans dwell on what and why, especially in those cases where the why seems to be changing as gaming culture changes.

So, I've come back to the question of what constitutes design more and more over the last year. I pretend to no particularly amazing insight into the universal human impulse for games, but I've had certain lessons brought home to me through sheer repetition and observation. I think I'm ready to make a stab at it.

# Defining Our Work

When we sit down as game designers and think about the work we do, there are a few things going on. We are imagining a particular audience with a particular set of expectations, from the reading level required to the style of game we're considering. We think about commercial elements and audience appeal: What will draw players in? And we think about immersion and replay value: What victory conditions or encounter descriptions are most compelling?

When I am designing a game, I am thinking about what set of rules will create an engaging experience of play for the intended audience in a new or existing mode or style of play.

Design is the creation of play experiences at a remove from play itself. That is, as the designer, your work enables new experiences in play for others. If you are doing it exceptionally well, you are inventing new game genres and new play styles; that is, entirely new methods, styles, and systems of play. You use

---

### Design is . . .

Design is its own discipline, but it always borrows and builds on other modes of creative work. Design is:

• art
• mathematics and probability
• literature and language
• geography and history
• the building of a field of play
• the encouragement of repeated patterns of behavior
• iterative rule-making to improve player competition
• rule-making to require player cooperation
• a fusion of exploratory play and mastery over time
• the study of player psychology and the conscious manipulation of behavior

The nature of game design is that it requires understanding many related fields. It's both a matter of syncretic thought and analytical or reductive thought. That's part of the appeal; in some games your work is a matter of pure geometry and probability and event timing, such as the creation of board game rules or arcade game rules where the shape of the play area and the appearance of resources and objects must be precisely calibrated to retain player attention, provide frequent stimulus, and permit a variety of successful strategies. In other game types, you must explain victory conditions, customs, landscapes, tools, and characters. These are less about timing and geometry and more about engaging a sense of wonder and discovery as the player uncovers layers of the setting and new challenges in the game. If you find yourself wondering whether you are solving the right problems, consider the list here and see what other approaches to the problem might cut through to improve the heart of the play experience.

---

technology, art, and your own vision of what it means to play to create that new game. Design includes the creation of new spaces to explore, and the creation of new rules and systems to govern play.

Each type of design—new rules, new experiences, and even new modes or play styles—requires a separate set of skills.

## New Rules

This is the simplest and most important element of game design: What are the rules of the game? What tactics do they enable? What odds do they set? What behavior do they promote or discourage? What emergent properties derive from the rules? Are the rules extensible? Are the rules complete and self-contained? Can the rules be summarized? Can they be programmed? What victory conditions do they require? What are the consequences of failure? How do they encourage repeated play?

Most of all, do they reward the player for skill, for mastery? Or are they essentially functions of time and money spent? Both approaches may be correct for different audiences; not every design need be a game of skill, as games on Facebook so amply demonstrate.

## New Experiences

Games allow us to imagine the impossible or at least the exotic, so fantasy and other genre games should enable new experiences: dragon riding, interstellar trade with hostile species, assassinations in the Middle Ages, or the seduction of a Bond babe in Monte Carlo. Even a relatively straightforward driving game needs to provide a complete experience of speed, control, and competition.

This property of game design is especially crucial for franchise games that derive most of their attraction over time: sports games, new editions of existing titles. It's vital that a designer can do "same but different" to keep a well-loved series, setting, or property fresh and engaging.

## New Modes of Play

New modes require an ability to imagine new styles of play: alternate reality games (ARGs), first-person shooters, roleplaying without a dungeon master (DM). New rules and systems are required to support those new styles of play— but for the most part, these new systems are variations on existing systems. It's rare that a truly original rule shows up, such as the deck construction rules that made **Magic: the Gathering** (MtG) a breakout hit. The other rules of **MtG** (resource management and attack/defense) were mostly variations on existing rules in other game styles.

If you can generate an idea on the level of **MtG**, refine it, and bring it to market, I've certainly got nothing to teach you. On the other hand, most of roleplaying and massively multiplayer online (MMO) game design is something else: the creation of play experiences within an existing rules framework or an existing game engine. That level of design is an area of the craft I've practiced for years, finding the pivot points within a complex body of rules and the richest veins of exploration and story potential in a setting. This is what makes definitions of design so difficult; it's many different types of work.

To me, design is less about engagement and immersion than it is ultimately about play. The time spent making decisions before, during, and after the game is only partly immersive. Certainly game design assists a player's immersion through the careful choice of rules and components, art for game boards and game pieces, cards, animations, flavor text. But in many games the visual and tactile elements are little more than set dressing. For example, the European style of game design (and the Hasbro style for card and roleplaying games, to a lesser degree) focuses primarily on rules design; art, graphics, and flavor are added later and may be fairly arbitrary. That approach works extremely well for board games and card games, less so for story games and roleplaying games.

> *"Game design is a function of human attention: getting it, directing it, and keeping it."*

## Design is a Bit Like Mind Control

Design is the conscious work done to manipulate the behavior of the game's players. This sounds worse than it is. You're trying to design choices and how those choices are presented to the players. A more realistic wording might be that game design is a function of human attention: getting it, directing it, and keeping it. A well-designed game commands the player's attention at frequent intervals, directs that attention to turns or events, and keeps that attention through various means such as social reinforcement, reward systems such as experience points (XP) and leveling, and even the timely appearance of in-game resources and materials (spawning for video games, the return of daily powers in **4th Edition Dungeons & Dragons**).

The better you understand the mindset of players and DMs, the easier it is for them to engage with your design. The more esoteric or niche your design, in other words, the less players will react as your design might expect them to. This is the nature of niche RPGs: they tickle the fancy of a minority of gamers, but they still scratch an itch that goes deep into the human id, to the reptilian drive to conquer, control, and master the world around us, to derive status and overcome enemies, to find food and resources for our tribe and family. Killing things and taking their treasure is—to my mind—a gaming variation on the hunter-gatherer culture that

defined human existence for 99 percent of our species' existence. No wonder it's
so compelling; it is bred in the bone.

## Setting plus Mechanics

Let's consider the value of setting and mechanics for tabletop roleplaying games.
The two are often discussed as if they were at odds, as if a player or a DM should
favor "crunch" over "fluff" (both rather misleading terms) or—more literally—
rules over flavor and story elements. This is a tragic mistake, because good design
is not about choosing a single design dimension and pursuing it until even the
most hardcore fans grow bored; it's about striking a balance between competing
needs for an enjoyable play experience for different audiences. Design in this
sense is about making the right trade-offs.

   In terms of the role-playing game (RPG) audiences (and most designers and
fans alike agree that there are several), I'd argue that generating a satisfying play
experience for these types of games requires design of the rules and the setting in
parallel. Games that fail to generate a sufficiently compelling setting will attract
tactical gamers and home brewers, but will not engage a wider audience that is

### Amateur and Professional Design

Game design is work done at a remove, that is, at a layer of
abstraction away from simply sitting down and playing a game
yourself. In particular, the work of design needs to consider
the needs of the audience, rather than your own needs as a
gamer, to be successful. Sometimes these two will overlap
heavily —that's certainly the case for DMs and many freelancers
in roleplaying game design—but it's not always the case.
And the more you cater to your own needs as a gamer rather
than to the needs of your audience, the less professional and
generally more "indie" your design will be. There's absolutely
nothing wrong with indie game design, but it proceeds from an
assumption that the audience is the niche player. When you no
longer see yourself as DM or audience, but design with them in
mind rather than purely for yourself, you've reached a certain
turning point in your career. Some game studios see this as a
failing, and assume that if you are not a member of the target
audience you can never understand that audience. This is
patent nonsense; most of the great video game designers today
are not playing twitch games, but this does not stop them from
designing such games. I had been designing professionally
for several years before I figured out this distinction between
audience and designer, and I'm not sure I could date it or show
you the product difference. But at that point, I stopped arguing
over trivial points of personal preference (well, mostly) and
started looking for techniques to hold two audiences (DM and
player) instead of one (myself as a DM).

interested in exploring a setting, specific character tropes, and telling long-form heroic tales. Games that enjoy a rich setting but fail to deliver rules that appeal to mechanical tinkerers, tweakers, and tacticians will likewise limit their audience, and furthermore will make it difficult to support the setting with expanded rules material.

Doing both well delivers the experience players want, but many designs fail on one leg or the other. If you can use an existing and well-supported rules set, you save yourself a great deal of trouble at the possible expense of fine-tuning the mechanics to suit your story and setting needs. If you decide to build out rules first and foremost . . . Well, that's the subject of another essay in this collection. It can certainly be done, but it weakens the end result if your mechanics need to cover everything from horses to spaceships and psionics to demon summoning and gigawatt lasers. Most successful RPGs specialize in certain time periods or genres, and indie games in some cases specialize in a particular plot line (operatic drama, zombie survival, or religious orthodoxy) or assumed a particular cast of characters (Dr. Frankenstein's servants, or mice).

Why is that? Because part of design is knowing to what degree you'll need to integrate setting and rules. If you already assume zombie survival as the default setting trope, you need weapons and survival gear rules, but the characters probably won't spend a ton of time using diplomacy skills. You can spend your design time more profitably outlining the stages of zombie infection or variant chainsaw rules. Different games demand different emphases. Board games are at one end of a spectrum where rules carry the burden of play, card games are somewhere on the rules-heavy side but with story-driven exceptions like **Legend of the Five Rings**, and miniatures gaming, MMOs, and roleplaying games lean further into the setting side of things. Failure to provide enough quests and backstory is unforgivable in a roleplaying-heavy style of play. Failure to provide short, crisp, and complete mechanics is unforgivable in a board game.

What style of play your audience favors decides how much time you spend on the core rules and how much time you spend developing the setting.

## Defining the Boundaries, Choosing Your Players

All too often, roleplaying game designs try to do far too much, and for years the industry largely abandoned the introductory book or box set that can be read and implemented by a new player. (It's making a comeback with the **Dragon Age** RPG boxed set and the 2010 **D&D** red box series.)

Those books set up the principles of gaming for people who knew nothing about roleplaying; their "what is design" core goal was to make difficult games accessible and to provide some sense of mastery to newbies. That's a very difficult design task and depends on a sharp eye for what carries a player into the game, engages them, and moves them on to master the next elements quickly. Defining the boundaries is crucial: You need to provide enough material for a player to get started while providing enough depth so that a veteran player isn't bored.

I'd argue the task is largely impossible. The **Pathfinder** RPG is 500+ pages long; it's newbie-hostile, and largely assumes that you have already mastered basic roleplaying concepts. The **4th Edition D&D** rules set requires that you subscribe to a paywall Web site to keep up with new releases and to have a decent character generator. Most players learn these games from someone who already knows them. The contradiction and the tragedy of it is that most veteran gamers disdain the idea of teaching newbies, and the intro boxes certainly assume that both the DM and players are novices. Certain war games and board games assume the same level of mastery: If you don't already have prior rules sets and components, you'll never understand the advanced version or expansion of the game.

So the first thing to do with a design is figure out who you want as your player. That single decision will inform all others after it, from the components of the game to the complexity and length of the rules set to the likely elements in an introductory adventure. If you can deliver what your player base wants, your design's odds of success increase hugely. Ignore the hardcore audience if your target audience is newbies, and vice versa.

## Victory!

One element we rarely consider consciously in roleplaying game design is the victory condition, though it is the single most important rule in almost every other type of game design. Without a well-defined victory condition, a game is not a game—and yet roleplaying games violate this principle. Or do they?

I'd argue that one way to strengthen an RPG design is by creating a set of victory or advancement conditions that reward continued or frequent play. **Dungeons & Dragons** isn't remembered for this element of design, but it has exactly this element: It grants levels to player characters. And there's a general goal of advancement in every RPG. I'd take this further and say that good adventures and setting all make implicit promises of what victory looks like. It's often no better than "stop the drow and save the kingdom" or "prevent Doomsday," but that's certainly a goal.

Even if your game has frequent rewards rather than a single overarching victory condition, I'd recommend that your find those reward moments and make them clearer, brighter, and shinier. It is almost impossible to reward players too much or too often in video games (positive reinforcement works). Use it in RPGs, not just in the form of gold and magic, but in the form of status, prestige, unique treasures, courtesans and admirers, and a sense that the heroes matter. What's the point of defeating dragons if you still can't get a beer at the pub? Make sure that heroes are acclaimed and rewarded both in and out of character.

# Your Invisible Ally in Game Design

In RPGs, game design is broader than in tabletop board games or even than in video games, because as a designer you must also enlist the DM as your ally. There's no RPG without a DM willing to run your system or your scenario, so you need to succeed in inspiring those who will spend the money on the system and setting, spend the time on mastering world and rules material, and spend the effort to construct and tell their own stories in collaboration with a gaming group. Not to mention cleaning up the house and putting out the cheese and drinks every week.

This is why writing dull-but-effective mechanics is a fairly big failure of design. If you lavish care on the mechanical elements to the exclusion of flavor, no one will bother to wade through your case-style rules to actually play the game. Most DMs will be looking for an implied setting at the very least, and most prefer a rules set that explicitly supports a particular world and/or style of play.

Likewise, if you worry only about the flavor and setting and fail to bulletproof your mechanics and rules, you may well inspire someone to play it, but disaster will ensue as soon as the game hits the table. As soon as the ludic experience of actual play falls apart around them, they will (rightfully) abandon your game system or house rule the worthwhile bits into another set of mechanics. Go too far in either direction, and you risk indifference on the one hand, and an unplayable morass on the other.

What makes a roleplaying design work, then? If I knew the answer and could make it plain I'd be a very wealthy man. The answer is complicated, and depends on three factors: audience expectation, surprise and originality, and what I will call heightened play.

## Audience Expectations

To absolutely no one's surprise, gamers are a diverse and rowdy lot who want a lot of conflicting things in their games: simplicity and play depth, great setting and easy customization, novelty and the comfort of familiar, conservative assumptions about the nature of high fantasy, science fiction (SF), or the like.

For the most part, you should ignore audience expectations.

You heard me. As a game designer, you will be asked often and loudly to deliver "same but different" game designs. That's fine if you are starting out, or if you are getting a toehold in the field. But if you really want to make a name for yourself, you'll fail to impress by just meeting audience expectations. This is clearest when you look at the career arc of most of the major pen-and-paper designers, but it's also true for video game and board game designers. Expanding on an existing design is a good way to keep Marketing happy, provide sales for a publisher, and cater to a fan base. It is not, in and of itself, a bad thing at all, and I've done plenty of such projects over the years, some of which I'm quite proud of.

The projects that really get you recognized as a designer, though, are the ones that don't cater to expectations, and that get you out in front of what an audience asks for. No one asked Luke Crane, "Hey, give us an RPG about sentient mice with a sense of honor!" And yet the **Mouse Guard** RPG was the entirely deserving winner of major accolades and a lot of fan enthusiasm in 2009, and the game has been a huge success by indie standards. Likewise most other hits for smaller publishers. Creating a core setting and a set of mechanics that supports it is the way to go.

Go big if you can.

## Surprise and Originality

So fine, perhaps I belabor the obvious when I tell you to give gamers what they don't yet know they want. Underlying that, I believe that what gamers really want beyond a faithfulness to a game's premise is a sense of surprise and originality. There have been dozens if not hundreds of major RPG systems in the last 35 years. There are thousands of board game designs. Why do another one? Because sequels suck, and because there's a chance that you'll do it better than it's ever been done.

Originality and surprise can take many forms. Reskinning an existing rules set to serve a new master is one road to success; look at **Blue Rose** and the underlying **True20** rules, for example, or the way that the **Call of Cthulhu** rules set has been reskinned in novel ways to support **Basic Roleplaying**, the **Elric** RPG, and others. And **Dominion** certainly reinvented the way card games work by fusing the deck construction of **Magic: the Gathering** with a non-trading-card-game set of components. Originality may mean fusion of two disparate elements.

Alternately, you may find a new mechanic that enables a whole new form of roleplaying, or a central conceit of how the gameplay progresses around the table that leans more in a particular direction toward story gaming, tactical gaming, or even family gaming. Wonderful! Design your heart out, and I hope that gamers everywhere embrace the new paradigm.

While on the one hand I do want to encourage designers, I have to sound one pragmatic note of caution as well: You won't start off with an opportunity to go big. Most publishers won't gamble everything on an unknown with a neat idea unless there's very good evidence that you can carry it off . In board games, that means your game playtests insanely well. In RPGs, it usually means you've got a track record of smaller titles and achievements. In video games it usually means you'll spend years supporting senior designers before you ever have a chance to lead an A-list title.

But watch for your chance, and keep notes for what you'll do when and if an opportunity presents itself. Chance favors the prepared mind, after all, and there's no reason you can't work on your rules design, setting design, board game rules set, or video-game treatment and story arcs even if there's no publisher in sight. Investing some of your time and energy into these sorts of "trunk projects" that you keep close to hand may pay off very handsomely when there's an open call, a staff job, or just a hole in a publisher's schedule. Maybe you can wow them with material generated right then (it does happen), but think how much better prepared you'll be if you have a notebook or a hard drive crammed with good material awaiting development.

## Heightened Play Experience

The part of design that I think is most fundamental is that of the heightened play experience. This is where I think good designers split from great designers, where immersion, story, mechanics, and originality all come together to lift a game from the glut of similar experiences to something special.

And it's devilishly hard to describe, but I think it boils down to concise language, escalation of conflict, and super-saturated style.

**Conciseness.** Part of the heightened play experience is a matter of emphasis, of honing down the language, the backstory, and the character descriptions into just a few key details that can be communicated quickly by a DM to players. The temptation for many beginning designers is to rattle on and on, and even many professionals are in love with the sound of their own keyboards clacking away. Resist the urge to just slather a design in text.

---

### Immersive Play

There's been a ton of discussion about immersion and its role in video games, from talking about flow (Everyone's got a theory—a few with actual data to support them!) to more obscure discussion about related topics like reward ratios, reading saccades, Skinnerian response, interface design, you name it. For the purposes of our discussion of online and tabletop roleplaying games, immersion is the sense that a player is deeply invested in their character or part in the game, and that they are playing that role with a sense of connection. Immersion seems like a red herring. It's different for every player, and as long as designers provide a wealth of options, and graphic designers and animators provide compelling images, gamers with powerful imaginations and even casual players will find a role they like and take to it. Immersion is important, but not central to design. Immersion is a consequence of good design practices at a different level: mechanical design, character design, and world design.

---

**Escalation.** At the same time, a great encounter design and a great adventure design both need to make every fight, every roleplaying encounter, and every trap and treasure matter. If it starts with a kidnapping, it had better end with mortal peril. If it starts with a plague, that disease had better be the fault of a villain or demon who can be confronted. Escalation is a critical element in gaming. If an adventure starts slowly (and it's okay if it does), it still needs to gather momentum over time. Even throwaway encounters should increase tension and emphasize the mood. To design for this means that you are looking at every character and encounter and trying to find a key element that is easy to communicate in the moment when the heroes encounter that element. Backstory is a waste of time for players in most fantasy adventures. Meeting non-player characters (NPCs) is good—if that meeting increases the level of tension in the scenario.

**Saturation or Pulp Roots.** Third and final, every single encounter should be in a super-saturated style. In photography and art generally, saturation refers to the depth or vividness of hues or pigments. They can be thin and watercolory, or they can be thick, saturated pigments like oil paintings. As a game designer, screw subtlety. It looks great on paper, but most of the time, it fails to translate across the medium of a DM to players. What you want is a richness of experience. The green knight shouldn't just be green; he should be wearing leafy armor, and his helmet crowned with oak leaves, and his eyes turn to acorns. The demon lord shouldn't just have horns and fire and claws; he should have horns of black poisonous smoke, with claws of adamantium, a whip of fire, and his entire body an embodiment of coals and wrath.

This isn't just a matter of description, though saturation in art usually is about the surface. For super-saturated, the depth of character, plot, and location should also be dialed up. Villains can twist moustaches, sure, but what you really want is a villain who rages against the world for a reason, not just because he's evil. He hates the order of paladins. Evil should be specific, not generic. Locations should be filled with devices for stunts and action, not with bland furniture and clichés. Nobody goes adventuring to be bored.

Yes, super-saturated design taken too far is over-the-top pulp stupidity. But the risks are greater if you fail to provide enough meaty adventure than if you provide too much. Consider for a moment the classic adventure **Dwellers in the Forbidden City**: It invented the yuan-ti, the aboleth, and the tasloi, plus gave us a whole lost city in a volcano's caldera. Over the top? Not really. The monsters are so rich and classic that they have survived four editions of **Dungeons & Dragons** (well, not the tasloi), and the setting is one that works time after time. The approach of pulp fiction is that everything should stand out, that subtlety is wasted, and that excitement is preferred over introspection. Games are a vibrant, participatory medium that demands action and color; don't waste your time trying to make them into something else.

# Conclusion

To understand games, you must study and master both the flavor and mechanical pillars of RPGs or your chosen specialty. You must pitch big ideas rather than incremental updates, because the incremental projects will keep your name out there, but will never gain you a reputation for big thinking. And of course, you must be prepared with a treasure chest full of design ideas for the day when a big opportunity presents itself.

The basics of game design are a variety of related areas of expertise, all used to create new rules, envision new play environments, and to generate entirely new modes of play in new gaming genres.

Within the RPG field, make sure your design supports concise rules and description, a planned escalation of tension, and a flavorful, saturated environment that compels players to engage with the setting and foes.

# 2

# Designing RPGs: Computer and Tabletop

## *Colin McComb*

B y now, we're all familiar with the gamut of computer-based role-playing games (CRPGs) even if we haven't played them all: the **Ultima** series, the **Fallout** series, **Morrowwind**, the various **Infinity Engine** games, MMOs like **World of Warcraft** and **Everquest**, and many, many more. As the market for CRPGs swells and more designers leave or consider leaving the tabletop market for the computer game market, it's worth considering the differences involved in designing the two media, what works, what doesn't, and what could be improved.

The primary reference manual for the design of a computer game is called the design document. The design doc outlines your system's rules, your game's mechanics, lists and descriptions of places, creatures, and people. It also contains art requests, sound descriptions, and guides for game music to help the composer set the mood. Each and every feature of each and every area requires specific and detailed information in order to create a playable game and an immersive atmosphere for the players. Unlike tabletop rulebooks, it is constantly changing and evolving as the game development progresses. It will not be final until "feature lock," the point at which the game's producer decides that nothing else will be added to the game, and all resources come to bear on testing the soon-to-be-final product.

For tabletop designers, the best way to imagine this is that you are building all the components of an RPG at once: rulebook, player's guide, creature guides, and the campaign setting, combined in a single document. The design document can frequently run into many hundreds of pages, especially for a game of any length or heft.

It might appear that there is a vast difference in the design between the two media. In certain senses, this is even true. However, in my experience, this difference can be summed up in two areas. The first is detail; the second is human intelligence and intuition.

# First Answer: Detail

*"You enter a 10-foot × 10-foot room here. There is an orc here. It is guarding a treasure chest."*

That's pretty simple, right? In a tabletop game, sure. But if you try to give this description to an artist and a programmer, they'll come back at you with a binder full of questions. For example, the artist will ask:

- What's the context? Is this in a dungeon, a house, a tower?
- What does the entrance to the room look like? Is it an archway, a gate, a curtain, or a door? If it's a curtain or door, what material is it made of?
- What does the room look like? Is it made of wood, stone, or metal, or something else? What's in the room?
- What does the orc look like? What is it wearing, how tall is it, how muscular? What weapons is it carrying, and what armor is it wearing?
- How does the orc attack? Are its movements fluid and sweeping or broad, hacking attacks? If the artist has to animate attacks and movement, this information is required up front.
- What does the treasure chest look like?

You'll need to tell the programmer essential details as well. This assumes that you've already defined the game style (first-person shooter, over-the-shoulder, third-person isometric RPG), and that you have previously established your basic game systems and monster stats in the design document. The programmer will want to know:

- Are there any constraints on the player's actions in the room? What are the clipping paths for the character—that is, where can the character move?
- What artificial intelligence (AI) set should the orc use: hostile, helpful, neutral?
- Are there any variations in the orc's routines? Does it have dialogues attached to it? Are there any action cues for the orc's behavior? Does the orc move around the room in a pre-scripted or random sequence?

- Can the treasure chest be opened? How? Does it require a key? If there's a lock, can it be picked? What sort of container is it? What does it contain: Should the program consult a random table or is there a specific set of items inside?

You get the idea—and this isn't even all that they'll want to know. A computer game designer must imagine the details a game master (GM) can invent on the fl y without the benefit of a targeted group of players and under the supervision of the rest of the development team. This puts the designer at an immediate disadvantage.

The designer's job is to get out of the way of the game—but first: to create the story; populate that story with friends, enemies, and other assorted creatures; assign treasures, quests, and keys; build the puzzles; and generate an internally coherent game system. In short, it's similar to tabletop design, but it's much more intricate and involved. There's a reason we see huge designer teams on larger AAA computer/console titles: We have story and character designers, level designers, item/shop/placement designers, mechanics/system designers, each of them focusing on a very specific part of the game play. While they may step in to help other design teams, most have a specific core competency, and they own that part of the game.

- What sort of benefit do we see from this attention to detail?
- We remove the necessity for a human game master, allowing players to play games alone if necessary.
- We can run complex equations more quickly. No longer do we need to rely on a single die roll; we can build intricate character/attack/defense systems that combine a variety of traits and skills to create a more realistic experience.
- We can run combats that might take all night in a tabletop game in a matter of moments, and create immediately comprehensible tactical situations.

On the other hand, we do see some serious drawbacks, and we as players have largely conditioned ourselves to ignore them or play around them. What are these behaviors, and what can we as designers do to improve them?

AI is only as smart as its inputs. The antagonists, though carefully and lovingly scripted, cannot act beyond the bounds of that scripted behavior. They cannot change their tactics to react to a surprising use of a spell or item by a player and, in first-person shooters, will frequently not react at all. The game may not even allow such deviation. Even if you want to do it, you just don't have the option. In real life, you can use a screwdriver, for example, to turn a screw, to defend yourself, as a drumstick, or to reverse it and use it as a hammer, though these latter three uses are not recommended. In a computer game, you generally have only one use for a tool: its designed use.

Computer games require chokepoints and a way to create the illusion of free will. If the players of a computer game decide to ignore the primary portion of the adventure, they'll soon find themselves with nothing to do. Further, they usually must gather keys, items, or complete puzzles in order to unlock other areas of, for instance, a town. Locking these areas makes a difference for character advancement, for tutorials to teach the player how to navigate the game system, and for game balance—not to mention the necessity of loading massive areas into the computer's memory—but they are strictures that make little actual sense in terms of the game world.

## Second Answer: Human Intelligence and Intuition

*"You enter a 10' x 10' room. There is an orc here. It is guarding a treasure chest."*

Sometimes it really is that simple. Do the players need to know the texture of the wall? Do they need to understand the light source in the room? What if they want to know why the orc is guarding the chest? If they do, the GM will be more than happy to make it up for them. The great advantage to tabletop gaming is that the depth of the answers to the questions depends on the imagination of the game master. You might call this "distributed design:" rather than spending precious words outlining every possible scenario, the designer can lay out a basic framework and trust in the game master to fill in the blanks in the manner that best fits each individual campaign.

This allows the designer to write more, to fill the pages with broader information and extend the reach of the adventure. Freeing up these pages opens the possibilities for serious and far-reaching epics, with potential detours across the whole of the campaign world. The tabletop designer's job is to ensure that the adventure adheres to the rules laid out in the system, to create an entertaining story, and to provide the tools necessary for the game master to run the game.

Yet our adventures still require us to create the illusion of choice for the players. If we want the game master to use our adventure, we need to outline plot hooks, story devices, and even mechanical inducements to lure the players into this web. If these fail, then at some point the game master may simply have to tell his players that the direction they want to go destroys the adventure he has prepared.

What benefits accrue from tabletop gaming? It provides a broader, more potentially interactive experience. Instead of being forced into a single storyline, the players can scrap the idea of the adventure altogether and strike out in a new direction. The game master may choose to integrate portions of the published adventure as necessary, but the players have far more choice in the fate of their characters. They can help create the direction of the story.

Tabletop RPGs offer better social aspects. Though online gamers can use headsets and communicate directly via voice over IP (VOiP) technology, the interaction is not the same. Computer games tend to require a sense of forward motion, a feeling that the players are making headway toward resolving their quest. In person, gamers are allowed to relax, to make jokes, to react to each other's physical presence and share the joy of the hobby.

The game doesn't end at a predetermined point, and the end of an adventure flows easily into next week's session. The players don't need to wait 12-18 months for a sequel, if one ever arrives at all.

Lastly, smaller audiences mean more material. It's no secret that the computer game market dwarfs the tabletop market. Ironically, this frees up creators in tabletop gaming to try new ideas, test new mechanics, and imagine countless worlds—the bottom line is smaller, so the reach can be greater. By contrast, computer games now routinely cost $10-25 million per title. With this much money involved, most developers can't even touch the envelope, let alone push it.

The drawbacks to tabletop games are visible and glaring. They require a group of friends and a scheduled time; it's rare and difficult to have a pickup tabletop RPG session, but a computer game is ready any time the player is.

The systems in most tabletop games are by necessity less powerful and less involved. Math, plotting, movement, scoring, and other essential record-keeping can bog down a game in no time if we designers aren't careful—we need to keep the rules comparatively light and the systems comparatively anemic if we're to allow our players to make any progress at all.

We have to rely on words to paint our pictures, while computer developers have teams of hugely talented artists to launch their ideas into full-colored glory. We have less reach and influence in the broad market. A tabletop game that sells 100,000 copies is a breakout success, while the same number at a computer development house might result in layoffs or the closure of the studio.

As computers become more powerful, we will likely see a growing ability in games to react to personal play styles and offer more open-ended adventures. The MMO world has already begun to replicate the social aspects of games, and while they cannot yet replace the actual physical presence of your friends, chances are good that someone's working on that. Does this mean that tabletop designers should try to emulate computer-based designs to lure that market back to tabletop? Or should we make a more permanent move into the computer game industry?

Ultimately, this is a decision that each designer will have to make for him- or herself, but regardless of which segment of the industry we choose, we should focus on delivering the single best positive gaming experience for our customers, to the best of our abilities.

# 3

# The Process of
# Creative Thought

C reativity is at the heart of good design, but it's an overused and sometimes over-mystified word. The work of creativity is different than analytical or physical work, but it's still a process that can be mastered. Here's one take on it, based on my own experience and that of a rather different mind.

This essay is a summary and interpretation of David Kord Murray's **Borrowing Brilliance** (Gotham Books, New York, 2009), which tries to systematize and demystify creative thought for the engineering and technical professions. In particular, Murray believes that creative thought can be taught and that you can become better at it with practice. I think almost any writer or game designer would agree; the proof is simply that creative work improves in quality over time. This is why, for instance, first novels are held to a lower standard than later work.

Here's my take on what Murray's approach means for game design, and especially adventure design. It's fairly densely packed, but I think there's a process and an insight into creativity here that's worth further unpacking and discussion.

## Origin of a Creative Idea

Creativity never happens in a vacuum. Everyone builds on what came before, and how you approach the work can make a huge difference in how good the final result is. For instance, some designers believe that creativity is paramount, and pursue the True Weird as their goal. Others find value in expanding the work of prior designers through canonical worldbuilding. These are two wildly different approaches. Both are generating creative work of different types.

Here are the three stages that represent the origin of creative ideas.

## 1. Defining the problem.

The first step is understanding what it is that you need to solve. For engineers and programmers, this is usually relatively straightforward: Identify the problem space, research it, understand it, and describe it. For game design and other less engineered pursuits, this stage is the creative brief. That is, what are you being asked to deliver, what audience will you address, what is the project outline, and what are the design goals?

In either case, you need to define a vision of what you're after. This can be a commercial proposition as well as a creative one. For instance, you might be looking to address entry-level players with a high-action, low-roleplay set of basic mechanics, or you might be trying to engage an experienced audience with a story-rich capstone adventure that builds on prior work.

> *"The core element of successful creative work requires reframing your point of view to approach the original problem in a new way."*

Know what are you after creatively and commercially, and define it for yourself at the start. Why? Because how you define the problem determines how you will solve it. Knowing the problem is knowing the foundation of your creative process.

## 2. Borrowing ideas.

If you think you operate in isolation from other designers, gamers, and the culture at large, you're mistaken. And worse, if you don't look at similar problems and systems, you are undercutting your chances of a successful design. You can get creative raw materials this way because, for all creative work, your materials are ideas. This isn't to say you swipe text and settings and so forth. Build up a library of resources that are both close and distant, and learn the options you have.

When you look to use ideas you find useful, it's best to borrow from distant sources; generally speaking, if you are writing a **Dungeons & Dragons** adventure, then swiping from other **D&D** adventures makes you a thief, whereas borrowing an element from board games or MMOs makes you smart. Borrowing from much more distant sources like theatre or history makes you a creative genius. Research the field, and then go far beyond that. I'd like to say that Open Design does this better than anyone else; the well of inspiration that patrons bring to a project is global, comes from all levels of experience, and is simply much broader than any single designer—even one at the top of his game at Wizards of the Coast—can hope to match.

It's worth mentioning here that creative work in this style goes back to an older formulation of creativity. That is, I believe true creative work is not about the artist or the designer; that's a modern aberration based on copyright maximalism and the notion of the auteur or the lone genius. To me, working with shared worlds and collaborative designs, this equation of creativity with an individual is largely nonsense. Individuals are products of their times and their culture and, most of all, are heavily influenced by their peers.

I take an attitude a little closer to the sciences. That is, creative work is about the work, which must copy and improve on what has gone before. Rules sets are a foundation. We build on them. Settings and shared universes are a culture that designers work within and build to improve. The creation of a better gaming experience is the goal, not the creation of artistic reputation.

Finally, it's worth saying that it's best not to fall in love with an idea or concept but to view the options fairly dispassionately. This is not to say that you shouldn't be passionate, but that there's a stage where you have to set that passion aside. If you are blindly in love with a particular idea or concept then you've stopped being creative with it, and it becomes locked in place. In my view, you need a certain critical disdain or at least objectivity toward ideas, an ability to abandon them.

### 3. Combining and connecting the borrowed ideas.

The real magic of creative work, to me, comes in the unexpected combination of the many notes, concepts, and materials you gathered in stage two. This is where you combine Hollywood-style narrative arcs with tax software (as Intuit did). Or you combine the insights of poker with economics (as Professor Nash did). Combine geology with biology and Malthus (as Darwin did). Or combine political science and network analysis (as Christakis and Farrow did). In each case, two different worlds at the start are a single element of thought by the end.

In the case of game design, finding such synergies might mean combining genre elements with non-genre elements, combining classical rhetoric with social skill challenges, or combining ancient saga plotlines with science fantasy elements. In each case, the core element of successful creative work requires reframing your point of view to approach the original problem in a new way: Reverse your encounter, change subgenre, combine history with pulp, etc. Brainstorm and jam pieces together to make them fit a narrative or to apply a matrix or triggers to a sandbox. For me, this usually means taking all the notes from stage two and puzzling how they fit together.

## Evolution of a Creative Idea

While creativity requires posing a problem, gathering ideas, and putting those ideas in unusual juxtapositions, it also requires time to ferment and time for your own take on the material to gestate. To me, the raw materials often seem like insoluble lumps at first—until suddenly they don't. Suddenly they seem like pieces of a whole. That requires incubation, judgment, and iteration of your creative approach—the next three steps.

## 4. Incubation.

Puzzling with the elements doesn't always get you very far. Take some time to allow combinations to settle into a solution. The first three elements of creative thought are about the inputs to your subconscious, but it's foolish to try to force everything to snap together in a massive rush. It might happen, certainly, but often it won't.

You might think of this as a creative block, but pushing the design process too quickly leads to errors that later need to be torn out. I find it more valuable to pause in your design process, to sleep on it, and sometimes to put it aside for weeks. The extreme case of this is Isaac Newton, who waited 15 years between the time he framed the problem before he came back to the calculus. But that's the pace of subconscious thought. I find that the best solutions are the ideas that spring to mind when I'm half-sleeping, or are the result of the classic shower inspiration—which is odd when you consider it. Why is creative thought advanced when you are focused on the mundane?

> *"If something about a design bothers you, figure out why."*

It's an element of the psychology of creativity; this is how your subconscious brings up possible ideas and solutions. In the early stages you are jamming ideas and possible solutions into your mind. The output from the subconscious requires you to turn off the stream of conscious thought and let other thoughts through—daydreaming thoughts. Sometimes that process is the fl ash of an instant, and sometimes that process is very long. It can, however, be helped, in an unusual way.

You can create opportunities for creative output by turning off your hurry and work and activity. Talk a long walk and give it a think. Get rid of TV, radio, your favorite MMO, or anything that requires conscious thought. Ideal activities are the ones that rely on muscle memory or at least no conscious effort, such as biking, knitting, meditation, or driving. It only looks like laziness; in fact, you'll find some of your biggest breakthroughs happen this way. It sounds a bit woowoo and New Agey, but I swear to you that time spent away from hammering the keyboard can be time very well spent.

## 5. Judging The Work.

Having a flash of insight is terrific (and it feels so good!), but it's not nearly enough. You need to get really critical of the results of that insight, and hold it up to comparison and discrimination against alternative solutions. That is, your stage of creative judgment should identify both the strengths and weaknesses of a solution. Brainstorms are a start in the earlier stages of combining, but you need to winnow out the best elements and discriminate between the viable and the foolish. Have a Steve-Jobs-level mania for what's strong and what's weak. If something about a design bothers you, figure out why.

Strong opinion and ego in design play in here; you will disagree with others, and that's normal. To win those disagreements, you need to identify not just that a given element is good, but why. How does it play into the whole? How does it solve a design problem? How does it improve the play experience? Or worse, how does it destroy the play experience? The creative process isn't about accept/reject based on your opinion. It's a debate.

I'd say that the Open Design discussions suss out weakness and find sources of design strength better than current publishing methods that rely on a small group of designer, developer, and editor, or even small teams of designers, writers, and quality assurance. The weight of many minds focused on results—or even just the knowledge of impending peer review—makes for sharper design because it finds more of the weaknesses and addresses them from many angles.

## 6. Enhancing.

The last stage is enhancing and iterating on the design solution you have. At this point, you eliminate the weak spots and enhance the strong through development and editing, ideally based on playtest results from the judging stage. Remember that creative thinking is about risk-taking; doing the same stuff will look the same as everything before.

> *"Every person comes up with ideas differently and works with them differently."*

A creative work will look a little odd; don't sand down all those corners, but find ways to enhance them and make sure that the novelty is still accessible to gamers who haven't seen it before. Your goal is recombining, re-borrowing, restructuring. Iterate until the final is a seamless whole.

For designers, this approach offers several advantages. It means you can talk about creative design in stages, and you can be self-aware enough to realize you haven't even figured out what problem you are solving, or you are circling around and around in the research/borrowing stage without ever moving on to combination and incubation. It means that in collaboration you separate out stages; you can narrow the focus to a discussion of the central problem or a discussion of what approaches to borrow, or you can brainstorm to combine and resort ideas. They are all separate things.

Likewise, particular parts of the process can be judgment meetings where the results of brainstorm and incubation are explicitly weighed and kept or discarded. Same with playtest discussions and sharpening the design. By then, it's clear that it is too late to introduce new raw materials for recombining unless you want to iterate the whole design process again (which you might).

## Making the Creative Process Work for You

Every person comes up with ideas differently and works with them differently, but these stages of creativity are fundamental. For my own part, I've found it useful to consider these stages with my most recent project, **Courts of the Shadow Fey**. It's a way to time your progress. ("Have I hit the problem statement cleanly? Maybe it's time to start borrowing ideas.") In the borrowing ideas phase this time out, I busily stacked up elements from **1st Edition AD&D**, from demons and fey in mythology, from 17th century rhetoric, from operatic history, and even from theatrical staging/scene trickery—I cast a broader net than usual, and found my own creativity pumped up as a result when I moved into recombining, outlining, and juxtaposing elements. And though I've been through the muddle in the middle many times, it never hurts to know that it's a normal stage of creative work. At this writing, I'm in the enhancing stage, drawing connections out between previously unrelated encounters to maximize shock value, to draw out the themes of the adventure—and just to make the whole as epic as it can possibly be.

I've found it helpful to consider my roadmap to the creative mind, some of it obvious, other bits less so. What's important about it is that identifying the stages helps you make a realistic schedule for your design work, helps you focus on what design problems or resources are most helpful at the beginning, middle, and end, and helps you consider what stages of the project you might want to spend extra time on to get the results you want. Writers and designers can spend hours talking about their process (instead of applying seat of pants to seat of chair and writing!), and I've done my share of procrastinating.

Now I have a better name for that—incubation—and I have a better sense of when it might be most useful: after borrowing ideas, before judging the work and enhancing it. I'm certainly glad of the results I've seen in my own work, and I hope that by ordering your own work into a sequence like that, you'll find your design work is faster, more organized, and more powerfully original.

*4*

# Design that Matters

E very volume of the **Kobold Guides** has tried to de-mystify some of the aspects of design. This time I'm going out on a limb.

I want to talk about art for a minute. Bear with me.

I know, I know: RPGs are entertainment, **D&D** is a great bit of escape from the mundane, and fantasy shouldn't poke its nose into the grownups' tent. This is what our culture tells us.

## Seriousness of Purpose

In the past, I've talked a bit about taking fantasy seriously, about making sure your design is plausible and meets genre expectations. That's important, but it's not the seriousness I'm talking about here. When I say that a really good designer should at least be attempting art some of the time, I'm not saying that every adventure or every rules set needs to be considered in light of the human condition. That's ridiculous, pretentious, and generally a waste of your time and your reader's money.

But I am saying that, like great fantasy novels or films, a great designer should at least be aiming at something beyond entertainment. Jonathan Tweet certainly did this with Everway, which came in for a lot of criticism (and poor sales) based on its visual and mythic style. But it was an attempt to broaden the audience for RPGs mechanically, to use a more collaborative and softer resolution system than

**D&D** did. It wasn't meant for the core hobby audience, necessarily, but it was meant to make you think about what roleplaying games are. **Ars Magica**, with its troupe style play of multiple characters in an upper and lower class, does the same sort of thing, restoring the class structure of the medieval era, with a fantasy spin. Another Tweet design, and a more commercially successful one.

These are game designs that broke new ground and changed the way later designers think about their work.

## Defining Success

But again, I'm talking about commerce when I should be talking about art. I don't mean something created in a coffee shop or some studio apartment by half-literate painters or anguished emo videographers. I mean stories and entertainment that withstand the test of time. For medieval fantasy as a genre, those include *The Lord of the Rings* (books and films), Jack Vance's **The Dying Earth**, and Robert E. Howard's *Conan* stories. Probably Michael Moorcock's *Elric* and Poul Anderson's **Three Hearts and Three Lions**. Looking at current writers, I'd put my money on George Martin's *A Song of Ice and Fire* to still be in print 50 years from now.

These are the stories that work in the fantasy novel world. What are the RPG equivalents? Well, the hobby hasn't been around for 50 years, but let's just look back 25 or 30 years and see what has been revised, rebuilt, shared, and made into canon. What are the core D&D adventure series? I'd argue that they are the *GDQ* series by Gygax, the *Dragonlance* adventures by Weis and Hickman, and a few one-shot bits of brilliance like "I6. Ravenloft" and Zeb Cook's "Dwellers in the Forbidden City" (which gave us the yuan-ti and the lost city adventure). Probably **Tomb of Horrors** as well, though the current Wizards of the Coast (WotC) design staff seems to disagree with me.

Since these are games rather than novels, we see the signs of art in mechanics and setting as much or more than we see character and plot as crucial. The introduction of the drow, of draconians and kender, of yuan-ti and tasloi are all elements of these designs that have become central to what we think of as high adventure, sword-and-sorcery gaming. Beyond **D&D**, some of these iconic fantasy tropes have since been swiped by **World of Warcraft** and other MMOs, just as minotaurs have been swiped from **Magic: the Gathering** and *Dragonlance*. Imitation and shameless swipes are signs of huge artistic success for a game designer and worldbuilder.

So we have one metric of success. Another, of course, is whether your adventure modules spawn ongoing fiction (as "Ravenloft" has done), and whether your design's mechanics have been taken up by later adventure writers, and whether you have created a whole new category of adventures.

# But Is That High Art?

Praise from one's peers and impact on future generations are definitely outward signs of success, but I think I'm still not quite as pretentious as I could be here. So I'll climb a little further out on this branch and see where that leaves me.

The praise and future impact are outward signs of the real success of those adventures. But I'd argue that those are symptoms of the designer's high art, and that the real reason the adventures are praised is how they work to appeal to us as gamers, emotionally and in narrative terms. They give us everything we want from our fantasy, and then a little more.

That "little more" is tough to nail down. Sometimes it's an unforgettable character (like Strahd). Sometimes it's an unforgettable place (like the "Vault of the Drow"). Sometimes it's a matter of the choices that the heroes are asked to make during play or the sheer challenge of the environment ("Tomb of Horrors"). If it were easy to pin down, it wouldn't be art, now would it?

Mostly, though, I think that great game design opens up new vistas of imagination for our play, offering new places to explore, new roles to take on, and an emotional connection to those imaginary people and places that we return to often.

> *"A really good designer should at least be attempting art some of the time . . . a great designer should . . . be aiming at something beyond entertainment."*

Some might argue that this is a function of the DM and his group of players, and that's true. But as a counterexample, consider the Lady of Pain from **Planescape**. She's a figure of mystery and the heart of the setting, and the DM doesn't actually get to play her that much in a properly-run game. She doesn't say anything. But I say she is a figure of art precisely because she is mysterious and her history largely unknown. **Planescape** is about mystery and layers of meaning and proxy wars among gods. If the central figure of the central city were just another big-statted brute or high-powered wizard, that character would have been a design failure. As it is, the Lady of Pain is an iconic figurehead who makes the setting what it is just by her presence and influence. That's smart design. That makes you think a little about the campaign, and what might be possible in Sigil. It is, in other words, inspiring.

Good design aspires to be more than mere story or mere mechanics. I think any designer who simply puts together a setting, sourcebook, or adventure to amuse is doing himself and the gamers who buy that book a disservice. While it's probably overkill to make everything in an RPG attempt to serve some higher art, designing without any attempt at a point of view and a deep impression is a sorry bit of hack work. There's plenty of that in the RPG field already—I won't name names, but you know the sort of hackfest and munchkinism I'm talking about. Why design for the lowest of the low bars?

Instead, good designers set up a memorable coming-together of friends against something a bit frightening. They strive to give the DM tools to make a mark on gamer's memory. Without shooting for the moon in a least a few sections of a book, you're just grinding out generic power fantasy clichés, which seems very sad work to me indeed.

## Let Me Tell You About My Character

I want all of my work to make an impression beyond entertainment. I know that the pay is going to suck. I don't care, because I like to think (and maybe I flatter myself) that a good adventure is a chance at joy, and a chance to laugh, and a chance to shiver when the beasts of ravening darkness come. We remember how it almost turned out all wrong, but one hero stepped forward and made it work out. Maybe a game is intense enough to keep us lying awake at night, thinking of the options for the next session.

This is why gamers are notorious for "Let me tell you about my character" stories—because when RPGs work right, they are memorable, and people want to share that memory with friends. It's not always possible to convey the magic to those who weren't there, but it makes me happy that RPGs have that power, the strength to make us say "That was so very cool. Let me tell you how it was . . ." That shared experience is what amazing design and strong DM skills get you. And that's what I shoot for in my designs. I want to give a DM the tools to make his or her players say, "Wow!" Not just, "Yeah, we killed monsters and took their stuff," but "That was the best adventure you've ever run."

## Ruthlessness and Personality in Art

To get there, you have to surprise people a little bit. Throw a curve ball. Make an encounter work inside-out. Turn a brawl into a hostage negotiation. Threaten the player characters' favorite mentor, barmaid, or magic shop owner; someone they already know. And make it personal. One of the lessons I learned repeatedly as a DM and that does translate to design is that you do the players no favors by taking it easy on the player characters (PCs). Yes, they may get lots of loot for little effort. In the long run, though, that's boring. Dilemmas, close calls, and villains who will do the vilest thing you can imagine are the ones that stick in a player's memory. Be ruthless when you design. Cheat a little to threaten what the player characters value, the way that **Wrath of the River King** threatens the party's gear and magic items.

They may curse you in the short run. In the long run, though, they will remember the hard times and the difficulties they overcame. Ruthlessness is required for your design art to thrive. Cowardice in design means always balancing everything, always giving the PCs an easy way out, always making sure that there is no chance of real failure. That's a recipe for boredom, and I don't recommend it. Finally, show your personal fears and quirks in design. Those are elements that should not dominate the adventure, but they make it distinctive rather than just another auto-generated corporate hackfest. My wife still raves about a hedgehog gardener NPC from literally years ago, because he was a hub that the party could return to again and again for information in a hedge maze dungeon. I'm still not sure quite what she saw in that NPC, but he was one of those personal quirks that worked, because folks hadn't seen it a hundred times.

There's a fine line between quirky and dumb, of course. Some mechanics are too quirky or complicated to work at all. Some stories are too niche or too weird to function. But consider a fantasy like Miéville's **Perdido Street Station**, or Ken Scholes' **Lamentation**. They are hugely powerful and successful because they aren't like what came before them. Take creative chances; it is the only way to make sure your design work is noticed and rewarded likewise. If some of those creative risks fail you completely, that's part of the price of trying something new. Fall down six times, stand up seven.

And there you have it, folks. I have taken my chances here a bit, trying to talk about something quite as highfalutin' as Art in the context of roleplaying games. I'll be curious to hear what folks make of it, either mockery or agreement. At the very least, you know why that weird little hedgehog is showing up in my next project.

# 5

# Seize the Hook

## *Rob Heinsoo*

This essay discusses principles I apply when I design new games. Since the focus of this volume is on roleplaying game design, most of my examples are from roleplaying games I love. I was the lead designer of the **4th Edition of Dungeons & Dragons** (**4E**), so the examples will often go into considerably more detail when they relate to **4th Edition**. But in my experience, I've found that these principles apply well to most types of game design: card games, board games, miniatures games, roleplaying games, and even video and computer games if you're lucky enough to get in on early design.

I'm most concerned with the mechanics of game design. If the game you want to design is like most other games, it will have a theme, physical or digital components, and written rules. The game's mechanics will consist of a set of carefully defined gameplay actions, component interactions, and information structures outlined by your rules. You can approach each game mechanic on its own, as something to be tinkered with and improved, or approach a mechanic as it interacts with all the other mechanics, the theme, and the components.

I've broken the essay into three nuggets of advice that more-or-less apply to the beginning, middle, and end of the design process.

First, design a game you want to play but can't because no one else has designed it yet.

Second, don't be satisfied with your design until you've found the key mechanical hook that captures the game's theme, creating an experience that's something like the experience being portrayed by your game.

Third, understand and follow through on the full implications of your game's mechanical hook.

## 1. Design a game you want to play but can't because no one else has designed it yet.

Corporations design products around what they think will sell. So do some writers and some extremely talented game designers. That may be a savvy move, particularly when you're deservedly confident in your creative powers and your ability to overcome designer's block and the obstacles that surface within every design. If you're starting out, or if you are more strongly motivated by internal creative pressure than business sense, you may be better off paying attention to the moments when you think about a game you want to play but realize that the game does not exist.

That moment may come while you're playing a game you love, then realize that it would be a better game if it had a different setting, different victory conditions, or had been designed for several players instead of only two. This process of riffing on what's already good is what I call the "Rolling Stones approach" to innovation, after the manner in which Keith Richards and Mick Jagger used to write songs together. Richards would start by picking out a tune they knew and liked, then they changed the song until they came up with something that sent them on a new path.

The Rolling Stones approach can work but, for me, moments of innovation come more often when I'm thinking about a particular group of people I want to play a game with. I get a clear vision of the game we would have the most fun playing together. Then I realize that the game I'm picturing doesn't exist. It's a good feeling: Now I can design it!

This social framework for your design vision can be a valuable tool. Writers learn to consider their audience, to think about the people they are writing for as if they are reading their work aloud to that chosen audience. As a game designer, you may be a just a bit luckier than a writer, because nearly all games are already group efforts or social experiences. It's a bit easier to know exactly who you are creating your game for: you and some friends who enjoy playing games with you.

Phrasing your goal in this manner is more important than it may sound. Our subconscious minds and insecurities trick most of us into giving up on creative projects too easily. Unless you're entirely certain of your abilities, that fear of failure can get worse when you envision your new game as a published product. Unconscious comparisons between your developing work and the published games you already love may erode your enthusiasm for your work. You're less likely to get derailed if your immediate goal is to create a specific game you'll be able to enjoy with your friends. You'll be able to figure out how your game can step out into public later. When you're starting, focus on capturing the joy you felt when you realized that the game you wanted to play with your friends was something you would have to design yourself.

*2. Don't be satisfied with your design until you've found the key mechanical hook that captures the game's theme, creating an experience that's something like the experience being portrayed by your game.*

Let's unpack this advice one piece at a time before analyzing some examples of mechanical hooks that worked.

## The Key Mechanic

The key mechanic is the most important element of a game design, the piece that sets the game apart from other games. In the best-case scenario, this mechanical hook ties so directly into the game's theme that it helps evoke a thrill (or other emotion) related to the experience that the game is based on.

Different genres of games have varying amounts of access to this best possible version of the mechanical hook. Some great board games, like chess, poker, and Reiner Kneizia's **Ingenious**, a color-tile playing game, aren't about anything other than their mechanics. But most of the best roleplaying games marry theme and the mechanical hook. The roleplaying experience lets players create a compelling story together. The shared experience becomes truly memorable when the mechanics perfectly reinforce the game's core story.

## "Don't be satisfied," he says . . .

Here is the good news: Once you start really working at designing games, you're going to come up with playable material. Really. If you're reading **The Kobold Guide to Game Design**, you've probably got enough experience to come up with ideas that will hang together well enough for dice to roll and pieces to move.

The potentially harsher news is that it could be a lot harder to get your well-themed mechanical design to be actual fun to play. There are a fair number of published designs every year that are clever, elegant, funny, or beautiful. But when you're done appreciating their aesthetics or their touches of clever design, the problem is that they're not that much fun. Designers who self-publish are probably most vulnerable to this problem, since the glow of getting a design to work can easily eclipse the fact that other people don't have as much fun playing the game as the designer does.

The single most common mistake is the same mistake writers make: getting fixated on an early idea or draft that seems to work so that you don't look for possibilities that might be better. It's not easy to stay open to the possibility that a good, early idea is in truth holding you back. But that's not the only angle you've got to cover. There's also the chance that ideas you're pretty sure are bad are somehow concealing worthwhile alternatives, somewhere behind their ugly surface.

As part of my creative process, I try to change my perspective about ideas I'm pleased with. I imagine that I'm tapping into a view from somewhere else in the multiverse. "Imagine I live in a world where this idea isn't the best possible solution. What other solution could there be?" Or "Imagine that this stupid piece of the game is somehow a good idea. If that were true, what would the consequences be? What would have to be true to make this a good idea?" When the trick works, new ideas that were eclipsed by earlier notions come out of hiding. The husk of the old idea falls behind.

## Match the Mechanics to the Experience and Vice Versa

Despite your best efforts, there's always a chance that the moment-to-moment fixes you discover through playtesting lead your key mechanic away from the original vision or theme of the game. This may not be a bad thing. If you're serious about doing excellent game design rather than about designing the perfect incarnation of one specific world or theme, it's possible that your newly mutated key mechanic is worth saving and that your original vision needs to change.

To use a blunt example, if your game about arena fighting ends up feeling bloodless and hyper-rational, you might have created a mechanic that suits battles between well-programmed AIs and their serially inhabited robotic armor.

I experienced this situation when I was working on the dice-and-cards system that became **Inn-Fighting**. I was originally designing a gambling game that would be played in taverns alongside **Three-Dragon Ante**. But that stopped making sense. The mechanic started working when I realized it wasn't just that the game was played in taverns, the game was also about people fighting in taverns. Much better.

## Key Mechanics that Work: Setting the Characters' Limits

**Call of Cthulhu** (**CoC**) is not my favorite game. I may be the only former Chaosium employee to say that I'm no fan of H.P. Lovecraft. But when I think of game mechanics that hook the players into the precise mindset of the characters they're portraying, I think of **CoC**'s Sanity check mechanics. Sanity starts high for most **CoC** characters. Like the people in Lovecraft's books, PCs start knowing little of the world's true masters. But as characters encounter traces of the supernatural and creatures from the Mythos, their Sanity steadily degrades, even if their "successful" checks prevent them from going into catatonic shock or psychotic reactions.

For a real world analogy, you can compare **CoC**'s Sanity mechanics to a statistic I love hearing quoted about veteran mountain climbers. People speak as if the number of times a climber has summited Mount Everest without oxygen is a good thing. Let's call it like it is: You don't want to be on a climbing rope with a guy who has gone to the Top of the World and sucked vacuum three times too many. Likewise, the longer a **CoC** character manages to dodge the shoggoths, the more certain they are to break down and take everyone along with them. These aren't the kind of hit points that come back.

So what can **CoC**'s sanity mechanic tell you about your own designs? First, it highlights the possibility that the themes of some games are best captured by limitations on the heroes. Most fantasy/adventure games focus on empowerment, but if the theme of your game is horror or final despair, it's possible that enfeeblement mechanics may be called for instead. The trick is making sure that the game remains fun to play.

The current flotilla of indie RPGs frequently dances along this tightrope. Some of its games nail desperate emotional states with grinding-you-down mechanics. They're not exactly the type of game you want to play often and that's usually deliberate. Personally, I prefer the indie game **AGON: Competitive Roleplaying in Ancient Greece** by John Harper. I mention **AGON** because it contains a subtle version of character limitation even though it's about high-powered Greek heroes who slalom through the monsters and myths of the ancient world.

I didn't understand **AGON** when I first read the rules. I noticed that as heroes took wounds in a given combat, they got weaker and weaker, becoming less likely to be able to dig themselves out of that fight, a death-spiral effect that many games blunder into. What I didn't pick up on right away is that there is a survival mechanism: A PC can climb out of mechanically hopeless situations by swearing oaths to the other characters and the gods. In other words, a Greek hero who wants to survive and conquer all enemies becomes more and more obligated to other characters and competing mythological entities. Heroes don't take permanent wounds; they take permanent obligations. It's a mechanical hook that shows that heroes' careers will be complicated by demands they could not have foreseen, demands that may place them at the mercy of one or all of their comrades. As a roleplaying incentive it captures the complicated lives of the Greek heroes wonderfully. And it's more fun than going insane.

## Key Mechanics that Work: Shaping the Game's Reality

Let's look at a more conventional roleplaying game experience, a game that was mostly (but as we'll see, not entirely) about empowerment. Steve Perrin's **Runequest** is the game that started the Basic Roleplaying system that gave birth to **Call of Cthulhu. Runequest (RQ)** was a streamlined system that had at least three subtle but effective key mechanics that came together to portray Greg

Stafford's world of **Glorantha**, a world permeated by the magic of ancient and eternal gods.

Runequest started with the assumption that every player character was capable of magic. In the late 1970s gaming industry, dominated by class-based systems in which most of the characters could only use swords and bows, RQ's battle magic system allowed every character to use points of Power to cast buff spells, minor or better-than-minor attack spells, and (praise be!) healing spells. In **Glorantha**, an adventurer who didn't know any magic was a deliberately crippled roleplaying experiment.

As an adventurer grew into a Rune-level character worthy of initiation into the mysteries of the gods, they had to sacrifice points of Power to gain rune spells. Magic wasn't just a free gift—truly powerful magic demanded sacrifice. Compared to the ever-escalating power curves of games like **AD&D**, **RQ** demanded sacrifice and cosmic responsibility as you rose in power.

And lastly, **RQ** modified its skill-based system with a groundbreaking book named **Cults of Prax** that detailed the myths, rituals, and beliefs of the worshippers of a dozen of Glorantha's hundreds of gods. Alone, the myths and rituals would have made the book a wonderful work of alternate anthropology, but each cult write-up included battle magic and rune magic that was only available to worshippers of the gods. Suddenly **RQ**'s skill-based system had something that functioned like other games' classes, but grounded in the game's deep cosmology. Nowadays it seems like standard stuff, but in the late '70s, Stafford's **Cults of Prax** was the first RPG product to take this tack—it created the player-oriented splat-book that came to dominate the **Vampire: the Masquerade** line, the rest of the White Wolf menagerie, and countless other games including both **3rd Edition** (**3E**) and **4E D&D**.

Roleplaying game splat books mix story and mechanical elements to give specific characters both powers that are fun to play and a heightened sense of their alternate selves. That sounds an awful lot like my goal of the perfect mechanical hook. In a sense, **RQ** opened any game that could support itself with supplementary material to the possibility that the mechanical hook could be repeatedly reinvented, a ritual act of publishing that shapes the industry and our game shelves.

## 3. Understand and follow-through on the full implications of your game's mechanical hook.

Sometimes a game's greatest strength is ultimately the reason it fails. A few good games might have been great games if they'd had the time and vision to grapple with the full consequences of their key mechanics. I'll discuss three opportunities that can become problems if you're not careful.

## Roleplaying Games Have Two Types of Participants

Roleplaying games have two types of participants: players and DMs. If all your effort goes into making a key mechanic that helps players have a great time but screws up the game master's life, you're not likely to find many groups playing your game. Unlike many other games, RPGs may require you to balance key mechanics aimed at players and key mechanics aimed at DMs. Of course, mainstream games have usually focused on the player's experience. Few mainstream RPGs have done much to provide key mechanics for DMs. Indie RPGs have recognized that hole and introduced any number of games that transform the experience of both player and game master.

In this respect, **4th Edition D&D** acted more like an indie game. We wanted to create a game that offered new key mechanics for both the players and the DM; innovating for one while ignoring the other wasn't going to be enough.

**Third Edition D&D**'s key mechanics for players and DMs had set the table for us. **Third Edition**'s most significant advance was to treat both the player characters and the DM's monsters with the same mechanical rules. In previous editions, only the player characters had Strength and Wisdom attributes. Monsters were ad hoc creations of the game's publisher, with very little advice for DMs who wanted to create their own monsters. "Wing it like we do" would have been accurate advice for previous editions.

**Third Edition D&D** advanced the art by showing that PCs, NPCs, and monsters could all be handled with (roughly) the same system math. DMs could spend their rainy-day-away-from-the-table time by leveling up monsters and designing NPCs that were every bit as detailed as PCs. It was an excellent system, although a bit strange because the arbitrary hit dice and attack bonus assumptions of earlier editions hadn't been revised; they'd just had a rational system of transformations applied.

**Fourth Edition D&D** took another look at what 3E had accomplished and decided that it was not necessary to treat PCs and monsters by exactly the same rules. After all, the PCs were the pillars at the center of the campaign, playing every week. New monsters showed up every encounter. If the PCs were doing their jobs right, few monsters lasted more than one encounter. So the work that DMs and the Wizards of the Coast's research and development (R&D) staff was putting into getting monsters just right with the detailed math of 3E was in many respects wasted work. There was a type of simulation occurring, a simulation that appealed to many, but the game wasn't necessarily benefiting, and DMs were either suffering or intimidated.

So 4E took the attitude that the DM's role had to be easier. The amount of information the DM needed to memorize or have on hand had to be cut down. Monster stat blocks needed to be simplified so that the DM didn't have to sift between minutiae that hardly ever turned up and important game-play mechanics.

For DMs, the key mechanic of **4E D&D** might be summarized like so: Hit points and attack bonus progressions were no longer arbitrary, so encounters played somewhat predictably at all levels; and role-based monster design helped DMs create fun encounters and adventures much more quickly. I'm not going to get more detailed about the DM-package which, to an ever-increasing extent, is backed up by the electronic resources available on the Dungeons & Dragons Insider Web site.

So what, then, of 4E players? They were offered a key mechanic that has turned out to be more controversial. I was tired of my 3E experience, when my favorite high-level Fighter turned out to be only as effective as his careful selection of magic items. The spellcasters in the 3E system called the shots and, although the game's storylines felt consistent, many campaigns stalled out about the time that the spellcasters' increasing power made the other classes irrelevant.

This could have been solved in many ways, including a radical rebalancing of spells' power levels. The solution James Wyatt, Andy Collins, and I were excited about was to give every PC an ongoing series of choices of interesting powers. Most every time you gain a level you select a new power or a feat. Every combat round you have an interesting choice of which power or powers to use. This was my nirvana of gritty combat options created by exciting, exceptions-based design.

In my case, the vision owed a good deal to **RQ** and to Robin Laws' **Feng Shui**, another example of a game in which every player character could be counted on to fight using interesting powers. Add exceptions-based design tricks learned from **Magic: the Gathering**, **Shadowfist**, and other trading card games. Add some lessons from computer games on ensuring that every character has a role in the party, and you've got a fair picture of 4E's major non-**D&D** inspirations.

## Do Your Resources Meet Your Key Mechanic's Ambitions?

We would never have set out with a design centering on 4E's key mechanics working for a company smaller than Wizards of the Coast. Exceptions-based designs take time and skill to design. Then, they take time to playtest and develop into balanced options. As a rule, most RPG companies can't afford true mechanical development. Most companies pay something for game design, trust the designer to test the game as much as possible, then pay an editor to work things out as best they can while putting the final book together. 4E's key mechanics wouldn't have worked for a smaller company.

One of my favorite games-that-didn't-quite-work-out proves this point. Robin Laws' **Rune** (no relation to **RuneQuest**) published in 2000 by Atlas Games, is a brilliant design stunt hinging around a key mechanic in which players take turns creating deadly adventures with an exceptions-based points system. Each player is a deadly Viking warrior, the type of savage bastard who becomes the stuff of legends if he doesn't become worm food first. The game's current game master isn't just trying to help the other players have fun; the game master tries to score points by doing as much damage to the PCs as possible.

This picture of unbridled competition, an unapologetic contest between the players and the DM, perfectly embodies the grim worldview of those chilly Northerners. Does the game get major points for a key mechanic that evokes the theme? Oh yes, hell yes! I love many styles of gaming. In one of them, I cherish buying powers with points and destroying my enemies. So I'm just the type of competitive player who grooved on the concept of an RPG that alternated pitting players against the rest of the group like Loki vs. the rest of the Asgardians.

But there was no way that the game could be developed so that all those point-based player and game master options actually make sense. **Rune** was playtested, but playtesting isn't enough. I started marking up my copy of **Rune** with arrows pointing up and down for things that I guessed needed cost revisions. Soon I just couldn't take it anymore: too many arrows up, a few arrows down—there was no way was I going to be able to introduce a game that was all about competitive play and point-buys when the point-buys were broken. So the exact type of player who was going to love Rune because of its key mechanic couldn't deal with the game because there was no way to deliver on the key mechanic's promise.

If your mechanical hook sounds great but you can't pull it off, your game can only succeed as a work of game literature. A few people may buy your game to have on their shelves because they think it sounds damn cool. But they'll be disappointed when play isn't as cool as the concept.

But if you're a roleplaying game designer, the ironically good news, specifically for you, is that you may not have to worry as much about questions of balance and development as other types of game designers. Most roleplaying games can afford to care less about balance than games like **Rune** or **Magic: the Gathering** because most roleplaying games allow players to cooperate. When one player character exceeds all others in a cooperative game, the others tend to rely on that character. Then they come up with game-world reasons why that character or power is so much better than anyone else. Eventually, people write game world novels that assume the power imbalance is the natural order of that world, and so it goes, until someone comes along and rebalances or re-imagines the magical order. Obviously this isn't ideal; you'd probably rather understand the implications of your mechanics rather than be surprised at the worlds that come out of them. But so long as your mechanics are fun, RPGs are a slightly more forgiving medium where balance is concerned.

## Know When to Moderate

Even if your key mechanic is good, you may want to temper its impact on your game in cases where there are secondary play styles that could be allowed to coexist with your primary player pattern. Perhaps this applies most to games that are revisions of earlier games. This may be on my mind because of my experience with 4E, since I'm having trouble thinking of other game designs that have the same issue. Or maybe the principle is a lot easier to see in your own work than when you're assessing other people's designs.

Yes, I love the effect of the power choices offered to every 4E player. As a key mechanic, it did exactly what we'd hoped for the game. But I regret that the original design didn't manage to implement a simpler class, or two, so that a few players could play a game that didn't require them to choose between lists of interesting powers. There are **D&D** players who don't care much about the full list of interesting powers that are available to them. Sometimes they're just into the roleplaying. They're definitely into joining their friends at the table, rolling some dice, cracking good jokes, and still making a positive contribution to the party's survival. A simpler class, or piece of a class, would give those players the ability to join the table and roll the d20 without caring about which power they were using.

Given that **D&D** is endlessly renewed by the publication of player-oriented splat-books, the smart money is on the likelihood that someone will address this gap in player-experience some day.

## Know When to Cut

You're starting out as a designer. You've got a design career ahead of you. You don't have to pack all your good ideas into one design, or even into three designs. This matters even more when your key mechanic needs space to flex its wings and your other ideas hinder the key mechanic from taking flight. You may have to dial down aspects of your game that arguably could have been just as good as the focus material that supports the key mechanic.

Again, **D&D** offers an example that's ready to hand. Once upon a time, early in **4E** design, the powers PCs acquired from their character class were only part of the equation. Racial powers were supposed to match character class powers for impact on your character and the game world. Throw in more powers in the paragon path and advantages that characters gained through feats, and you had an overcrowded character sheet.

As we fleshed out the character class powers, we recognized that class was capable of handling all the heavy lifting. Class powers mattered and made sense as the principal way that players thought about their characters. Racial powers still worked, but it turned out that they could still have a big impact on the game if each PC had only a single exciting racial power.

Fair enough. But not all of us had accepted the biggest consequence of the move to interesting character powers. The major source of **3E** character power that had to be severely pruned in **4E** was magic items. We had some good ideas for how magic item powers might work: They worked too well! Yes, magic items are an important part of **D&D**, framing many adventurers' aspirations, allowing players to fine-tune their characters, and pumping up the sense of the world's fantastic history. But the character classes were already doing a great job of throwing around awesome magic. When every character has the choice of dozens of interesting powers, there isn't room for magic items' powers to compete with character class powers.

*"Cutting good ideas doesn't dispel them forever."*

I'd never been a fan of the way in which non-spellcasters in 3E could end up defined as composites of their magical items. And since I knew the choice was between compelling character powers and a full arsenal of magic item powers, I focused on making character class power compelling.

Cutting good ideas doesn't dispel them forever. If you keep track of your draft s and flag worthwhile ideas that have to be cut, you'll often be able to use the ideas in a later design. Cutting a good idea can pay off when it is competing with too many other good ideas. Give all the elements of your design the amount of attention they deserve and you'll have several designs to your name instead of one overstuff ed curiosity.

## A Strong Hook and Strong Follow-Through

Find a mechanical hook that thrills you. It may come to you in a bolt of inspiration. It may come to you after many false starts. Either way, keep searching until you find something that you suspect will set your game apart from all others.

Then follow through with the hard work that provides your hook with a full game to live in. Yes, even with the best mechanical hook, it's going to take a lot of work to finish a game. The good news is that if your hook really is good, it's likely to make your work easier, opening new approaches and ideas that keep you entertained. If you end up feeling like you're doing drudge work, you should ask yourself whether the work is necessary, or whether the audience will also be bored.

If the finished game ends up sitting on your shelf, scarcely played, you probably didn't succeed. If the game turns out to be something you and your friends play often, even with simply playtest components, you're either a skillful game designer or (much less likely!) a charismatic demagogue. Either way, you've got potential.

Every design will teach you new tricks. Like writers who return often to pivotal themes, successful game designers have a way envisioning new ways of using key mechanical hooks; what worked once can work again, if phrased in a way that the audience perceives as new.

The worst outcome is that you give up before you finish your game. You learn less this way.

The best possible outcome is that you will design a great game, then manage to launch it out into the wider world. If you enjoy that best possible outcome, guess what happens next? Pretty much the same thing that happens if your game design doesn't quite work out: You start your next design, taking what you've learned and doing your best.

If you're having fun, keep designing. The world continually surprises itself by its need for great new games. With a good hook and some hard work, you'll help.

# 6

# The Infinite Onion
## Creating Play Depth

S ome game designers would have you believe that they are powerful
authorities with a lot of secret knowledge about the world. And it's true
that game designers are generalists with good math and language skills,
and skill with both syncretic work and reductive analysis. But design is a process
of invention, and so it always proceeds by fits and starts. If there were a simple
formula for it, everyone could do it. So all that deferring to authority is a bit of a
scam.

Here's the truth: Sometimes, I don't know what I'm doing with a design. And
that's okay, really.

This is a normal stage of design, the stage I think of as playful discovery. It's
not that I don't have ideas (ideas are the easy part!). It's that the ideas I have don't
work together smoothly. For instance, the character motivations don't all click
in the backstory. Or an encounter is sort of boring tactically, or it playtests badly.
The things that I find exciting may be elements that the playtesters find pretty
routine, or even too easy. Resource management may be completely out of whack.
Nobody's first draft of rules is perfect—not Richard Garfield's, not Sid Meier's,
not Gary Gygax's. No one's.

# Design as Layering

A large part of the design process, for me, is about making the pieces fit. I call this process layering, or lacquering, or making connections in the design. Erik Mona talks about the technique in his interview in **KQ#1**, and most of the better designers I know depend on it. Build a prototype game. Playtest. Fix. Iterate.

There's no substitute for spending time with a design and working it from many angles. Over time, you find more and more of the plot holes in an adventure, or more of the mechanical holes in a new subsystem, or more of the power-gaming rules abuses when a new creature or type is combined with existing material. The more complex the game is, of course, the longer this process takes.

> *"Sometimes, I don't know what I'm doing with a design.*
> *And that's okay."*

With adventures, I usually think of "outline, revision, first draft, playtest, second draft" as the minimum requirement. That gets me a manuscript that has enough interest on every page that a publisher can hand it to an editor and get something out of it. I've written faster in the past, and I have always regretted it.

# Playtest Types

I'll make one further statement on process: hands-on design is just as important as mediated design. That is, you can't always count on editors and playtesters to find the flaws that you care about. They'll find most of them. They'll find flaws you would miss. But whenever I can make the time, I like to playtest the material myself, as well as having it playtested externally.

An external playtest is always (rightly) lauded as more likely to find the gaping holes that a designer mentally "fills in" during his own playtest runs. That is, he applies the rules that are assumed to work a certain way, or adds in the unwritten NPC reactions crucial to an encounter setup.

Those are flaws you won't find yourself, so I think external playtests are crucial for revealing your blind spots. For instance, they helped pinpoint the need for improvements to the investigation/clue structure in **Blood of the Gorgon**. They nailed the need for better treatment of the maelstrom in **Six Arabian Nights** and led to a partial redesign of the nightwing in **Empire of the Ghouls**, not to mention the revisiting of game balance on several encounters.

# The Perfect Game

But doing a playtest myself gives me another kind of data. It tells me what isn't working in the "ideal game" that I am striving for with a design. That Platonic ideal of a game is sometimes a spark that inspires me (such as the clockpunk of

Tales of Zobeck), or it can be an attempt to match a particular genre tradition (such as the use of faerie lore in **Wrath of the River King**).

In an adventure, this is usually tone or theme or roleplay elements that external playtesters may or may not pick up on. In a rules set, it's usually about gauging player reaction to a new mechanic. Is there excitement or is playtesting it a chore? How much sizzle does that mechanic really bring to the game? Even a boring mechanic can work flawlessly in mechanical terms. But if it's boring me at the table, or cycle times are too long, I need to know.

This is a long-winded way of saying some encounters are written in rough form knowing that they must be rewritten, trimmed, expanded, and improved. But every encounter and every rewrite should bring the resulting design closer and closer to that ideal that a designer carries around as a target for a particular project. Sometimes I get very, very close to that target indeed. Sometimes I miss by miles.

*"Good design isn't a road with milestones you can tick off until you arrive at Done."*

And the difference between the two is usually time. Rushed projects almost always lack the connections between parts that make the whole worthwhile. Whether those are mechanical connections or story connections doesn't matter. Anyone can string together a set of dice tables and character generation systems. Anyone can put together a quick set of location descriptions and monster stats. But to rise above the level of "just another rules set" or "just another crawl," there needs to be a little more to it.

# What-If Design

The time I spend examining design permutations and drawing new connections is the game of what-if. What if the spellcasting mechanic feeds back into the hit point mechanic? What if the mounted rules use the same action points as unmounted combat, but in a new way? What if the archvillian changes over the course of the story, jumping body to body? What if the stories are all set in a shared world that ticks to a devil's timetable? What if the King of the Fey got really, really angry, and the only way out was to placate his even more evil sister? What if...

So that's where layering comes from for me. Asking "what if" 100 times, and throwing 90 of them away. There comes a point where the number of choices is paralyzing (usually fairly early in a project). And there is a point where the number of choices is really already determined, and it's a matter of trying to keep things pointed in exactly the right direction.

Once rewrites start to feel like I'm drifting from the goal, I know I'm done with a project, and it's time for editors and developers to take it further. When "what if" turns from a tool into a problem, and each new "what if" starts to annoy me, it's done.

While I suspect I have the right answer, I want playtests to support that view. If they show me that players are getting out of the design what I hoped, then further "what ifs" will degrade the value of the design. Further playtest may overload it with features, subplots, backstory, subsystems, or chrome that seems valuable.

That temptation to overdesign is deadly; you wind up with lots of design junk. Avoid adding too much stuff. Good games are pretty simple at their core, and good adventures are not too convoluted. Leave exposition and backstory to novels and films. Concentrate on action, connections, and setting that gives players exciting things to do.

## Conclusion

When people ask me about the process of design, that's where I start. Take two or three or ten ideas, and see if they connect in new and interesting ways. Layer them together with what-ifs, test that in playtest, and repeat.

Good design isn't a road with milestones that you can tick off until (ta-da!) you arrive at Done. This is why publishers who manage creative types like artists and designers sometimes go quietly mad. It's not easy to wrap a schedule around layering and connections.

In my experience, good design is more like an infinite onion, layers of junk and variables, and better and better approaches to a goal. A goal that, in most cases, you never quite reach. But that's the joy of it.

# 7

# Fortunate Accidents

T he things I talk about so often in design—the matters of design discipline, writing every day, using outlines, sticking to word counts, and meeting deadlines—are all important.

But sometimes luck and serendipity have something to do with it as well, and I find this is especially true when dealing with collaboration. People misunderstand and miscommunicate about shared settings and shared ideas.

And that's a great opportunity. Some of my favorite design moments come from that, and one of them just showed up today in the ongoing work of map labels for the Zobeck map. The list included the Moon's Grace Temple, the Moon Temple, and the Temple of the Dawn Goddess, in three different districts of the city. Now, these are all ways to refer to the Temple of Lada, the Golden Goddess. And originally, they were all meant to be a single place.

But the list made me think: "Why should there be just one temple of each god in a city? That's ridiculous!" And in fact, you never see this in the real world. Temples to the same god appear in many parts of the same city. Even in pagan times, there was more than one temple to Jupiter in Rome.

So, likewise, this kicked off some thoughts about the gods and temples of Zobeck. There may be just five main gods and two lesser ones in the Zobeck pantheon, but that doesn't mean just five main temples and some lesser ones. And the map reflects that.

I love these moments in design, when what seems like a mistake becomes a feature that sets a monster apart, or makes a map richer and more detailed, or makes an NPC worth talking to.

You got any favorite "splendid mistakes" from your campaign or your games? Visit the Kobold Forum (www.koboldquarterly.com/KQForums) and let me know.

# 8

# Basic Combat Systems for Tabletop Games

*Colin McComb*

Nearly every game you'll play has a dispute resolution system. Dominoes uses a simple numerical comparison; Rock-Paper-Scissors has an elementary matrix; checkers and chess follow prescribed rules to determine who takes what piece and how. For role-playing games, chances are that you're looking for something with a little more heft.

Any time you create a system, you should keep your end goal in mind: What do you want your system to do? If you're looking for speed, a quick-and-dirty combat system is for you—but you'll have to accept that rules lawyers will find loopholes and exceptions. Naturally, you'll want to minimize those holes, but if you spend your time designing a system that closes off every workaround you can imagine, you've just removed "quick-and-dirty" from the equation, and are instead creating a real combat simulator—and that's well beyond the scope of this article.

Likewise, if your preferred combat includes a battle map, detailed movement, and careful placement of miniatures, you're looking for a more representative combat system. You'll want to add a variety of rules supporting movement types and how they relate to combat, and you'll want to have more detailed discussions of attacks, armor, defense, and damage. In short, you're looking for a way to create an engaging and in-depth combat system.

For either route, you'll need to create some basic parameters. I've included an example system at the end of this article. Feel free to use it, modify it, and write to let us know how you've tweaked it. Comments are welcome at the Open Design forums at www.koboldquarterly.com; you'd be surprised at how often designers drop by to respond personally.

Your first concern is meshing your dispute resolution with the rest of your game system, to make sure it flows naturally and smoothly. If you use dominoes as your character generator and skill checks, you should seriously consider the use of dominoes as your combat resolution as well. Having five different ways to resolve issues may be entertaining to design, but it's a nightmare to play (unless you're playing Calvinball, in which case all bets are off).

You may want to design the combat first and generate the rest of your rules around your combat system; that's fine, but be aware that you will need to test, re-test, and smooth your gameplay with each new addition to the rules you create. Your elegant system may turn into a lumbering monstrosity if you don't exercise caution; every variable you introduce has the potential to throw the whole thing out of whack, and bolting new pieces on to address those unbalancing issues introduce issues of their own.

## Attack System

With all that said, here's a checklist to help you generate your own basic combat rules set. First, you'll need to establish how to hit.

- **Determine your resolution system. Deadlands** uses poker chips and playing cards. **Dungeons & Dragons** uses a d20. Amber uses storytelling and ranking comparisons. **Shadowrun** uses dice pools with target numbers, with players rolling large numbers of dice to match or beat a 5. What's your method? Remember that you want your combat system to be portable across your design, so pick something that has broad applicability. Is this an opposed check? That is, do both the attacker and the defender take part, or is the attacker the only active participant for each check?

- **Figure out your probabilities and outcomes.** You don't need to be a mathematics genius to know basic statistics. You do need to know the basic probabilities of your chosen resolution. For example, do you know the average roll on a d6? What about a d10? What about flipping a coin? (Answers: 3.5, 5.5, and 1:1. You should also know that probabilities and odds are two entirely different creatures. See the sidebar.) Once you've figured out the probability for your system, make the average your base chance.

- **Your base chance** is an attempt by an average person using average weaponry to hit another average person with average defenses. This number may go up or down in your system depending on the modifiers you choose for this number—but remember that the more modifiers you include, the slower your system will run. If you want your characters to be superheroes, your chance for success will rise—say, to 60/40. Conversely, if you want a grim system where failure is expected (such as **Call of Cthulhu**), or a system with frequent lethal hits (such as **Bushido**), turn the success rate down to 45/55 or even 40/60.

- **Pick your modifiers** (if you want to include any). Your modifiers can be either positive or negative, and can include:
  - **Character traits**, such as strength, speed, wits, proficiencies, skills, and experience level.
  - **Attack types**, including ranged, melee, armed, unarmed, to subdue, or to harm.
  - **Weapon modifiers**, including reach or range, damage type (or damage type as compared to specific armors, since certain weapons are more effective against certain types of defenses; note that damage type in this instance is used purely for calculating to-hit modifiers), magical or technological bonus, or size.
  - **Target's protection**, including magical, armor, speed or agility, or natural protection. You may also consider defensive modifiers, such as Parries or Dodges in the **Basic Roleplaying System** as part of your combat system; this is a great way to include the defender in an opposed check, if you so desire.
  - **Movement/mounted modifiers**, such as horseback, from a car, or in flight.
  - Other modifiers, such as **concealment**, **surprise attacks**, **terrain type**, or any other modifiers that you think would be appropriate to your system. If you're aiming for a level of significant detail, you may also choose to provide a modifier to target limbs and extremities.
- **Test it!** Make sure that the system can scale as your players become more proficient, and that more skilled characters can hit more frequently or more accurately than less skilled characters.

---

### *Odds and Probabilities*

Odds are measured as chances against compared to chances for; probability is total chances compared to chances for. For example, let's say you have six cards. Five of these cards are black and one of them is red. You have five chances of drawing a black card and one chance to draw a red card. Thus, your odds of drawing the red card are 5:1 against (or 1:5 for). To calculate probability, you simply take the entire pool of cards (6), and ask how many red cards are in that pool. Thus, your probability of drawing the red card is 6:1

---

# Timing System

Next, determine your timing system. That is, who attacks, and when?

- **What is the unit of time?** How long does each segment of attack/defense last? Timing determines how much action each player can realistically take in his or her turn. Make this time too long and you'll have players complaining that they could do so much more than this in real life; make it too short and they won't have any time to complete an action.

- **How much action will you allow?** When do players declare their actions, and what sort of actions can they perform? What proportion of each time segment do you allot for each action? **Fourth Edition Dungeons & Dragons** allows a minor action, a move action, a free action, and a standard action. You can create something similar, or allot action points with a set cost for each action the character wants to perform: reloading, movement, dropping an item, drawing a weapon, speaking, spell casting, whatever. If you choose to use action points, you'll need to include Action Point expenditures for each action the characters might undertake. You can generate your own system as well, but be sure not to overload it with possible actions: create broader categories so you can generalize specific actions into those categories.

- **How do you determine the order of action?** Do you require an initiative roll? Random draw from a deck or stack? Choose a method that is similar to your resolution system. Again, you can choose modifiers from the list above for appropriate action modifiers: speed, magical or technological bonuses, luck, experience level of the characters, and so on.

- **Outline the order of actions**. Do you require players to announce their action before or after the order of attack? Do certain actions (such as speech) take precedence over all others, or do they depend on the player's order in the order of action? This is a judgment call you'll have to make depending on the style of play you want for your combat system.

- **Test again.** Make sure the action flows the way you want it to flow, and make sure that your testers enjoy it as well. Take notes and iterate your system as necessary.

## Attack Scale, Duration, and Defense

Now that you've determined your dispute resolution system and your timing system, it's time to begin the action: shots fired, spells cast, melee engaged, enemies grappled, or disengagement and flight from the foe. This is where you find out if your system works in dealing and returning fire—but before you can dish out the consequences of this action, you'll need to determine a few other factors about the sort of attacks the players are making.

- **Area of effect attacks:** These attacks cover a broad area and can potentially damage more than one person. Is this splash damage, with the damage reducing the further one is from the center of the attack, or does it deal damage equally across the area? A fireball from **Dungeons & Dragons** covers a set area, while a lightning bolt from the same system travels in a straight line; those standing to the side of its effect receive no damage.

- **Personal attacks:** Does this attack affect only one person or thing, regardless of who else is nearby? Any melee attack with an ordinary weapon would fall under this umbrella, though certain attacks with larger pole arms or swords might hit more than one target.

- **Combined effects:** Can the attackers combine their attacks or lend support to each other to improve the damage, such as with the stances in **3E D&D** and later? If you allow this, you need to make sure that these abilities do not chain together to create an unstoppable team—aiding a comrade in combat should come at a cost to the helper, whether in speed, his own defenses, or his turn to attack.

- **Defenses:** Does the target have an additional chance (beyond the dispute resolution system) to evade damage or reduce the damage? For example, are they allowed saving throws against a breath weapon? **GURPS** allows for "Active Defenses" like Dodge, Parry, and Block, and the difficulty of the check has nothing to do with the success of the attack. You could go this route, or you could choose to have an active opposition. That is, the attacker rolls to hit, and the defender rolls a defense, and the person who succeeds by a greater margin wins that particular contest. You might also consider an attack matrix, as used in **En Garde!**, in which the players plot out attack routines and then cross-reference against each other's attacks to determine the outcome.

- **Duration of the effect:** How long does this attack deal damage? For example, is it like an acid attack, that keeps eating away at the target, and when does it stop dealing this damage? If damage is ongoing, it might affect the target's attacks, spellcasting, further defenses, or even incapacitate the target altogether. The effects you choose can have undue influence on the course of combat, and players may focus on weaponry that emphasizes ongoing damage to the exclusion of all others if you do not limit the effects.

## Consequences of Combat

Finally, you'll create the results and consequences of the action. This portion will mesh closely with your character generation and equipment rules, because it corresponds closely with what your characters do and carry, and how much damage of any sort they can sustain before they die, fall unconscious, automatically surrender, or otherwise end the fight. Some considerations include:

- **Permanent damage**. This is damage that will take time to heal, absent magical or advanced medical techniques. This is damage intended to maim, kill, or otherwise cripple the target. Most weapon damage falls into this category: If you hit someone with an axe in **Warhammer FRP**, you are most likely attempting to end their life, and the damage you do reflects that.

- **Temporary damage**. This damage is of the blunt weapon, unarmed combat, and subdual variety. The target can shake it off, heal within a few hours, and be otherwise functional without the aid of additional healing. Grappling, punching, striking, and kicking by non-expert martial artists, or striking with the fl at of a blade or a sap, generally results in temporary damage. You may want to create your system in a way that each attack that deals temporary damage also adds a small amount of permanent damage. A shot with a blackjack still has the potential to cause brain damage.

- **Character modifiers**. Certain types of damage may target character traits: weakening, disorienting, making it harder for the character to attack targets. Use this damage type carefully, and explain thoroughly whether it is permanent or temporary. The effects of a knock to the head can fade, while brain damage is significantly harder to heal. Likewise, a pulled leg muscle can slow a person down for a short period, while a knife to the Achilles tendon does longer-term damage. Both **3E** and **4E Dungeons & Dragons** provide for "conditions," effects that limit movement, open vulnerabilities, or create penalties on various attack, defense, or skill rolls.

- **Movement modifiers**. Speaking of knives to the Achilles, your damage may include ways to cripple or slow opponents. Some damage will be permanent, as noted above; some might be as simple as caltrops in the boots, requiring opponents to take off their footgear or suffer a movement penalty. This kind of damage segues into equipment damage.

- **Equipment damage**. Sometimes characters will want to target their enemy's equipment, or a piece of machinery, or a door, or some other inanimate object. The rust monster from **Advanced Dungeons & Dragons** is a classic example. You may want to include a summary of how equipment and inorganic material suffers damage, and how to repair or replace it. Again, this may generate too great an encumbrance on your rules, slowing them down, which is why I come back to the next step.

- **Test!** You want to be sure that all of your damage is consistent with the style of play you want. Do you want quick and fatal combats, with potential one-shot kills, as in **Rolemaster**? This is fine if your character generation is not a long and laborious process; however, if you expect your players to become involved and invested in their characters, you will want to ensure that they have at least a decent chance of survivability in a combat appropriate to their experience level. Remember that all combat requires record-keeping, and the more caveats, modifiers, and damages you include, the slower your combat system will run.

Your consequences should include instructions on recovering from each specific damage type. If the target cannot recover from this damage, or the damage requires extensive rest, recovery, or repairs, it's essential that you outline this as well.

The most important goal of your system is the reliable entertainment of your players. Your combats shouldn't be punctuated with cries of "But that's not how it works!" or "That could never happen!" Your players should be so engrossed in the game that they are willing to overlook the occasional hitch and bump; if you've managed that, then you've done a good thing. Congratulations, and good luck.

# Our System

In the interest of full disclosure, I note that I've violated the cardinal rule of this essay: I have not thoroughly tested this rule system. However, as an example and using only this essay as a guide, I created this system in under a day. If you're planning on putting a system together for widespread public use as the base of your RPG, you really should put more time into it.

## Goal

Our goal is to create a moderately involved combat system for a near-future campaign setting with increasing but not automatic lethality. We want something we can play relatively quickly—that is, a single combat won't eat game night—but not so quickly that we have to invent the actions and the outcomes ourselves; we want some guidance. We also don't want to keep exact track of all the locations of the characters.

## Dispute Resolution

Our basic system uses d100 (2d10) so that we can correlate the results of any attempted action with a percentage chance. We can also roll d10s to generate smaller increments of actions, skill traits, and so forth. Using firearms, attackers must roll above 55 (that is, a 45 percent chance), modified, for their attack to have a chance of hitting. If the target is wearing armor or moving, the rate of success drops dramatically.

Unarmed or melee combat requires an opposed roll, referencing the appropriate melee/unarmed skill, with a base (unskilled) chance of 40 percent; whoever succeeds by the greatest margin wins that contest.

## Attack System

Because we're using d100, our average roll will be 50.5. We want an opposed check only for close-in combat, with both the attacker and the defender taking part. We will offer combat modifiers for the following:

## Trait bonuses

Our character generator is a point-buy system, based on an average 50 ability, with the players using points and swaps to generate scores above average. We'll offer non-cumulative bonuses to unarmed combat for an Agility trait 60 and above (reserving the damage bonus for Strength 60 or above). We'll also offer bonuses for ranged combat with the Reflexes trait above 60.

- **60-69**: +5
- **70-79**: +10
- **80-89**: +15
- **90-99**: +20
- **100+**: +25

## Improved Skills

We offer three different levels of skills. Our skills include attack and defense modifiers. Our list of skills includes but is not limited to: Quick Draw, Pistols, Long Arms, Submachine Guns, Karate, Judo, Wrestling, and Bareknuckle Brawling. Our unarmed combat skills will allow defense rolls as well as attack rolls. Characters must purchase skills, and then may purchase ranks in those skills.

- **Proficient**: +5 to roll
- **Skilled**: +10 to roll
- **Expert**: +15 to roll

## Armor

Armor includes Kevlar Vests and Body Armor. Kevlar grants a +15 to defense against firearms, and -5 to movement checks. Body Armor is +25 vs. firearms and -15 movement.

As noted above, we will allow the target defense against unarmed and melee attacks by using the various unarmed skill styles. Movement modifiers include:

- **On-foot:**
  - Walking: -5
  - Jogging: -10
  - Running: -15
- **Mounted** (bicycle, motorcycle, horseback)
- **In-vehicle** (speed)
  - 10-30 mph: -10
  - 30-60 mph: -25
  - 60 mph+: -40

Range modifiers will depend on the weapon; long arms will have a better modifier for distance shooting range than pistols, and pistols and shotguns will be far superior in close quarters.

## Timing System

Our system will use a ten second action round, and characters will have a number of Action Points (AP) that equal (Reflexes + Agility)/100, rounded to the nearest 10. Actions will have an AP cost ranging from 1-10 AP, and may be reduced by certain skills or traits. Unarmed attacks cost 2 to 4 AP each; using a gun 3-6 AP; movement 1 AP per 10 feet.

We want to keep our combat fluid, so we don't require the players to announce what they're going to do ahead of time. Instead, they have a chance to react to what the other players are doing.

The combat round works on the countdown method. That is, at the beginning of each combat round, every participant announces the actions he wants to take, rolls a d10, and adds his AP and any surprise or initiative modifiers he might have. This number is called the Action Score. The highest scorer goes first (a tie goes to the higher Reflexes), performs his action, and subtracts the AP expenditure from that action. If his Action Score is still higher than the others, he can go again; otherwise, the highest remaining Action Score takes a turn, subtracts the AP cost for a new Action Score, and play continues in this fashion.

## Attack Scale, Duration, and Defense

A variety of damage is available for attacks. We'll have grenades and rockets available, which will cover diminishing splash damage in a radius. We'll have personal attacks, both armed and unarmed. We will not allow combining effects for combat except for melee combat—when, for instance, two attackers combine to hold and then hit their target. Our system considers most kinds of aid like this to be more disruptive than helpful (if someone is trying to wrap bandages around your arm or inject you with a stimpack, it's going to throw off your attack).

As mentioned above, we will have active defenses for unarmed combat, and a chance for the target to dodge, parry, or block unarmed or melee attacks with an opposed roll; the person who rolls the greatest margin over their chance of success wins that contest. We'll add damage bonuses for high Strength with these kinds of attacks.

We will also allow appropriate defenses against area effect damage, requiring modified checks against Reflexes (e.g., to duck out of the way of shrapnel), Agility (e.g., to dodge behind cover), Fortitude (e.g., to resist acid or poison gas), and so forth. These defenses and the durations of their effects will be specifically outlined in our equipment lists.

## Consequences

We will be including the various forms of damage outlined above in our system. We want to be able to beat enemies unconscious, to blow up their cars and their houses, to cause damage in all its myriad forms. To do so, we need to establish what it takes to bring a person down.

Our system relies on Health Points. Each character starts with a base of 30 HP, with a bonus derived from the character's Fortitude score. She can buy additional points with skill points.

Characters have both temporary and permanent HP, and they are equal to one another. The character's temporary HP can only be as high as the permanent pool; if a character has only 5 HP left due to gunshot wounds, he can take only 5 HP of temporary damage before falling unconscious. Any time a character reaches 0 HP, he falls unconscious. Any permanent damage below -10 HP causes death, and temporary damage below -20 HP is also fatal (people can be beaten to death).

Our "one shot" mechanic works like this: Any time a character causes damage, he rolls the dice as indicted by his equipment or unarmed skill. If he rolls a 10 on one of the dice, he rolls for damage with that die again and adds that number to his damage; this continues for every 10 he rolls. We're doing this in order to reflect lucky shots; we want to our players to recognize that every combat could be fatal.

Rest and healing are the surest routes to recovery. Temporary damage heals quickly: within 1d10 minutes, the character regains 1d10 HP. Every ten minutes thereafter, the player rolls 1d10 again. Rest, icepacks, and bandages can all restore additional temporary damage.

Permanent damage requires first aid kits, medical care or the Doctor skill, and rest. It returns at the rate of 1 point per ten minutes, and may be hastened by artificial means as well.

# 9

# More Empty Rooms

## Simplicity, Playfulness, and Deliberate Omissions in Game Design

I've been thinking a lot lately about the hideous compulsions that game design sometimes reveals in our hobby. Gamers and game designers seem to include a statistically-above-average number of collectors, completists, rules lawyers, and know-it-alls—the people who can tell you every iteration of every rule and every character over 10 or 20 years of publications. On the one hand, this is wonderful, and collecting, rules knowledge, and strong memories for detail are all positive character traits—to a point. Taken to an extreme and sometimes beyond that extreme, gamers and game designers seem to drift well out of the range of usual human pastimes and into obsessive-compulsive behavior. These positive characteristics cease to enable joy and entertainment, and instead become off-putting, self-defeating, and harmful to friendships and sociability.

Game designers are not immune to this general trend, and some games display their flaws as virtues. I'm here to tell you, there's room to do excellent game design without completeness, without rules expansion, without a need for encyclopedic design. Indeed, each of these elements should be part of our hobby, but there's a dangerous tradeoff in going too far. Let's consider the options, and what we gain and lose when we privilege either completeness or simplicity in design.

# Space and Emptiness in Games

I have relatively few regrets as a game designer but one of them is not putting enough empty rooms in an adventure from about 8 years ago: the "Fortress of the Stone Giants" in the *Rise of the Runelords* adventure path was loaded with monsters and encounters and, yes, a fortress full of giants. Packed with them and their allies, in fact. And this looked great on paper, until I read the write-up about it that said, "No room for the party to rest, fight after fight, sort of grindy," and that comment really struck home.

> *"RPGs at their best allow us to explore wonderful, glorious, and profoundly weird environments. There should be room for oddness that doesn't involve combat."*

Part of what I loved about early **D&D** adventures was the combat and the thrill of finding treasure. And then there was the third element: pure exploration, the sense of wonder, the thrill of discovery. All the talk about how to design a fun game, and all the emphasis on providing a design with a sense of mastery from power characters—that's not wrong. But it misses something important. Tabletop RPGs at their best allow us to explore wonderful, glorious, and profoundly weird environments. There should be room for oddness that doesn't involve combat. Puzzles. Runes that don't figure into a key or a lore check. Statues of forgotten figures, strange shrines that stand mute, and places that give players the creeps, without ever checking hit points off a character sheet. That's mystery. That's space for imagination. (And yes, also a place for the party to rest up and heal, and recover spells). Combat after combat, encounter after encounter, the sameness of a combat-heavy approach turns to ashes eventually, just as a diet of nothing but ice cream gets old pretty fast. Designers should make way for wonder.

More than that, smart designers should plan for it. And it is entirely possible to plan for that sense of wow and awesome. Games are about rules, but they should also be about the unexpected, the epiphany, the sudden realization that, "Hey, I just noticed . . . " There should be room built into RPG environments to accommodate that. It's up to the designer to place those hooks for others to discover.

So consider this my plea for more dusty corners in RPGs and more open territory in rule sets. Here's why and how to expand that beyond adventures to other rules areas.

# Creating Space for Play

Our compulsions are a problem. Too much combat, too much emphasis on magic or melee or treasure is a mistake. Those are the foundation stones that are important and obvious, and it's easy to overuse those tools because they are the ones we know. Allow me to propose five additional tools, each of which allows for a wider field of possibilities and encourages players to try something crazy and entertaining. They aren't the only ones possible, but they are a start toward a richer form of design.

1. **Playfulness:** Design elements of your game world, adventure, or sourcebook that are impish, trickster-ridden, confusing, contradictory, or at least puzzling. If everything is straightforward, if every relationship between monsters and villains is straightforward, life is less interesting. What if the river troll has an unrequited love for the elf queen? What if the dragon is allergic to gold? What if the bridge is sentient, or made of floating teacups, or the bridge is rigged to collapse when a large mass (say, a giant's very large mass) steps on it? What if the orc is a bard with a silken voice? What if the cleric of the sun god is also a werewolf, and the treasure of the dwarves is cursed by the god of greed? Don't throw away or subvert all of the traditional tropes of fantasy; that's just a mess. But consider designing something off-kilter and letting the GM and players find the humor and potential in it.

2. **Breaking the Rules:** Some monsters and some treasures should simply ignore the standard rules. They should be rare, but nothing says "wondrous magic" like an item that does something the rules say is impossible. Be sure to include a limit to the item, lest it take over a campaign: the fading charges of a bygone era, the single-use item powered by a great wizard's soul, the holy avenger blade that lasts only until it slays the big baddie, then crumbles to rust. Alternately, include such overpowered or laterally-powered items in a one-shot adventure like "The Exorcists" in **Kobold Quarterly** #18—even in a one-off, players will delight in things they shouldn't have.

3. **Simple Side Systems:** A reward system based on speed, status, stealth, highest poetry or history skill check, best arrow, or enchantment magic could all be pretty simple to build. I included these sorts of challenges as part of the Birch Queen's Fair in **Wrath of the River King**, and players seized the opportunity to shine in the skills that have always been part of their character, but that were never given a moment to breath in melee.

4. **Rewards for Laughter, Leadership, or Teamwork:** Games are fun. Why the heck don't the reward systems in more games explicitly reward teamwork or laughter or the most entertaining player at the table? True, maybe the entertainment is its own reward. And maybe the player who diligently writes up the session notes each week is satisfied with her contribution in thanks and kudos. But man, as game designers we really should be able to gamify the rewards for this better than we do right now. I would love to see a leadership mechanic that rewards the player who

always rounds up the troops for game night with an in-game henchman, a hireling, a title, a Diplomacy or Intimidate bonus, a morale bonus, or something similar. Out-of-game behaviors affect our enjoyment of the game, but are rarely recognized. Games encourage certain behaviors (I call it "mind control by design" elsewhere in this collection). We should be broader in what we encourage and offer rewards for more out-of-character behaviors than most RPGs currently do. Speaking of which . . .

5. **Treasure for Kindness, Mercy, Stealth, or Healing:** The rules for any RPG reward certain things in the game. Those rewards force certain behaviors. For **D&D** and **Pathfinder** and a host of others, killing or defeating monsters is the primary road to advancement, so characters kill and defeat monsters. I'd be delighted to see more games that offer XP rewards equal to or great than the monster-killing rewards for saving the hostage, showing mercy to the defeated black knight, and healing the ancient sage struck down by the black knight. Likewise, the player who solves the puzzle or puts together the clues should reap a tangible reward. I'd like to see rewards for stealth, seduction, fast-talking, character knowledge, or solving mysteries built into certain adventures. All of these get some nod from existing fantasy RPGs, but . . . it's shaky at best. We can do better.

All these cases would need to be made clear to players in the setup ("This adventure is about stealing the Dragon Orb of Harkesh without being caught."), and rewarded in the final with XP and advancement. I know it's easier to design a dungeon crawl with monsters and treasure. But we should design more variety in play styles to attract a broader range of players.

## The Price of Too Much

In addition to those five thoughts for new tangents and variety in design, let me argue for a moment against the sheer weight of our hobby's core rules and mechanics. Consider the strength of two versions of the Pathfinder RPG. The first version of the **Pathfinder** RPG is a 576-page behemoth, the so-called **Pathfinder RPG Core Rules**—completely inaccessible for a beginner, and daunting even for the casual RPG player. The second version of **Pathfinder** RPG is the **Beginner Box**, a much more approachable boxed set with 2 slim-but-colorful booklets and a stack of pregenerated characters. The larger rules volume is always harder for beginners and, like every hobby, RPGs need new players and a welcoming approach that anyone can master. I think the advantage here for the beginning player is pretty obvious, so I won't belabor the point, but why limit this to beginners? An entire movement of RPG design in the indie realm and in rules-light system such as the **Dragon Age** RPG have ditched masses of hardcovers for a few thin books.

The question is, why?

First, let's understand that a portion of the appeal of gigantic books of rules and masses of complexity is that exactly: they discourage newcomers and casual players. The rules are a barrier to entry; they say you can't join our subculture unless you are willing to prove your seriousness by reading these tomes. At a certain age, I think that's no barrier: if you have a lot of time on your hands, reading the big books of rules is a delight in itself. Better than that: Having read and mastered a complex set of hundreds of pages of rules provides a sense of achievement and mastery. It feels great knowing that you have figured out the "Massive New RPG Rules Set."

But what does that barrier cost us? Why do gamers sometimes graduate from simple beginner boxes to complex shelves of books—and then abandon them for simple systems with strong adventures? I think the answer may be that, at some point, the game's design complexity and the burden of completeness makes it harder to find players because the rules themselves are so off-putting.

The hardcore will always want the more complete and complex system with all nooks and crannies covered. But that approach makes the game harder to play, because there's more lookup time. It stifles further growth in the hobby, because if everything is covered in the basic rules, there's no point in writing clear, modular expansions of the rules. Or rather, an approach centered on completeness stifles individual expansion: it seems that people will always publish splatbooks and add-ons, but if the core rules are complex enough, the amount of homebrew rules needed is smaller than otherwise.

Some people will argue this is a virtue: homebrew rules are sometimes poorly thought-out, unbalanced, or full of bookkeeping and drudgery. But I'd argue that generating your own monsters, spells, and variant classes is part of the joy of RPG play: the people who play by core rules only are missing some of the fun.

People abandon over-designed systems for simpler ones that give them room to breathe. An over-engineered car may be perfectly safe or the fastest car on Earth. Neither of those options is likely to appeal to anyone as a commuter car. That commuter car has a drink holder and a radio, and gets decent mileage at a price someone wants to pay. A RPG system that offers some complexity without completeness hits that sweet spot as well. And that sweet spot is different for different players at different times in their gaming careers.

## Paralysis as the Price of Complexity

Finally, there's the design problem of decision paralysis. I've seen this mostly in some game of **4th Edition Dungeons & Dragons**, where it stands in marked contrast to the retro **2nd Edition AD&D** game I've been playing lately. A player's turn comes around, they look at their dozen At-Will, Utility, Encounter, and

Daily powers—and they dither. And they can't decide. And they haven't thought through their Minor Action, Move Action, and Standard Action.

By comparison, other games say, "Roll 3d6 to hit!" or "Roll damage for your spell and mark it off your list!" The constrained nature of the choices of a simpler rules set mean that a player is never confronted with many options during a combat or even during a roleplaying encounter. There are fewer tools available in their toolbox, so making decisions about which tool to use are easier. And allocating resources and making the right player decisions is part of the cognitive burden of an RPG, in addition to staying in character and exploring the environment. The more options you have, the harder it is to be sure that you are making the right call.

If your game is simpler, it's easier to make the right call. That's the great advantage of the streamlined rules sets. You spend less time managing your character, and more time interacting with the game master or your fellow players, getting into your character, poking around looking for treasure, or thinking up a clever scheme to outwit the bad guys. It's a tradeoff; you'll have fewer choices when it's your turn to act. But you'll also have more freedom to try something outside the rules.

## The Price of Simplicity

Not everyone loves simplicity in RPGs, of course, and it does come with its own problems. So let's consider the rules-light approach to RPGs for a moment. It has its own virtues and problems. Many indie games provide only the most basic resolution mechanics, and assume that players can sort out any special cases. The **Dragon Age** RPG, the **4th Edition Dungeons & Dragons** red box, and the **Pathfinder** RPG **Beginner Box** all assume that the first boxed set will just get you started. Rules are present, but minimal. If Steve Jobs had designed an RPG, it would look a lot more like one of these. With rounded corners, peerless use of typefaces and layout, and dice offered as $10 optional accessories, probably.

Designing for less weight of rules means designing more for general cases, and ignoring corner cases. You can see this clearly in the **Dragon AGE** System, where everything uses the same resolution mechanic, and attacks are made unique through the use of stunts. The stunts provide variety and excitement to the mechanics, and interest in the results of a die roll, but they don't show up every turn.

Compare this with a **4th Edition D&D** power, which always has the same effect, and must be chosen from a list (decision paralysis again), and then multiple effects must be resolved. It just takes a lot longer for a player to complete their combat turn in **D&D** than it does in **Dragon Age** or **AD&D**. And that longer wait time between your turns means two things: 1) combats feel slower because each player spends more time waiting to act, and 2) players can stop paying attention at the table when it's not their turn (despite **D&D**'s attempts to mitigate this through powers that react to other players or that affect the whole encounter area). The game bogs down at the higher levels when more decisions are required.

## Simplicity as a Disastrous Problem

So where's the problem in simplicity? Simply put, more elements of the game must be adjudicated by a GM or done on the fly. The rules don't cover it, so... make it up. This is appealing to some players (mostly veterans and those who enjoy improv or freeform gameplay), and it is annoying others (often newer players, but also those who prefer complete rules coverage to avoid arbitrary decisions by a GM).

The greater problem in simplicity is that the game can feel shallow and your options as a player or a GM are limited. There's no robust skill system in AD&D. This is a great opportunity for roleplaying the fast-talker, but whether it works or not is purely up to the DM's ruling or a house rule.

As another example, there's no support (or no absolute requirement) for using miniatures and grid maps in many RPGs. This is great for speed of play (try it and see) but terrible for providing a richness of tactical options. Some players love the ability to model the combat space, and use it to their advantage or to pull off incredible heroic moves. Anyone coming to a relatively minis-poor game like **AD&D**, **Fiasco**, or **Call of Cthulhu** may rightly bemoan the lack of complete tactical support and the paucity of combat options. It's ridiculously simplified compared to a game like **Champions**, **4th Edition D&D**, or **Pathfinder**. Depending on the audience, of course, that's either a strength or a disastrous failing.

## Conclusion

Simulations and storytelling, whimsy and completeness, are all elements of a successful RPG design. Where a design falls on that spectrum of completeness versus simplicity, and where it falls on the spectrum of combat-simulation versus tactical richness versus narrative power is always a choice for the designer. Consider expanding your range of options and leaving hooks and tools for playful mayhem or humor in your game levels, adventures, or settings—and leaving some empty rooms simply as a source of mystery and room for exploration.

A crowded and complete design might be just what you want. But sometimes, the players remember that one room where nothing happened.

# 10

# Fantasy Realism

I hate the common critique of fantasy adventures and settings that they are "not realistic enough." At the same time, I totally understand. The critique is not about realism. It is about depth and plausibility.

A realistic setting does not have wizards, 20-pound battleaxes, or half-naked Amazon elves. Or giants, dragons, or beholders. Or anything fun, really.

A fantasy adventure has all those things, plus flying carpets, cloud castles, clockwork monkeys, and earth elementals of pure diamond. If you present these things in a serious, respectful, and coherent way, it wins over more fans than if they are munged together haphazardly. The magpie tendency to want to do everything cool is a powerful force. As a designer, you must resist it.

Or rather, you must channel it. Choose only the shiniest baubles, and make them fit together in a new way that astounds all who see it.

## Serious Fantasy

Fantasy literature has a weird image among the mainstream. Some people still believe, despite all evidence, that fantasy is just kid's stuff of wee goblins and faery princesses—essentially escapist trash ever since the Brothers Grimm. Others believe, despite all evidence, that fantasy is pernicious soul-eating rot. Harry Potter is accused of witchcraft or Japanese tentacle porn anime is accused of indecency, quite understandably.

These are fantasy junk food. The Grimm stories are bowdlerized folktales; Harry Potter is a vigorous hybrid of boarding school novel and fantasy clichés.

And the anime? Teenage boys have needs. Apparently tentacles are big in Japan. I sense I'm getting off track.

What I mean to say is that every genre has its introductory, broad-audience writers, plus its more obscure variants. The perfect example of the serious strain in fantasy is Tolkein. He devoted a lifetime to scholarship, to genealogies, linguistics, alphabets, and sagas. He wrote heavy action-oriented material at times, and light-hearted songs and pastoral characters at other times. He always took his of subcreation very seriously. That's why his books come with appendices. There's something primally satisfying about a fantasy world that says, "This could have been. This is grounded in sagas as deep as oceans, and this world will never end."

Tolkien did that. Middle Earth still resonates as one of the great touchstones of literature. Fantasy can be compelling, but only if its power is respected rather than treated lightly.

Does **D&D** do this? It's arguable either way. Do the smaller indie press RPGs treat fantasy with respect? I'd argue that more creatively successful games do so, and less creatively successful games don't. Certainly financial success is not correlated with depth or serious treatment of the subject.

> *"There's something primally satisfying about a fantasy world that says, 'This could have been. This is grounded in sagas as deep as oceans, and this world will never end.'"*

Not everyone is interested in Big Serious Art Fantasy. And that's fine. I'd argue, though, that the settings that thrive and find new readers over long periods build on a foundation that take their premises fairly seriously. Laughing at your audience is a recipe for failure. Laughing with them is a sure sign of shared vision.

## Respect for Players and Setting

Success in RPG fantasy comes from treating your characters and setting with some respect, even if it contains light-hearted portions or humor. If the whole thing is an elaborate punch line (Terry Pratchett's *Discworld* notwithstanding), who will remember it in 5 hours, much less 5 years?

What does this mean in practical terms?

A setting should have a scale, characters, and conflicts that match the real world to some degree. Large empires don't spring up from the dust. No magic can change the nature of the human heart, either its noble impulses of bravery, kindness, and generosity, or its weaknesses in greed, cruelty, and abuse of power. That's really what makes tabletop games shine, when they do shine: the human element.

Which means both the light and the dark side. Don't cop out and make cardboard villains. Don't let heroes weasel out and become mercenaries time after time. A great setting requires heroes to step up and be counted. I've seen a lot of that overplayed as cheesy. I've seen it ignored in favor of Monty Hall loot dungeons. A little basic respect for the intelligence of NPCs and monsters usually solves the problem. Creatures in a good setting act in their own interests. Even goblins seek some way to better themselves, even if they go about it by cattle raiding, kidnapping, and banditry. If they act the way raiders, kidnappers, and bandits acted in the past, they're more challenging for the players, and more credible. That's the trick of good NPCs. Stupid NPCs may be easy and fun for heroes to slaughter, but they don't build respect or depth for the setting if that's all the adventure offers. Tougher, smarter foes do more than make a combat stronger; they make a setting more credible as well.

## Coherent and Plausible

To show respect, you need to actually know something about history, geography, religion, myth, and the medieval period. You need to think about how pieces fit together. And you need to make some choices. The kitchen sink approach (while perhaps good for sales) makes for garbage settings.

Both *Forgotten Realms* and *Eberron* suffer from trying to put all possible flavors on the map. This makes them useful as sales tools, because everyone can find something to like. Designing for them is annoying because there's no consistent framework to use as a fulcrum for logical extensions. Or rather, you have your choice of logical extensions—you can justify whatever you like: the settings include fantasy technological states, Dark Ages regions, riffs on Eskimos and jungle adventure, everything. The logic of extending the kitchen sink is simple: everything is available to the designer, so hard choices are never required. Every area on the map is identical in terms of rewards for various play styles, and every culture has a certain sameness. This is convenient, but unlikely.

When gamers say "unrealistic," they usually mean "implausible even in a fantasy context." They mean a kitchen sink of ninjas with lasers, pirates with magic wands, and dragon folk with breasts, all in the same world. Sure, it's fantasy. But most gamers draw the line somewhere.

I'm not saying that every designer needs to be a historian and every setting should be a gritty historical grind. That would be dull. If you design a wild pulp Hollow Earth setting, it would pay to understand both the real science and the genre conventions, and to read a few of the foundation novels. Dinosaurs would fit right in, but **Men in Black** probably would not.

I guess I'm saying lazy designers piss me off.

The game design that swipes a historical trope and reinvents it in a fun, approachable fantasy way that doesn't exclude people who don't know the background impresses me. The reinvention of the golden age of piracy by the **Pirates of the Caribbean** is one example; the reinvention of the samurai epic by **Legend of the Five Rings** is another. No one would claim those are "realistic," but they are plausible and internally consistent. They are serious about the genre they work within, while subverting and expanding it with other strains of fantasy.

So, "realistic fantasy" still makes my teeth hurt, but yeah, I know what people mean. I want what most gamers want, namely fantasy that puts down a few markers of style or explicitly excludes some subgenres, to make the most of what it does have. Give me fantasy I can believe in, not fantasy that is convenient to a designer, set designer, or novelist. Work for internal balance. Fans will respond to the plausibility and resonances you create, taking echoes of that logic into a thousand fanfics.

---

### What are we really doing here?

A few patrons made two great points in response to this essay. The core job of a DM is never about worldbuilding or maintaining a complex narrative; the core job is retelling stories that have been around since mankind first gathered around a fire and spun a yarn. What people like to hear is not a carbon copy, but another take on a few key elements that everyone knows.

If you remain true to the tradition or genre, players will forgive implausible things. In a swashbuckling pirate game, for instance, juju zombies, mummy horror, monkey islands, and even "Lost World" elements all fit the overall themes and tone. Plunder your genre tropes, and that genre's "realism" is yours by default.

The audience expects realism from the type of story you are telling. If you make it clear what genre the players are in at the very start, you set their expectations. They'll give you lots of leeway regardless of what might be plausible in some other subgenre, but you need to live up to those expectations. Switching genres halfway through asks for boos and disappointment.

---

# 11

# Designing Magic Systems

*Michael A. Stackpole*

Back in the late 1980s, I attended a computer game developer's conference put on by Electronic Arts. I'd been invited to go by the folks at Interplay Productions because I was working on **Wasteland** at the time. I remember sitting in a conference room, where everyone was introducing themselves. Again and again, the programmers said, "I had this really cool way of handling [packet exchanges or some other bits and bytes stuff], so I designed this game."

I remember thinking that having a cool programming trick was insufficient reason for designing a game. A game should be more than just data manipulation.

When I look at magic systems in games and novels, I get the same feeling as I did at that conference. Too many people see magic as a great vehicle for special effects. The *flash* and the *bang* are what they focus on, which means they have a magic system that simply does not work. This is truer in novels than games, since game designers need to make a stab at having numbers add up, but even being forced to do the math is not enough to save most magic systems from being lame.

Magic is, at its base, really very simple. It's all about *probability* and *temporality*. Consider the following example: A piece of kindling wood has a high probability of burning. A wet piece of seaweed has a low probability of burning. Magic, then, would be a way of raising the probabilities so that either item will burst into flames. Clearly, in a well-balanced system, making the wood burn will require less of an effort than making the seaweed burn.

Temporality comes into play in a slightly more complex way. If you want the stick to burn *now*, that requires one level of effort. If you want it to combust completely—releasing a lot of energy—right *now*, that would take an entirely different level of effort. If you want it to ignite at a particular point in time—a delayed *now*—we have yet another level of effort. And if you want to permanently enchant something, that requires a lot of effort, whereas having the enchantment kick in only some of the time—like beneath the light of a full moon—or when acted upon by outside forces, it might require a bit less of an effort.

Once you have a grasp on these basic concepts, you realize a number of things. First, every bit of magic in games and books adheres to *probability* and *temporality*—though not always very elegantly. Second, most magic systems fail to sufficiently balance effect with effort. Third, the window dressing is just that: window dressing.

A quick look at something as ubiquitous as magical weapons shows how this works. A weapon that is "plus 2 against Dark Races" is just a weapon that has been enchanted, so there is a 100 percent probability that it will do greater damage to Dark Races. A sword like Sting, from *The Lord of the Rings*, has a permanent enchantment that causes it to glow in the presence of Orcs—100 percent probability of glowing for an infinite amount of time.

The third point, the one about window dressing, is where most designers (and writers) begin to head off the rails. They tend to think that what they're doing is unique and wonderful. It might well be. The fact that it is different from what others have done does not separate it from *probability* and *temporality*, however. A designer may decide that his magic system is based on the magic user's ability to subdue and exploit demons into doing his bidding—thereby accomplishing the effect he wants. Having a demon tear enemies apart is really no different than casting a fireball that smokes them; the magic simply raises the probability of death for the target to 100 percent. The mechanism by which death is dealt may make the game flashier, but the fundamental blocks upon which the magic system is built remain the same.

The big fail, when it comes to magic system design, comes in the area of *balance*. As I noted above, bigger and better results require greater efforts. The bottom-line balancing mechanism in magic systems is *limited use*. The simplest example of this method is that any magic spell is consumed when it is used. This is consistent whether the mage employs a prepared item, or casts (and then forgets) a spell, or must dutifully make a sacrifice and worship a capricious deity to be allowed to use a spell again. The slightly more advanced method is a spell-point cost system, where the mage incurs a cost (Strength, Vitality, Life/hit points) to cast spells.

I'll admit a marked preference for the advanced method. It makes the cost of magic readily apparent to players and readers. In my *Crown Colonies* novels, firearms are fired by magic, and combatants, depending upon their stamina and skill, can fire a limited number of shots before they fall exhausted. Using larger weapons, like cannons, can literally kill gunners by draining them of strength. In that world, any magic use results in physical damage, like bruising. Because the effects are cumulative, characters have a chance to contemplate what the results of their continued action are likely to be, and face a choice between being heroically dead, or alive and disgraced by running from combat.

In any magic system, a balance must be struck between effort and effect for the system to be entertaining and provide dramatic tension. While a simple spell-point cost system works well to establish this balance, it lacks some of the more interesting window-dressing aspects that provide mystery and wonderment to games. Moreover, providing means to lower the costs for a desired effect rewards experienced characters and quick-thinking players—good things to do in a game.

For the sake of draining complexity from what follows, I'd like you to imagine a magic system in which everything in reality falls into one of five elemental groups: Earth, Air, Fire, Water and Wood. Rather obviously the five groups could be expanded, but we'll work with a limited palette for this series of examples. Ideally the groups in your design would be drawn from elements intimately woven into your world.

Things which could be employed to mitigate the cost of a spell are:

**Components**: Any component that could logically be used in an enchantment would be placed into a group. For example, a salamander is often considered a creature of fire. Let's say, in your world, healing spells are also grouped as fire because they rekindle the spark of life. It would be possible, then, for a wounded warrior to consume all or part of a salamander and, for the next couple of hours, the effects of a healing spell would be increased.

Balancing that positive effect could be accomplished in a couple of different ways. For the next day and a half his sweat would exude a faint scent of salamanders, which attracts lizard-men and drives them slightly crazy. Or, remaining in the magical realm, while he has salamander in his system, he's far more susceptible to spells based in *water*, the opposition force to fire.

**Style**: Mages educated by one school of thaumaturgy might have greater skill in casting certain classes of spells. For example, an Academy on an island might turn out mages really good at water-related spells, providing a natural advantage with them but difficulty with fire-based spells. Conversely, a student who studied under a Master whose cave is on an active volcano might have learned a lot about fire, and not much about anything else. So, casting spells and using components with which the mage is most comfortable will cost less, and is balanced by an increased cost (or decreased level of efficacy) for spells from outside his wheelhouse.

**Knowledge:** Spells can be grouped in other ways from the elements. When I was working for Flying Buffalo, Inc., I created the 8 Cs of Magic. All spells broke down into one of eight classes: Combat, Conveyance, Clairvoyance, Construction, Conjuration, Curative, Communications and Concealment. It would make sense for a murderous mage to have concentrated in Combat and Concealment, whereas a kindly mage might have focused upon Curative magic. Having skills in these general areas would demand that the magic system is integrated with any skills and experience systems in the game.

A *package deal* is a logical grouping of magics that work well together for a particular occupation. A sailor, for example, might know spells that splice ropes, can reconstruct spars, and help in navigation or moving a becalmed ship. Providing access to those spells at a more proficient level would make sense, especially in a campaign setting where roleplaying is rewarded over roll playing.

**Arcana:** Arcana would function a lot like Components, but are best if handled with a significant degree of mystery and delayed effect. Let us say, for example, that a mage knows a symbol for fire from the ancient language of the Thaumaturges (a nearly forgotten race of mages who were giants and heroes and who died out because of a massive war between them). He knows that if he draws it over the site of a wound in salamander blood, it really boosts the effect of his healing spell.

The balance here is that its employment—which is likely learned through experimentation—has unintended consequences. The patient, for example, might become far more susceptible to the cold. They might develop a skin condition which involves scaly skin. These would all be things which, when they come to a head, will generate a lot of drama.

**Preparation:** Having a character take the time to prepare potions, spells, and enchantments outside of an adventure is something I favor. This is likely based out of my learning to play RPGs through Flying Buffalo's solo adventures. Being able to spend money, buy components, combine them, roll some dice, and come up with a magic item is a great way to kill time between games. While a Game Master will have to supervise (or trust) the player creating these items, it's a great way for the player to experiment. To whit, he can report to a GM what components he used, how much time (and gold) he was spending on the effort, and what his *intended goal* for the concoction was. He makes any die rolls the GM calls for, and the GM can note the result. In this case, he'd tell the player whether or not he'd succeeded; and then would note for himself any added/unintended consequences of the effort. A smart GM will also note *why* he modified the result so, if the player likes it, he can work to duplicate the effort.

**Timing:** Werewolves are the perfect embodiment of this factor. Great magic, but it only works at certain times.

**Location:** Oracles, shrines, temples, ancient ruins, and altars can be locations where magic can be strong and used more easily. Conversely, hostile environments might limit or even negate magic use.

By combining any or all of the above mitigating factors, a designer can create a pretty robust magic system without getting overly complex. By just giving a mage a spell-point reduction equal to his level number for any factor that applies (with everything costing at least one point), simple addition and subtraction is all that's required to make it work. Conversely, increasing the spell-point cost if they want to push things for a greater result also works.

**The Whiff of Death:** Magic, and truly ambitious efforts at it, should always contain a chance of injury or death. Spell-point systems have that built in, for the most part. Most systems also allow for a saving throw mechanism within certain spells—either for the target to avoid damage, or the mage to increase damage. Failure to make such a roll by the mage, or a spectacular success by the target in avoiding damage, can and likely should rebound harshly on the mage.

Random dice rolls are not the only way to introduce this element. Say a mage finds an artifact which allows him to cast spells at a reduced cost. With research he may pinpoint spells where it will be especially effective. Likewise, he might uncover spells where it harms him—though not many players will heed veiled warnings couched in terms of legends. Setting up story-based balance points does require more work on the GM's part, but builds more mystery into the world.

Effective and fun magic systems can be dressed up any way you like. By balancing your system, not only do you prevent it from overwhelming your game, but you give your players more mysteries to unravel, which is always entertaining. And that, after all, is what makes gaming magical in and of itself.

# 12

# How NOT
# to Design a Magic Item

As a judge for the RPG Superstar contest (twice), I have to admit that I have seen more than my share of fan-designed magic items. And the majority of them are perfectly reasonable items for a home campaign, but don't meet the level of Superstar design. What does that mean? It means standing out from the crowd through the originality, strength of mechanics, and unity of design that makes an item demand attention from DMs and designers.

What I hope to share here is the inside scoop on how to design a competitive item in a contest of any kind. The general principles apply to anything similar: monster-design open calls, design tests for WotC jobs, item contests or open calls from other companies, submissions to magazines. There's a difference between designing for yourself and your players, and designing for publication. And there are also very specific things to avoid when designing magical items.

## Gimme an Excuse

First off, the basics. If the contest offers a particular format (such as, say, following **Pathfinder** RPG style for items), then it is in your best interest to follow the rules of the contest. It amazes me that some people submit a Superstar item without following the guidelines, because in any contest of this size, with hundreds or even thousands of entries, judges are really not looking for the gems on first reading.

We're looking for an excuse to reject your item.

Yes, judges are bastards. We have to be. There are so many submissions, and not enough hours in the day to read each one in a flattering light. Frankly, I'm not interested in putting the item in a flattering light. That's the designer's job: to make the item compelling. But putting it in the wrong format is one strike right off the bat.

Another strike is poor grammar, bad punctuation, and lack of writerly craft. If you can't write your way through a couple hundred words of item description, why would anyone trust you with a larger project? Your work would be hell to edit, so it gets rejected on that basis.

These are two things that are very easy to fix. Follow the rules, and ask someone to review the language if your English skills are not stellar. Don't give the judges an excuse to reject you out of hand.

## Design Choices: *Boredom*

But, I hear some readers exclaim, I followed the formatting requirements and I did fine with the text. Why didn't I win?

Formatting and basic English are just the start. Judges are really looking for a magic item that inspires them, that cries out to be part of a big adventure, that makes them smile with glee at the thought of this item in the hands of a potent PC or villain.

> *"It's a joy to see someone go absolutely right over the edge, flap their wings a bit, and bring back a bit of game design fire stolen from the heavens."*

And yet, so many of the items are solving mundane problems that most heroes don't have. Or at the very least, non-heroic problems: food items, shelter items, maps and navigational items. Those are all fine for an adventure hook or extended wilderness campaign, I suppose, but they're not all that interesting. These utility items have their place in the game, but no one gets that excited about a Leomund's tiny hut or a create water item. I think of these as camping items: boots, tents, lanterns, everful canteens.

To stand out in a slush pile or a cattle call, you need a hook. You need a bit of flavor that makes the item sing. It could be appearance, a new power, or a killer name. Sell the sizzle on the item; make it sexy. This is not the same as gonzo weirdness for its own sake. We'll get to that.

## Design Choices: *Spell in a Can*

For some reason, many contest entries focus on divination, like the mass of augury coin items we had in the first RPG Superstar contest. These items aren't original and aren't all that flashy. I'd love to own one in the real world, of course, but that's not enough.

It's not just augury and divination items. The problem is a general one: repeating something already in the game is inherently balanced, but also dull. So unless you have a great twist, avoid designing what the judges generally refer to as "a spell in a can." That is, one-shot items might as well be a scroll or potion. Those single-shot items are great when you're a player, but they're pretty dull stuff, mechanically speaking. You can dress them up with a bit of flavor, I suppose, but the level of originality is pretty low on these. Why would anyone hail a *lightning bolt*-shooting necklace as great design? For one thing, there's already a *necklace of fireballs* in the game. For another, the item is just an overgrown wand.

## Design Choices: *Swiss Army Knife*

Some designers attempt to get around the spell-in-a-can angle by just giving the item multiple powers. And this is often a fine way to go, but some people don't know when to stop. An item that grants *command, hold person, fireball, cure serious wounds, prayer, cone of cold*, and *stoneskin* sounds pretty exciting from a player perspective. But it's doing several completely unrelated things, and that weakens it quite a bit. It's meant to solve too many disparate issues for players, both combat and healing and defense.

This design would be better served if it were split into two items, one divine item for *command, hold person, cure serious wounds*, and *prayer*, and one arcane elemental item for *fireball, cone of cold*, and *stoneskin*. They still wouldn't be great items from that list alone, but they'd start to trend toward a unified design.

I suppose there are exceptions to every rule, but any wondrous item that goes beyond four or five powers is immediately suspect. It begins to look a lot less like a well-designed and fine-tuned item and more like a player wish-list. Wish lists are for Christmas shopping; they should not be the organizing principle for serious item design.

It's very rare that a well-designed item uses more than a handful of powers. And the best items don't just replicate skills and standard spells; they do something original.

# Design Choices: *Über Items and Breaking Class Abilities*

Clark Peterson likes to talk about "über items," meaning overpowered junk that is a player's wet dream and a Dungeon Master's nightmare. If the powers lack any coherent theme other than raw power, the item is definitely a loser. That is, designing an item that does everything well is a terrible design strategy. Wondrous items are not meant to solve all of the problems a game might provide. On the contrary, they are meant to provide focused power around a theme or to extend a character concept.

And this is where designers also get into trouble.

> *"The time and class restrictions are there for a reason . . .*
> *keeping the game enjoyable for all characters."*

Some items grant a free class level, do away with the need for rest for spellcasters, or grant class abilities. These are all big, big, big mistakes. The time and class restrictions are there for a reason, serving overall play balance and keeping the game enjoyable for all characters, not just the ones with overpowered items. The scale of rewards, even at epic levels, should never overshadow core class abilities, and items should never make it possible for one character to take over the function of another class.

In other words, granting better turning abilities to a cleric is fine, if powerful. Granting undead turning abilities to a rogue is just a mistake, de-valuing the cleric's contribution to the party and blurring the lines between classes. Same story with barbarian rage, wizard spells, or sneak attacks: these abilities can be enhanced but should not be granted by a wondrous item. Maybe an artifact could do it, but they come with their own costs. Overall, I think you'll find that the game plays better if characters have mastery of their role, not other classes' roles.

## The Gonzo Factor

Some items are just plain weird. They summon eldritch things, they break a game rule in an interesting way, their descriptions are squamous and rugose and likely crepuscular: robes filled with eyeballs, chests full of mechanical men, undersea contraptions with lobster claws. **D&D** has a tradition of some weird stuff.

I'm of two minds about it. If you have the talent, it's a joy to see someone go absolutely right over the edge, flap their wings a bit, and bring back a bit of game design fire stolen from the heavens. If you don't have the talent, it just comes across as overdone, weird, and perverse design, possibly excessively showy or unusable.

It's largely a matter of taste, and as the culture vultures say, *De gustibus non est disputandum* ("There's no accounting for taste" to you and me).

I'm probably as guilty as anyone of doing occasional gonzo bits (the Shining Children of Thassilon from **Pathfinder #4** break a few rules around blindness and fire and ranged touch attacks to generate a particular reaction of fear among players, and the ghoul necromancy tends toward overblown prose in **Empire of the Ghouls**). It's fun to design this way, but it's a risky strategy in a contest. Clinton Boomer has the knack for it and rode that knack all the way into the finals of the first RPG Superstar.

If you've got it, run it with. But know that it's not going to suit everyone's taste, and it could flop completely.

## Pricing, Cost, and Balance

I don't want to underplay the importance of numbers, either. The bonuses, charges, uses, and creation costs of an item need to be correct. However, obsessing on the numerical side of things is only partly a designer's concern. In fact, it is secondary to having a great core concept for the item to begin with, and errors or omissions in this area are relatively simple fixes for a developer or editor to make. Which isn't to say that these mistakes won't cost you. Forgetting to include the proper spell in a construction entry, making an error in calculating cost, or failing to balance an item so that it works for the most likely levels of play are all serious mistakes, and count against you. The rules for all this, though, are out there in the **SRD** and the **Pathfinder** rules. Read them, know them, and use them.

## Flavor

Finally, beyond mechanics there are the intangibles of flavor and feel. It's absolutely true that the look and feel of your item matters, starting with the name. The "Idol of Bladderwort" is not quite as cool an item to own as the "Black Stone of Devesh-Nar," to my ears. Mordenkainen's Magnificent Mansion is a much more compelling spell than Morton's Hidden House, and iceberg is a better spell name than crushing snow mountain. Based purely on the names, of course.

A good name and a cool description won't save bad mechanics (and vice versa, of course). Yet some designers submit entries that are mechanically wonderful and totally devoid of soul, spark, or any animating glimmer of life. If you are designing primarily from the mechanics to the flavor (which is absolutely as valid an approach as the reverse), you need to be sure that you have given the item enough personality to keep the reader's interest long enough to digest the mechanics. If there's no personality, an item design has failed, no matter how wondrous the mechanics underneath, because no one will read it long enough to appreciate the worth of its rules.

# Conclusion

So, as you can see, there are many hurdles leading up to a successful item. The easiest ones are formatting and clean prose. The hardest are style and flavor decisions that every designer may treat differently but that define your work as your own.

As an example of glorious design, consider the portable hole. It has style, it has solid mechanics, and it does something that no other item does. It's a classic of **D&D**, giving rise to no end of stories and retellings. Best of all, it solves a core need for players and is widely lusted after by adventurers. A success on every front. Go forth, and create items just as wondrous!

# 13

# Location as a Fulcrum for Superior Design

S ome adventures start with a villain, some start with a monster list, or a big event meant to Change Everything about the campaign. Those are all fine ways to start design for a setting and a story, and I'd say they work for fiction superlatively. But for RPGs on the tabletop or on the screen, sometimes those elements are second.

Yes, the main ingredient for me to design a worthwhile adventure is a worthwhile location.

## Why Location?

There's a simple reason that location matters so much in an adventure design: It's the only story element that a game designer really controls. The heroes of the story are controlled by the players; they can go and do anything, do everything out of sequence, fight all the roleplay encounters, and talk their way out of all the fights.

They probably won't. But the players are definitely out of the adventure designer's control. They lead the adventure plot points through their decisions, but they aren't something you need to consider at the highest level.

The DM, by contrast, controls all the non-player characters and monsters, a cast of characters that you as the designer have a lot of say over. The villain, the henchmen, their motives, their stats, and their locations are all determined by your design. But I'd say that from my own experience, many Dungeon Masters don't run them as written. They improvise. They tweak, they mold and rename to match their own home game, to shoehorn it in. That's fine—well, that's great, actually—they're making the experience better for the players. But the voice, the impersonation, the details of all those characters, even their tactics, stand or fall based on how the DM feels about them. Sometimes he'll run them by the book, sometimes he won't.

The setting, though—well, that's different. As the game designer, you control the maps, the area descriptions, the flow from one encounter to the next. The dialogue, the choices of plot by PC and villain—those aren't yours to command. But the sequence, the map, and the locations are all elements that are the foundation of an adventure, and that most DMs rarely change. (Why buy a cool castle or dungeon with a map if you need to redraw the map?)

So, how can a designer make the most of this control over setting? In three ways: the ideal adventuring location must be exotic, it must be plausible, and it must be worthy of heroic investigations.

## Exotic Lands

Having proposed the case for the importance of location, here's the first of my three critical ingredients: an exotic setting.

Damn few gamers want to see the wide-open prairie grasses or the well-kept crops of a peaceful kingdom in their fantasy game world. They'd rather brave the fetid Last Swamp, a place infused with the ghosts of a slaughtered army, or perhaps fight their way up the Snowy Mountains, a chill place with towering cliff s where heroes can leap from cloud to cloud on their way to the giant's castle. Going someplace where normal people would fear to tread does two things from the gameplay perspective: 1) it proves their character's heroism by daring to go somewhere difficult, and 2) it gives the whole venture, in the end, an air of accomplishment.

Now, I'd argue that the accomplishment is almost entirely illusory; do any but the most anal-retentive and novice of Dungeon Masters bother to track every pack of rations and enforce every penalty of climate, disease, and terrain? Probably not—there are monsters to throw at the players! But having strange scenery does provide some degree of heroics in those who venture there, and it makes it easy for the DM to increase the threat level with lava, avalanches, and other location-based elements.

Choosing a locale with some style is a smart design choice. It's loaded with peril and totally subjective, but I think it's fair to say that making your fantasy setting bold and brash pays off in what it implies later: the cover art, the combat setups, the terrain effects, and even the sense of a journey and exploration of the frontier or the wilderness—all great themes.

## Exotic People

Now, exotic locales are much more than just geography, of course: Different cultures, different classes, and different lifeforms can all lend an air of the exotic far more effectively than the desert climate or the Fire Swamps of Bajor.

For instance, modern gamers certainly prefer the exotic over the homegrown, and designers tend to place modern-day adventures in exotic lands as well. That is, a gang of Masonic elders and redneck mercenary PCs might enjoy Vegas or Cairo more than Muncie or suburban Dallas. Yes, it might be fun to add vampires to your hometown and play that out, or nuke Miami and see what sort of mutant apocalyptic landscape your players might enjoy, but those are exceptions. Most players would rather visit Victorian London, Communist China in the Cold War, or the Incan Empire at its height. Go big in the real world.

And do the same in fantasy. The heights of the Elven Court, the mysteries of the dwarven Cantons, the world of cloud pirates, or an empire ruled by vampires—there's no reason that fantasy shouldn't immediately grasp hold of strange cultures, customs, languages, and people. Yes, the scenery is fun to describe, but this is smart design for other reasons as well. It provides incentive to explore, to ask questions, to learn the ways of this new place, to not make too many assumptions. An exotic environment rewards players who are curious, not just those who have optimized their damage per strike. A player can be both a tactical mastermind and intensely curious why the halfling empire has never been conquered from without. Provide both elements as a designer, and the DM is grateful and the players are enthralled with the setting.

## Plausible

While I've just finished praising the exotic, I'll now contradict myself. The exotic is a tool, but it is so very easy to abuse. Fantasy has stereotypes for a reason: Those stereotypes work, they are grounded in the fantasy traditions of literature and gaming, and they are accessible to newcomers. Yes, dwarves love beer and elves drink wine, dwarves are smiths and elves are archers and work mithral and ancient magics equally well. The trouble many designers get into is an overemphasis on weird for the sake of weird. There's a point where flights of fantasy turn into Alice-in-Wonderland oddities that are . . . disturbing? Hard to describe, certainly.

Now, if you're going to cut against the grain on those stereotypes as a designer, more power to you. But I'd offer two cautions to anyone discarding stereotypes in order to make the adventure more exotic. First, the further away you move from the tropes of your genre, the more original you are, then after a certain point, the less anyone will care about your wild originality. The audience will follow you to new and wonderful; most will stop at the border of weird. Indeed, fantasy gamers are inherently conservative in their fantasy tastes.

*"The ideal adventuring location must be exotic, plausible, and worthy of heroic investigation."*

Humans in general and gamers in particular want "same but different" rather than "wildly original" in their stories and entertainment, and roleplaying games are no exception. The most original creations may be more acceptable to your audience if you give them a new name and a standalone role in your world: deryni rather than psionicists, kender rather than childlike kleptomaniacal halflings. After a certain point—and as the designer must know where that point is—your dwarves aren't dwarves anymore, they are uvandir (see Kobold Quarterly #12).

Likewise, if every city is a shining wonder of magic and pure eldritch power, the DM will wonder why he paid good money for a boring utopia of mega-magic. You need to change up the scenery in an adventure to keep it interesting. Slums can be exotic and exciting, full of their own customs, their own hierarchy, their own ability to make noble, well-fed adventurers feel like fish out of water. Or if the PCs are all gutter urchins, perhaps a visit to the harsh, orderly orphanage of the Knights of Undying Light will change things around; being asked to stand vigil all night will play havoc with a young guttersnipe's usual nocturnal habits.

The idea for all these directions is simple. Give the Dungeon Master someplace new, someplace that must exist in a fantasy world, and do a better job of describing how it works and who its people are and what they want than the DM could do on his own. Give that world a sense of both strangeness to make it exciting and a sense of familiarity to keep it accessible—greed, familial loyalty, and the urge to power are universal constants, for example. This is what I mean by plausibility in setting. It must be simultaneously different, and yet not so strange that the players cannot come to grips with it. A setting built on the customs of Mesoamerica may be fascinating (see **Empire of the Petal Throne**, for an example), but it will never be a mass market success, and the audience able to appreciate will always be a small one.

Make your story universal enough that everyone sees their own life reflected in it. Even if the orphan is a gnome and the city is gold rush camp in the ruins of a dwarven settlement, the collision of a child without anyone in the world and a place driven purely by money should still connect with DMs and players who have seen something of the world.

The role of setting can ground the larger issues. The orphan isn't in trouble unless the environment itself is hostile—so make sure that it is visibly hostile. The more you emphasize two or three elements of the setting—through read-aloud text, through maps, and through NPC or area descriptions—the more likely it is that the DM will pick up those elements and relay them to the players. A few short details can make all the difference to bring the setting alive.

## Worthy

Finally, there's the matter of worthy settings. What the heck do I mean by "worthy" locations? This one's the hardest to define, but let me see if I can sharpen up the concept.

Heroes only get so many chances to go on an adventure. Many characters in RPGs die horribly, and even in a game with *raise dead* and *resurrection* as everyday occurrences, there are still *disintegrations*, dragon's *acid blasts*, and lava pits that leave nothing to raise. And gamers only have so many hours to spend gaming so, as the designer, it is incumbent on you not to waste either heroic lives or player time.

> *The place the heroes go must be worthy at a mythic level: where ancient blood was spilled, sacrifices were made, where the gods themselves reached down and changed the course of history.*

Make those settings count. A dragon's lair should be feared for miles around, not unknown and unremarked. A dark lord should live in a kingdom or at least a fiefdom of his own, because his evil seeps into everything around him. Hiding a dark lord in a dank basement somewhere is just . . . an underwhelming milieu. Think Hollywood, in other words. If you're planning a finale for an adventure, consider your setting the way a Hollywood location scout would consider it. What's most effective for the adventure you're trying to tell: the squalid tavern down along the moldering docks, or a charred jungle full of the haunting cries of ghostly parrots, or a madcap festival of halflings, half-besotted and half-stuffed with food while devils scheme around them? Any of those might be the right setting for a different type of adventure. Think about where you'd set the final scene—and then go one better.

Here's where worthy become a little tricky, as location bleeds into plot and character. If your villain is found at the top of a crumbling keep, then make sure that keep has connections available for the DM to hook into his party. Perhaps they found an earlier clue that one member of the party is related to the bloodline that built the place. Perhaps the wizard's skill with the arcane revealed that the site is metaphysically dangerous: Too much magic here may release something buried under the castle walls, something ancient and worse than their present foe. Perhaps the castle is where the paladin or his squire fought to defend his order against overwhelming odds, and lost.

In other words, an ideal location has some connection to things greater than the characters themselves: to their family, their institutions, religions, history, and even their place in the metaphysical world. This is why Joseph Campbell goes on about the hero leaving civilization behind, going into darkness, and returning triumphant. The place the heroes go must be worthy at that mythic level: It must be where ancient blood was spilled, sacrifices were made in a great cause, where the gods themselves reached down and changed the course of war and the course of history. That sort of setting is a frame worthy of the deeds of the current player characters—and if you've designed it right and the DM is on the ball, that sort of setting creates a frame worthy of new heroic tales. Make that setting rich, and deep, and you'll be surprised at how DMs and players respond. Never think of location as just window dressing, or just a sequence of squares and fields of fire. Never design it as an afterthought.

Make it worthy, and the adventure itself will resonate with some of that sense of depth and importance and heroic story. That's location's role in design.

*14*

# Worldbuilding

*"To make a Secondary World... commanding Secondary Belief, will probably require labour and thought, and will certainly demand a special skill, a kind of elvish craft. Few attempt such difficult tasks. But when they are attempted and in any degree accomplished then we have a rare achievement... indeed narrative art, story-making in its primary and most potent mode."*
—JRR Tolkien, *On Faery Stories*

Worldbuilding is an enormous topic. In fact, all forms of it can be distilled down into a few principles. I did that every summer in June for several years at a worldbuilding seminar for authors during an event called Writer's Weekend. It covered all the usual elements: setting, characters, logic, and throwing rocks into ponds.

Ponds, you ask? Yeah, they are a useful analogy for scoping this sort of work. Bear with me. I have five more general points to address first.

## Point 1: *Gaming Ain't Fiction*

The worldbuilding I do with those fiction writers tends to be all about the telling detail, building the world from the character out (or building the character from the setting), directing reader attention to just the parts that matter, and so on. None of this works for gamers because, as a designer, your first audience is the DM, not the players. Even if the DM likes the worldbuilding, you have little control over how it gets bent, twisted, spindled, and mutilated to suit a homebrew, or a corporate campaign setting, or some combination of the two. So your worldbuilding had better be bulletproof.

What do I mean by bulletproof? You need to hit a very particular sort of middle ground. For fantasy settings, it needs to be the-same-but-different, a tricky target if ever there was one. If you build a clichéd set of elven havens, hobbit shires, and dwarven mines, nobody will give a damn. They have seen it before. Likewise, if you build something so odd and exotic that the only way to understand it is to read it all, play the simulator, and chart some graphs, well, not many people will follow you there either. For settings like Jorune, Dark Sun, Spelljammer, Empire of the Petal Throne, or Blue Planet, you may have a small but devoted hardcore following. That's the best you can hope for.

The trick is that you must offer a core concept that's easy to grasp and fun to play once the shiny cool factor has worn off. Bulletproof worldbuilding starts with a big idea that is so cool, other people will import it wholesale into their homebrew. They will make room for it in *Eberron*, the *Realms*, *Greyhawk*, *Freeport*, or *Ptolus*. This is easier to do with an adventure or region than a whole campaign setting. What's that big idea? That is up to you; it's your world. But if you look at **The Free City of Zobeck** or the **Empire of the Ghouls**, it is pretty obvious what the setting hook is. Your hook should be just as clear.

## Point 2: *Genres, Action, and Big Ideas*

What do you want the world to do for players and for the DM? Ask that question when you start worldbuilding. What it does for the designer or the corporation should always be secondary.

Think about your goals and touchstones in genre terms. Is it steampunk or power fantasy? Is it dark fey kingdoms or low-magic intrigue? You know the kind of big choices I'm talking about. This approach has limits: most genres are already familiar to the reader.

You might try melding multiple genres, but you will weaken the setting if you try to do too many things at once. If you want a historical, ethnographic setting (drawing on, say, samurai Japan or mameluke Egypt) you are looking at a lower magic world. If you want a Manichean world of pure white and black, with heavy emphasis on magic, ancient gods walking the earth, and wizards in different colored robes, that's tough to build with a gritty, low magic approach. Choosing one of these approaches enables certain heroic actions (gunpowder, or combat feats, or chaos magic) and eliminates or reduces others. Druids and rangers in an urban campaign can work, but it's a lot harder to make it to work well. Every choice carries wide-ranging consequences.

Naomi Novik's *Temeraire* series melds genres well, blending Napoleonic nautical fiction with dragon fantasy. Likewise, Harry Potter melds the traditional English schoolboy story with traditional fantasy. The goal is to find two genres that complement each other. TSR's *Steel & Bone* mini-setting combines the

Vikings as honorable barbarians and a race of intellectual necromancers who venerate the past. Other examples include the nautical and space-faring fantasy of **Spelljammer**, the Cold War and Cthulhu mythos in **Delta Green**, or the combination of planar/time travel and Hong Kong action in **Feng Shui**.

You can create your world large enough to contain multitudes, as in the kitchen-sink approach of *Eberron* and the *Realms*. This creates problems, which I'll get to in a minute.

I use an alternative way of thinking about big ideas in worldbuilding, namely that worlds are verbs. You can describe city streets, architecture, and the typical tavern all day long, but what matters in gameplay are the actions of the inhabitants and the resources of the setting. Are the NPCs cowardly? Make it plain that no one but the PCs is going to save this town. Are the NPCs too bloodthirsty? Make it painfully obvious that they're going to war and a lot of innocents will die, unless the PCs stop it.

Think of the main type of action that you want to enable (whether that's pulp adventure, sword and sorcery, or musketeers vs. necromancers). You can build places, organizations, and characters that support that conflict. With that idealized action in mind, you can quickly find whether a cool new idea helps your setting or just muddies the water. It's a streamlining tool.

There is a time to be coy with your readers, and to give yourself room for future growth in the setting. When you are laying down the foundation conflicts of the setting is Not That Time. Spell it out. If someone asks you for the two-sentence description of "What is it all about?" you better be able to give it.

## Point 3: *Hide Your Work. Bury It Deep*

Science fiction writer M. John Harrison said (and the resulting discussion on ENWorld at http://www.enworld.org/showthread.php?t=193738 might be worth your time):

> *"Worldbuilding is dull. Worldbuilding literalises the urge to invent. Worldbuilding gives an unnecessary permission for acts of writing (indeed, for acts of reading). Worldbuilding numbs the reader's ability to fulfill their part of the bargain, because it believes that it has to do everything around here if anything is going to get done.*

> *"Above all, worldbuilding is not technically necessary. It is the great clomping foot of nerdism. It is the attempt to exhaustively survey a place that isn't there. A good writer would never try to do that, even with a place that is there. It isn't possible, and if it was the results wouldn't be readable: they would constitute not a book but the biggest library ever built, a hallowed place of dedication and lifelong study. This gives us a clue to the psychological type of the worldbuilder and the worldbuilder's victim, and makes us very afraid."*

Fairly harsh. He's largely right, as far as fiction is concerned. You don't want big data dumps in a novel or short story, though many writers find they need to do worldbuilding in text that never appears in their novels. Those notes are cut early, but they have served their function: to help the writer map out the logic of the setting. In good fiction, the reader shouldn't be burdened with that.

Games aren't fiction. In an RPG, the requirements are different: the world-building in **Empire of the Ghouls** isn't necessary to the adventure. It is necessary to the DM, who needs tools and backstory to carry an adventure when it goes off in unexpected directions. A novel or story controls the reader's point of view; a game session doesn't and can't control the player's point of view, so there needs to be some kind of fallback.

> *"As a freelance rule of thumb, keep your backstory and worldbuilding down to 10 percent of the total word count of any adventure if you can."*

Setting up fallbacks goes on with good worldbuilding. A lot of material fades into the background. A DM reads the sourcebook or skims the relevant material on an institution, class, or society, and uses that to power the storyline, either through their adventures based on the backstory, or through published adventures in whole or part. Worldbuilding should not be dropped on players in big lumps. Dropping it on DMs in large, weighty tomes seems to make everyone happy: it defines setting for the designer (allowing you to establish shared ground), it explains material that the DM wants for context, and it doesn't interfere with the player's focus on their characters and heroic action.

But it can be a problem. A DM showing off his worldbuilding to players who just want to get on with the story does not serve his audience well; he's too self centered to address the characters as the primary source of action and drama in the campaign. Do the worldbuilding you need to set up a story, then do the same thing novelists and story writers do: bury it deep in a research file.

If you do, you will have the satisfaction of knowing all the secrets. The players just want to skim the cream of all that work, just as readers skim the surface of setting in a novel. Readers and players are there for characters first, setting second. As a freelance rule of thumb, keep your backstory and worldbuilding down to 10 percent of the total word count of any adventure if you can.

# Point 4: *Logic of the Setting*

Internal consistency is crucial. The logic of the setting should be ironclad. Once you set up the rules, never break them. If the moon goddess is the villain in your campaign, keep her that way. Switching her into a sympathetic role halfway through loses all the credibility you have built up.

The upside of consistency is that players know what to expect. The downside is a smaller palette to play with for any one world or campaign. You may love both historical simulation and anime, but combining the two won't work to either's advantage. At best, different kingdoms operate under different rules or expectations (the way the Moonshaes are quite a different tone than Waterdeep, or that Khorvaire is not the same as Aundair).

This kitchen-sink approach is the default for the main **D&D** settings (despite my earlier grousing), and it's not entirely bad. Every DM finds some part that appeals to them. The weakness of the kitchen sink is that, by trying to appeal to everyone, every one of its flavors becomes muddied. The players will want to use elements from all over the setting. Your Aundairian wizard knights will stand arm-in-arm with Khorvaire's undead captains and the Silver Flame's prissy paladins. If you mix styles and flavors too often (within the same adventure, say) you dilute the overall campaign tone. Certainly, it's a price you might be willing to pay; just be aware you are paying it.

**Empire of the Ghouls** has a simple, consistent logic: it is all about cannibalism, about sick hungers and undead power-mongers and the weird ecology of the underdark. Switching into a light-and-fluffy or humorous tone won't work, even for a single encounter. That undermines all the work. This doesn't mean that your players won't find humor in the scenarios, NPC names, their own actions or failures. That is not the same as throwing in a goofy stoner pseudodragon, an undead hobbit minstrel, or a set of exploding smiley-faces. While those might be fine in an April Fool or light-hearted adventure, you need to know the logic of your adventure and stick with it throughout.

## Point 5: *Empire of the Ghouls*

Speaking of the Imperium, how did that worldbuilding start? What is the logic? It is a strange setting, so I'll just say a few words about it.

The logic of **Empire** derives from something that Dragon editor Roger Moore said to me in, oh, 1994 or 1995, namely "Wouldn't it be neat if ghouls or something ran the Underdark?"

To which I said, "Heck yes, the undead should definitely be kicking drow butt. I'll write up a proposal." Little did I know how obsessed I would become with it (four drafts, I think, to keep the word count down). Or that it would take a year to write. Or that it would be so well received. It's dark, what with the cannibal, claustrophic, drowning, and generally morbid elements that permeate it.

The setting has a fun "what-if" logic, giving ghouls more power, more magic, a society, civilization, and culture. "Kingdom of the Ghouls" managed to do a lot of that in its 22,000 words or so. The logic of the premise is easy: ghouls gain food or offspring every time a foe falls. They march and work tirelessly. They fight with a *paralytic touch* and with power equal to drow or dwarves, but without needing silly things like clean air or water. In a hostile environment like the underdark, their undead state is a huge advantage.

The ghouls seem likely to succeed in their dreams of conquest. Naturally, they also reflect a lot of things that I layered on as important to the flavor, such as remembering their prior lives (giving them access to skills and magic of the surface), tying them to shadow energies, advanced necromancy, and a martial and quasi-feudal social structure.

**Empire** takes all of these things further. The society has been around longer, the scale of the empire is bigger, and the goals are more than just the conquest of the underdark. They now have domesticated animals (giant carrion beetles), an underclass (the beggar ghouls), a more complex lifecycle (with bloated, sated, and bonepowder ghouls), and professional legions to fight for the imperial center. The class system is still fairly fluid, and clawing your way to the top is most ghouls' goal. But the society is more complicated and interesting: multiple strange cults, more varied equipment, specialized magic, the slave system with deadmind powder and guardian wraiths, the backstory of consolidation of the Hundred Kings, and so on. The mechanics are different, the flavor is much richer, but the logic beneath it all is based on the same what-if.

I'm confident that the adventure itself could have been published without the backstory chunk. Working up that level of detail is great. Much of it is not visible to the PCs except though Knowledge and Lore checks and discussions with NPCs. Both are narrow channels. One of the beauties of publishing with Open Design is that I provide all the additional material that people want. Maybe not all of that backstory will work its way into each DM's adventure, but it's there for everyone if they need it.

## At Last! Pond-Oriented Worldbuilding

Finally, back to throwing rocks into ponds. I imagine the pond as the size of the worldbuilding project. The rock is the place where the party arrives and changes the world in some way. The trick is to write only the section where the rock lands, or at least to accommodate any option. You can do this in one of three ways:

1. You can shrink the pond into a rock-sized area (that is, you narrow the size of the setting) 2. You can guide their hand (railroading the plot) 3. You can offer the players a huge pond, so that no matter where they land, the effect is a small splash (a commercial, kitchen-sink setting).

My recommendation is you keep it small to start.

The world really only needs to be big enough to envelop the actions your players take, and to show the first ripples. Think about how many areas you need to detail/fill with water for a world to work like that. Ideally, it's just the space right under the rock where the players meet the world, plus little ripples nearby. In fiction, that's exactly the amount of worldbuilding you need, as John Harrison suggests, since the author guides the reader's viewpoint every step of the way. In gaming, you need a margin of error to account for player actions and decisions. For most campaigns, you get the most dramatic campaign with a narrow focus. Any splash seems larger in a smaller pond than in the ocean. With a narrow focus, the only worldbuilding you need to do is what the DM and players need for a very limited time period: the first few adventures in a campaign setting. For the most powerful impression, avoid the kitchen sink. Stick to a particular genre, a particular conflict, a particular kingdom, and make it matter (see Ed Greenwood's essay, "On the Street Where Heroes Live").

## Set-up

I recommend setting clear limits on character types: ask players to stick to a subset of the core classes. Barbarian, ranger, druid, and bard define a setting—and so do fighter, paladin, cleric, monk, and wizard. If you make 31 flavors available, be sure that your players will try to use at least that many ("I'm a half-dragon Aundairian wizard with halfling scout levels"). I exaggerate, but not by much. Likewise, you may get a more focused party (and tighter connections to other setting elements) if you restrict PC races to human plus one or two others. Zobeck, for instance, is really about humans, dwarves, and kobolds. Everything else is a bonus.

## Tight Focus

Most of what constitutes "worldbuilding" in RPG products is padding, things that give a sense of the setting without being in any way useful to anyone. Padding makes it sound more negative than it really is; flavor, short fiction, and epic histories all add to the reading experience, to the broader understanding of the setting, and to the DM's fun in running the game. Just because something isn't "useful" doesn't mean it's not fun. You can build a huge pond with waterfalls and bridges and duckweed and streams. But don't be surprised if your players stick to their own little lily pad.

As a hobby, worldbuilding eats up as much time as you want to devote to it. If your time is limited, direct the vast majority of design time squarely at the gameplay elements, such as flashy feats, deadly monsters, dangerous terrain, new spells. I don't just mean crunch, of course: plot twists, planned set pieces, handouts, lines of dialogue that reveal crucial information, or the details of traps and treasures are critical ways to show what the world is like. As long as the players will see it, it's worth your time. If you have time left over to write a creation myth, a centuries-long history, a set of extinct creatures, or a lost form of magic, great.

To avoid either overdoing the backstory or undercooking the flavor, nail your worldbuilding early. Use a one-sentence bit of logic for the world or each major region. Keep a set of actions in mind that fit into that narrow tube called "Playtime at the Table." Know your big idea, your tone, and your story goals, and let things proceed from that. If you are good at improvisation, I would say spend your time on plot and tone, and ignore the historical, the mercantile, and the mechanical sides of worldbuilding.

The easiest method starts with a single village, city, or kingdom. Deliberately ignore the rest of the world until the party asks about it or is ready for it. "I'll tell you about that next week" is always an acceptable answer. Invent the ancient empires and the lost form of magic when the party is ready to go find their dungeons and loot them. Then have the new magic burned into their brains by the last surviving ghost of their archmagi. But leave the epic sweep out of all your initial plans. Epicness shows up on its own soon enough, if your villains and their current plots get most of your attention.

## Conclusion

Players find a world irresistible if it offers them immediate hooks to act heroic from the first time they gather together, and just enough detail to keep them coming back. DMs love a setting if it offers them endless stories to tell, without the minutiae that just clutter their ability to keep a campaign moving.

Action is your secret friend in worldbuilding: set (real or figurative) boulders on top of cliffs, leave levers for the DM and players to pull, string high-tension wire between the major factions—and trust that the gamers' experience will do the rest. Your ultimate worldbuilding goal is always to create a powder keg that the heroes inevitably explode or preserve through their actions.

## Worldbuilding for MMOs

A patron asked, "How do you think the creative process differs for massively multiplayer online role-playing games (MMORPGs)? From a design perspective, it seems like the worst of all worlds. You need to start out with a (nearly) complete world from the get-go, expecting that every nook and cranny, every hook, every NPC will be explored by the players."

I know a lot of MMORPG designers who used to be RPG designers. Their complaints show some of the differences.

The main thing is the built-in limitations of the launch code; the game starts as a collection of well-defined (or if you prefer, heavily railroaded) adventures. Art assets are hugely important; if there is no animation of the action, you are stuck writing around it.

At the same time, MMORPG designs are really about the hundreds of small set pieces (the quests), plus enabling players to set up and play among themselves (guilds). The crunch is, oddly enough, secondary to the art and software assets and what the engine enables.

Some of the paper RPG designers seem to enjoy the highly scripted nature of MMORPG design (trigger/asset/text string, repeat). Others seem eager to find ways around those limits. Which sounds a lot like the WotC/indie split in tabletop design.

# ENHANCING ADVENTURES

# 15

# Crafting a Dastardly Plot
## *Ed Greenwood*

ometimes, roleplaying campaigns can be like the lives of drifting,
directionless teenagers: This adventure (purchased by the DM from a
gaming company) happens to the players, and then that one (also bought)
befalls them, giving them until the next gaming session to prepare for, yes, yet
another ready-bought adventure.

So brave adventurers get hit with X and then with unrelated Y and then with
also-unrelated Z.

All of which hardly seems much of a recreational getaway from one-darned-
thing- after-another real life, does it?

Nor is it really much of a "campaign," which in its older, military (and tabletop
military gaming) sense, meant a series of battles and skirmishes that made up the
same unfolding conflict in a particular country or "theater."

## The Whys of Adventuring

To put it another way, a heroic life—an adventurer's life—has direction, meaning,
and purpose. Mere warriors may just fight to resist whatever the world hurls at
them, but adventurers set out to remake (or at least influence) the world around
them by striving, through battle and diplomacy and other deeds, to Change
Things. That is, to alter the land they're in, and perhaps the region around it, by
what they do.

So adventuring player characters, if they seek to be heroes—or tyrants or criminal kingpins, for that matter—seek to be agents of change. Change, that is, they hope to control or at least steer, to reach goals they find desirable (as opposed to overthrowing kings only to end up transforming several happy, prosperous neighboring realms into a vast lawless and devastated bandit territory, roamed by opportunistic monsters and inhabited only by the desperate who are unable to flee the area).

## Awash In A Sea of Plots

Enter plot. Which can be said, in its simplest form, to be the script or outline of a story. A bestselling novel, unless it is gang-written by a group of writers all playing tug-of-war with each other, will probably have a single plot. It may be convoluted, and it may be festooned with subplots and diversions, but a professor examining the finished tale should be able to discern and write down "the" plot of the book.

Which can often be reduced to a string of statements following this rough model: "Protagonist (major or viewpoint character), finding self in this situation/ dilemma/challenge, seeks to do or achieve X, but faces Y, so Z happens." Though there may be several protagonists (or a major character set against several minor ones) at work in the same story, and much conflict between them, a plot can be derived from all the narrative sound and fury.

This is not necessarily the case in roleplaying adventures, where many plots may collide. Every player character can be a major protagonist, and follow—or try to follow—their own plot. Some of them may make things up as they go along, rather than devoting much time to strategies or tactics, but if they're pushing for specific things, what each of them does can be labeled a plot.

Not to mention the metaplot, or over-arching situation and chain of unfolding events (these countries are at war, World War II in particular, and "as our story begins, the Allied forces have just been swept from the face of Europe, and—") described by the DM when providing the background setting, and the various dark and devious plots of the non-player character villains (also played by the DM) seeking to frustrate the PC heroes.

## Shackled By Story

Unlike a novel or short story, where the goal is to entertain but there's only one ringmaster (the writer) choosing the road to that fun that the tale takes, roleplaying sessions should allow and encourage the players to shape the unfolding story. Their entertainment is lessened when DM-provided carrots and sticks are too obvious, and slain—or at least forced into gasping, staggering life support—when the sequence of events feels "railroaded."

There's momentary satisfaction in smashing down a door, finding the Lost Gem, or finally shoving your sword through the Dread Deathheaded Dragonmage, but lasting satisfaction in roleplaying is felt by players when they achieve something meaningful, when they change the world in some small way, or take a clear, gloat-worthy step toward achieving an ambition. Players want to have an important or even dominant hand in the storytelling, and how a DM structures unfolding play should give player characters choices and something important—that feels important, even if it's not saving the entire world, every time—to do.

> *"Bring on the railway track with the bound captive, the mustache to twirl, and the scheme to endanger the World As We Know It."*

Until a DM knows the motivations of individual players very well, player characters are rarely going to do what a DM wants them to do. Novice DMs may write out endless "flow charts" of "if players get the gem, then this, but if they don't, then that" possibilities, but it's more fun for everyone (ever seen a sports game made up of teams that haven't practiced together beforehand? Often chaotic, but usually wild fun) to keep that to a minimum. If the metaplot a DM has worked out absolutely must reach a particular outcome (this king dies, that castle gets destroyed), the DM should work out three ways this outcome can happen before play begins, and if PC actions look likely to prevent that outcome, adjust matters so the PCs are distracted or pinned down doing something major and important (so players don't feel cheated) in one place or with one NPC while the outcome occurs in another place.

In short, fiction plots end up "set," but roleplaying plots must stay flexible, and are best kept hidden, so the players either know or feel as if their characters are determining the plot.

Often by foiling the dastardly plots of other characters.

## What Is A Dastardly Plot?

So "what the villains are up to" make up the "dastardly plots" that provide resistance to PCs in most fantasy roleplaying campaigns, forcing them into adventures, and are the plots that concern us there.

Yes (cackle), bring on the railway track with bound captive, the mustache to twirl, and the scheme to endanger the World As We Know It. Those sort of dastardly plots.

Any scheme hatched by a villain, from a ruse to frame PCs for a petty crime and so take them away from blundering into, or stopping, other schemes already being enacted by that same villain, is a "dastardly plot." Something as small as a secret, unwritten agreement among trade rivals not to price-war with each other at a village market, or something as great as treason against a wizard-emperor who is to be not only deposed, but slain, destroying the stability of magic over half a world and unleashing long-bound (and therefore ravenously hungry) dragons from their lairs.

Those greater plots last longer and have more influence on play. They mean more, present stiffer challenges, and of necessity are more complicated and take more time to uncover and (try to) thwart. As a result, they are what most people mean by "dastardly" plots. The "silent no-compete over the melon cart" may be just as nasty or profitable, but it's just not in the same world-shaking league.

Yet merely defining dastardly plots is hardly the point. We need to get at what makes any plot juicy and memorable, what makes it bring a campaign to thrilling life and get players excited and eager to either join and further the plot (overthrow the hated monster tyrant, and free all the human slaves!) or to uncover and shatter it (the rebels are really shapechanged monsters, and if they overthrow the king, they'll eat us all in the bloody civil war that inevitably follows!). So we're after the desired elements of a truly dastardly plot.

> *"In any robust fantasy roleplaying campaign, the DM will arrange to have at least two, and usually four or more, plots on the go all at once."*

That is, the features of the sort of plot we want to create—if we're the DM or players in an intrigue-filled campaign whose characters are trying to craft their own plot—if we want to have some lasting fun and build some memories of real achievement, by either following and successfully carrying out our plot, or expose and destroy a foul plot and take care of the dastardly villains behind it.

There is, mind you, no perfect plot, no single truly dastardly plot. If there was, everyone would know it, it would already have been done over and over again until the few survivors arranged things to guard against it ever happening again, and it would therefore provide us with almost no entertainment at all. So you'll find no Perfect Recipe here. What you will find is how to stock a kitchen with juicy ingredients to craft your own killer plots.

## The Truly Dastardly Plot

A truly dastardly plot has both mystery and menace. It must imperil and challenge the PCs (or the PC foes, if PCs are behind the plot), and it must surprise or attempt to mislead them or at least have unknowns they must figure out (by investigations that will inevitably draw them into adventures most people would prefer to avoid, the traps and encounters that are the meat and drink of the fighting side of a roleplaying game).

A dastardly plot shouldn't be easy to figure out. If it's obvious due to the situation (the very elderly king is dying, and six factions all vie to grab the throne, each led by, or controlling as a puppet, someone of royal blood who has a claim on the crown), then it should incorporate some Plan B and Plan C contingencies, fallbacks to be put into operation when things go wrong. (If the dying king anoints one royal as a heir, and it's not the royal of your faction, kidnap and hide that heir right away, keeping them incommunicado and powerless and spreading rumors of their death the moment the king dies—but keeping them to use if "your" royal gets killed in the strife that follows.)

These contingencies should all have been arranged beforehand by someone who thinks deeply or deviously enough to impress the players (once those players begin to see what's happening), and more importantly to enable the plot to survive collisions with the hostile plots of others.

Oh, yes, other hostile plots galore. In any robust fantasy roleplaying campaign, a DM will arrange to have at least two, and usually four or more, plots on the go all at once, even before any PC plots get hatched and going.

There's nothing wrong with plunging players into a bewildered state where they thought they knew everything that was going on in the happy kingdom their characters have grown up in, but realize that skirmishes, battles, disappearances, robberies, and monster sightings are suddenly occurring all around them with bewildering rapidity and in astonishing numbers, and they haven't a clue why, what triggered all of this, and which way to jump and swing swords next, to try to restore order. Or even to try to figure out who's a friend, and who's just a smiling foe.

A superior dastardly plot—obvious or not—should also involve some conspirators whose identity or whereabouts are unknown, and perhaps some impostors (so when PCs triumphantly kill the Pirate Lord, they discover the next morning that the real Pirate Lord is laughing at them just as triumphantly from halfway across the kingdom, and they've really killed some poor wretch— perhaps the realm's Chief Justice, or a kindly noble who has long sponsored the PCs—who was magically transformed to look like the Pirate Lord). Look at the number of Shakespeare plays that involve mistaken identity and impostors. Look at why so many of his characters pretend to be someone else. Some of the reasons are silly, but some can readily be re-used. These sort of deceptions—or any deceptions—tend to make plots last a lot longer, lead to lots of confusion and running around/adventuring possibilities, and force players to think or speculate as well as hack at whatever's nearest.

## Don't Forget to Spice Things Up

Which brings us to the specialized ingredients in our plot kitchen; the spices, if you will. (No, this isn't the "sex" chapter; this time, we're talking a different sort of seasoning.) DMs, know thy players. Players planning on spinning plots of their own, know the NPCs or other players you want to deceive or defeat.

What do they find irresistible? Do they like—or hate—puzzles? Being frightened? Can or can't they resist chasing anyone who runs away, or hacking at any slithering, tentacled monster they see lurking in shadows? Maybe they long to be accepted as truly noble by the snooty nobles, or have the princess say "yes" to their entreaties. Perhaps they want to swim in rooms full of gold coins, or have the power to control all the merchants in a kingdom, to set fashions or "own" powerful locals so those powerful people leap to obey their every calmly-murmured command.

Find their buttons, then craft plots that push those buttons. Or as an aunt of mine once put it, "Make those marionettes dance!" Tailor your plots to what your players or in-game foes want more of, or can't resist.

That doesn't just go for the lures that will drag others into your plots; that goes for the rewards the plots should yield them along the way.

Like a movie director, you're trying to arrange things so the action will arrive at moments when the players around the gaming table shout in triumph, or sit back grinning in satisfaction. When they solve the riddle, or finally catch and kill the marauding bandit, or (please forgive the cliché—things are clichés because they work, over and over again, remember) rescue the princess. It's your campaign, after all. The only people you have to please are your players (or fellow players). When they get bored with rescuing princesses, it's time to stop. (And be sure to slap them with a few double-crosses along the way, such as discovering the hard way that, unlike the others, this particular princess is a megalomaniacal tyrant, and "rescuing" her has set her free again to terrorize the world and everything in it, and it's all your fault.)

The important thing is to know what your players—all of them, because tastes may vary widely from one end of a gaming table to the other—will find to be satisfying rewards. Give them those rewards. Not too easily or too often, but often enough that they want to come back for more battering each gaming session. You are, after all, doing this for them (it is to be hoped).

# When We Grow Mighty

Yet when we have triumphed again and again in adventures, and risen to become the meanest you-know-whats in the valley, what then? If no Masked Terror of a foe can ever hope to match us, what plots will then seem dastardly?

The easy—and so, too often used—solution is to build a super-monster, a godlike colossus of a Leviathan Uberdragon, so we go toe-to-toe against someone simply stronger. This forces us to get allies, or trick the Uber-Foe into a situation where we can collapse the castle onto it.

However, there are two less popular and therefore more attractive alternatives. One is the Temptation Plot, where we the successful veteran face something that tempts us into folly (godhood? An emperorship?). A lure that may fool us into overreaching, so longtime foes can rush in and crush us when we fall or are made weak.

The other is the mirror of how we must fight the Uber-Foe. It might be called the Uber-Conspiracy, or Fighting Many Tiny Foes. It's when many nobles, or merchants, or monsters in an area all work together to be rid of us, and we find ourselves betrayed by those we thought were our allies, or too weak to ever dare to challenge us, or whose numbers we never thought we'd ever face in seemingly endless succession. The time when we must either find some brilliant new road to victory, or learn the old, old lesson from before we were mighty: it's time to run away, if we would live to fight another day. (When Conan once more loses it all and flees into another land to start all over again, alone and coinless.)

## What We All Want

In life, everyone searches for meaning to it all, for some guidance or some sign that we're doing the "right" things, or what's right for us. We want to succeed, and we want things to make sense. To have a plot.

Yep, we want life—and the lives of fantasy characters we play—to have plots. Yet easy and clear isn't satisfying. To have some real sense of achievement, we must clear up doubt, solve mystery, and overcome some stiff challenges. We have to struggle against dastardly plots—and win.

So our truly dastardly plots can't be hopeless, unsolvable, or unbeatable. Yet they must be formidable. They should have twists and surprises, misdirections, and blind alleys, and yet offer clear moral choices (so the characters involved, and the players behind them, can feel right about what they choose to do) and tactical choices (we can't be everywhere at once, so we have to choose to rush to the deserted castle or the dockside tavern—which is the Masked Terror more likely to visit?). This lets some failures along the way not be all our fault, yet lets us own the successes because we chose to go up against the Masked Terror at all.

And because the world needs someone to go up against Masked Terrors, and they seem in all too plentiful supply, choosing to do so can never be bad.

# 16

# Challenge and Response

When I'm thinking about challenge in design, it ain't about challenge rating (CR) or experience points (XP) totals.

The fundamental unit of adventure design for RPGs and MMOs is the encounter, just as the fundamental unit of text in fiction and screenwriting is the scene. Until you master the encounter, your adventures or quests will always fall flat. Isolated, episodic, unconnected encounters can grow dull and repetitive, but surely not every encounter needs to connect to a larger plot or narrative. So, how to construct encounters organically, and let story or sandbox options grow from the base up?

One way to think about encounter design is in purely mechanistic terms. You don't know anything about the Dungeon Master who will run an encounter, or the players and characters who will try to beat it. But you do control the presentation of the challenge and how it works out.

That is, you can present a stimulus to the game and predict the likely paths players will take to overcome it. If you predict the player actions well, you can avoid discussing cases that are best left to the GM to decide, and you can offer follow-ups, which can be the difference between an okay encounter and a great one. I'll discuss follow-ups in more detail at the end of this essay.

The setup could be as simple as saying, "You see a goblin" or as complex as, "You find a heavy, locked book in the abandoned room." Those two particular examples show two extremes on what I call the Action Spectrum.

# The Action Spectrum

The easiest way to think about an encounter's place in the spectrum is, "How likely is this encounter to kill a character immediately?" It's an assessment of threat. Another way to think about it, though, is, "How does this encounter further engage the characters in the plot?" The book discovery mentioned above seems innocuous, but it might score very high on the killing-PCs scale if the book title is "Rituals of Diabolism" and the book is found in the chamber of the king's mistress. And the book has a silent magical alarm, and so on.

Encounters on different portions of the action spectrum require different challenges and setups. Let's run through the six most common types, from highest action to lower action.

## 1. Combat

Everyone knows what a combat encounter is: any situation you have to fight your way out of. This could be an ambush, a duel, a toe-to-toe slugfest, an arena fight, or a running battle through difficult terrain or long stretches of dungeon or castle halls. These could all be discussed in a separate design essay on combat encounter design. But because they are the most common and most familiar type of encounter, I'll pass over them for now; they are vital encounter types and deserve a full treatment on their own.

## 2. Threat and Negotiation

Though we usually think of combat as the most exciting type of encounter, I'd argue that the encounters with the greatest tension are actually the threat and negotiation encounters. I call them "almost-combat" encounters; they are hostile but one or both sides hasn't quite decided it's worth fighting.

In this situation, the challenge presented to the players is someone or something that is powerful, non-threatening, or interesting enough for them to hold back from attacking immediately. A party of 1st-level characters meeting a demon might fall into this category, or a party of any level encountering elves in the woods, or a PC on watch who hears a voice in the woods but cannot see the speaker.

> *"Most players . . . assume that any monster they meet is meant to be destroyed. Finding out the hard way that some encounters . . . could overmatch the party is an interesting twist."*

In these cases, the encounter can be designed to maximize the fun by obscuring the difficulty level (such as the hidden speaker), by providing an unexpected foe (the elves), or by clearly signaling to the players that they are overmatched (such as the major demon and the minor heroes). Combat that could wipe out the whole party may make the players do more than hesitate; they may wet their pants in fear, offering bribes or other concessions to get out of a fight. You have to lay it on pretty thick, though, to get that reaction. Most players, especially in **3E**, assume that any monster they meet is meant to be destroyed. Finding out the hard way that some encounters are written in more of a **1E** or **2E** style (where encounters could often overmatch the party) is an interesting twist. The hidden speaker is usually a conduit for negotiations with a Big Bad Guy, offering terms or threatening dire reprisals if the party does not cooperate. It's common for the players' reaction to default to either tricksterism or heroics.

By "tricksterism," I just mean that the party uses social skills, bluffs, or a well-constructed lie to make the BBG's minion go away, or even reveal information that the party needs (see Information Gathering, below). They outsmart the voice through conversation and leverage, threatening something or someone dear to the villain. This can result in a standoff or in the hidden speaker making a few somewhat hollow threats. The encounter ends without a strong resolution, unless the hidden speaker actually does return with reinforcements, or carries out whatever threat he claimed would befall them.

Heroics, by contrast, is great for keeping the spotlight on one or more players, but it should come with a price. The hidden speaker may have ranged attacks that can't be countered, he may unleash hellhounds when the party defies him, he may follow through on his plan to annihilate the paladin's beloved warhorse. By no means allow heroics to come cheap; it makes the villain less despicable, and it cheapens the players' efforts. Heroics are the response that you might want out of a particular encounter, but that does not mean that the players should be rewarded for making the right play. On the contrary, things should get more difficult for them. This is why they are heroes, after all.

## 3. Chase

While chasing down a villain is a great action scene in films and books, it's a lot less so in video games or RPGs. Movement is inherently less exciting than combat, unless the movement involves lava, rivers full of crocodiles, or rafts sailing down deadly rapids.

That being the case, make sure that when you challenge a party of heroes to chase down a villain, it really does require big successes. Work up the average party success rate with, say, a Ride or Climb check (Athletics or Acrobatics in **4E**). Then make sure that 60 percent of the party will fail any given check. In three or four rounds, you'll likely be down to a single hero trying to catch the pyromaniac/ diabolist/ slaver. Then, require a secondary skill to bring him down, such as a Jump from one horse to another, an attack while climbing, or a confirmed critical skill check (as described in **Kobold Quarterly #3**, "Up the Action!").

While players can turn down the chance to participate in a chase scene, it's relatively easy to goad them into it. A phrase like "The orc courier takes the wand from the dead necromancer and sprints toward the boat by the river" is a good start. A phrase like, "You make the Spot check just in time to see the orc captain slip into the darkness. He's heading toward the main army camp!" might be even better. You know your players' hot buttons; use them shamelessly to start a chase.

## 4. Terrain and Devices

Traps, environmental hazards, alarms, and even watchdogs can fall into this category. The challenge is that the terrain can harm the party or summon watchers if the PCs aren't careful. It's lower on the action scale because the party can always choose to walk away; there's no active threat. The best solution is to always pair a terrain, trap, or device with an engineer, gong-ringer, or monster that is at home in that terrain.

One type of terrain is usually plenty, though you might place obstacles within that one type. Put rocks and whirlpools in a rushing river, for instance, or put some islands of safety in a pool of thin-crusted magma.

Don't forget your terrain in the heat of running an encounter. The two easiest ways to be sure everyone knows about it are to mark it on the battlemat or to use an index card or other terrain stat card. Hand it to one of your players if you like. Finally, you can combine terrain with most of these other types: a chase plus terrain is especially entertaining, and so is stealth plus terrain.

## 5. Stealth

The stealth encounter type is all about tension and release, so you need to ratchet up the danger one notch at a time. Each time the party gets past a guard or a monster, they are putting one more obstacle between themselves and eventual escape. Each time they blow a Move Silently check or inadvertently trigger a magical alarm, the odds increase that they cannot recover by silencing the area or knocking out a minion.

Work with this. Put weak creatures at all perimeter pickets, and put stronger creatures on patrol paths or in chokepoints. Make the characters aware that their disguise or magic is fraying after a combat; eventually, all that blood spatter will give them away.

Time is a powerful addition to stealth encounters of all kinds. Stealth takes time and caution; time pressure prevents the party from dawdling and beating the encounter through dull, repetitive, but effective tactics (scry, invisibility, silence, etc.). When dawn comes, when the army awakes, when the temporary damping of the magical wards is over, the party will be discovered and must flee or fight. Remind the players of this time limit frequently.

Some groups do this all the time. **Call Of Cthulhu** adventurers probably spend at least 60 percent of their time in various forms of information gathering, from witnesses, books, court records, letters, and the like. In **Dungeons & Dragons**, the value of information is still high (wouldn't you like to know exactly what monsters are in the dungeon?), but most play-group styles minimize the role of reconnaissance because it is time-consuming and/or involves only a single player.

This is foolishness on the players' part, but unless they have a military background they may not realize just how profoundly dumb a lack of recon really is. One possible solution is that the deadliest encounters come with what I think of as an antechamber or waiting room encounter. This is a meeting with a creature or clue that says, "Big fight ahead! Figure it out; it won't be a cakewalk!" Yes, you are signaling to the players that an encounter is deadly. Eventually, one hopes, they'll figure this out for themselves before they lose a lot of PCs.

For instance, if the party must defeat a batch of evil druids, they might have an earlier encounter with three or four ettercaps who serve the druids and who are all too eager to brag about their masters' strength. More than that, though, it's best if these pre-encounters mention the numbers or the general invulnerability of the foe. You might not give details, but if a minion brags that his master walks through arrow fire and cannot be slain by mortal hands, the party may choose to spend a few spells or skill checks figuring out the likely immunities and resistances. If not, well, you've given them fair warning; let the heroes' corpses fall where they may.

---

### Discovery and Reveals

While the "Ah-ha!" moments can be really satisfying from a campaign arc perspective, they do not necessarily occur at moments of high drama. They could be very dramatic (and certainly I'd recommend that if possible), but they could just as easily fall into the party's lap, kicking off or redirecting an entire adventure. Adventure hooks, clues, and climaxes can all fall into this category.

For instance, learning the identity of a smuggler or the awful fate of a young noblewoman could easily come from reading a book, intimidating a witness, or bribing a courtier. The information itself has a huge effect on the storyline and future PC actions, and you want these scenes to be successful ones to keep players engaged. But in terms of spell-slinging, sword-thrusting action, not so much. Don't underestimate the preparation required for these scenes; if they fl op, your adventure might have to be shelved, or you might need to do some hasty improvisation. Consider the likely Q&A, and just how much information the players need to follow the story elements.

---

There's a second problem with these sleuthing encounters: they're often dull—poking at documents, or deciphering dusty script, or quizzing some archivist. How do you make the actual information-gathering scene interesting? While divination and class abilities like Legend Lore or Gather Information can make these scenes mind-numbingly mechanical, it need not be so. Open Design adventures make frequent use of player handouts, because having something tangible focuses player minds on that element of the story or mystery. Your own handouts are easy to throw together with a very small bit of prep work.

And of course, documents can have guards, owners, and keepers who must be appeased or outwitted. You can force the party to seek out lorekeepers, scriptoria of arcane knowledge, or wild-eyed hermits who have survived meetings with such foes.

Unfortunately, this runs close to the realm of rampant clichés: everyone is a bearded wise elder, or the tome is dusty and hidden in a dungeon or ruin of some kind. Consider using an unexpected lorekeeper character to hold the vital clue. For instance, if the survivors mentioned above are a maimed paladin and his tiefling mistress, they'll make an impression. If a talking polar bear was once a member of the evil druids' order and has now been banished—well, he's not the average conversationalist, especially if the party needs to climb over pack ice to question him and placate him with a few tasty seals.

## Follow-ups

I recently ran my "Madman at the Bridge" city encounter at Paizocon. It's a fun "ticking time-bomb" encounter that starts with a drawbridge that is stuck open, and some misbehaving machinery. The PCs are sent to fix the problem and find some missing engineers.

But of course this scenario quickly spirals out of control, with alchemical fire, insane clockwork guards, a gnomish plotter and his undead servants, and so on. The final encounter starts as a simple fight against a kobold zombie, then escalates to include the gnome wizard, and then escalates further when it's clear that the entire structure the party is standing in is about to suffer a massive boiler explosion that will destroy the bridge and maybe a chunk of the city and some innocent bystanders.

This adventure winds up as rather more than a simple Turn Undead check. By going from an easy victory to a fully engaged party to a party with more threats than it can deal with, you put the players under ever-increasing pressure. Typically, that's where a good group of roleplayers will thrive and come up with some clever solution to the overall problem. A bad group will fall apart and the mission will fail. I'd recommend that you let them fail, especially if they did not do research, information gathering, scouting, or character preparation for the major fight that is clearly approaching. But adventure failure is a topic for another day as well.

# Conclusion

While combat encounters get most of the glory, you can make other encounter types more prominent and more successful to improve the overall strength of your campaign. By pushing players in social situations, dilemmas, and nonstandard challenges in addition to a healthy diet of heroic combat, you give every class and every player a wider range of responses. Or, the way I prefer to put it, you give players more ways to be heroes.

> ### *Open Design Editor Bill Collins Comments on Chases*
>
> "Impromptu chases can be fun especially when it looks like a villain/enemy/opponent is about to get away, but someone wounds them—improbably and from a distance, but it works. The difficulty with a chase scene in d20 is magnified by the rules which suppress a free flow of dialogue to get the players standing on their feet and the adrenaline pumping. I ditch initiative and ask players to declare actions from left to right. Spells can enable easy escape or capture, so if the option is there, I include a couple of lesser individuals in the chase who the party can catch and interrogate later, and who can bear the brunt of a web without the PCs feeling cheated out of a clever move. Rules lookups during a chase scene really are anathema."

# 17

# On the Street Where Heroes Live

## Bringing Towns to Life in a Fantasy Campaign

### *Ed Greenwood*

*"Tired of dungeons? Well, then; head into town, where the action is!" The grizzled caravan merchant grins, displaying decayed brown teeth, and points down the road. Just the other side of yonder ridge, waits . . . yet another town. How is this one any different?*

Right now, the new town in the campaign is just a name on a map: a place where the PC adventurers want to resupply, get healing, buy some better weapons, and see if they can somehow sell six basilisk scales and a severed leucrotta paw that doesn't smell too good. The DM wants to hit them with The Secret of the Fanged Temple, from a magazine he bought at the last convention.

Obviously the town is a necessary place, but it is still just a name on a map. Let's call it Yonder. Despite the waiting nastiness of that fanged temple, the GM secretly wants the PCs to stay for a bit so he doesn't have to frantically map and create faceless town after faceless town along this road they insist on riding along, no matter what, heading nowhere in particular.

How can he make Yonder come to life? It should be memorable enough that the PCs will want to tarry, without turning it into a grim-foreboding, over-the-top Hollywood movie set.

# The Basics

First, consider the bones of the place: the main-streets map and major industries. Then think about the creeks, wells, and horse ponds; bridges; mills; market square; major intersections; castles or grand buildings of any sort; and notable landmarks such as gibbets, leaning tavern signs, sites of never-failing magical motes of light that dance or appear to burn, and hauntings. Name an inn or other place to stay, note the bed rates, stabling, what food and drink the PCs can get, and the name and looks of who will serve it, and start playing. It's not subtle but, on rare occasions, sufficient unless the PCs are being chased through it at top speed by something deadly. The only way to shirk these basics is to enshroud the place in impenetrable fog, install an officious local watch to keep PCs from exploring, and provide the PCs with just exactly what they most need (imagine a handy inn next door to a temple of priests waiting to heal). If that's what Yonder provides and you tempt the party with at least one local treasure tale, the adventurers won't stay long.

The tale might be "Folk are being murdered by a flying knife that can get into the most tightly-locked chamber," or "The king's zombie chasers are here, destroying the undead that keep crawling out of the ruined castle—and looking for whoever keeps causing them to rise and walk." With the local innkeeper or tavern master installed as the tale-teller, complete with colorful looks and accent to match, they'll see the hook and be out of town by sunrise.

Yet if there's no fog nor chase, you will certainly need more. Look and feel, for one thing: what does the place smell like? What's the skyline? Is Yonder a small forest of smoke-belching forge chimneys, or is it a cluster of overgrown shacks huddled around a way-stables, a shrine, and an all-goods shop? Are the streets dirt, cobbles, or something more formal? Do they wind as if they grew that way, or are they laid out in a deliberate design? Are they deserted, or bustling, or bristling with uniformed lawkeepers?

Think up a few faces and names of those lawblades or shopkeepers. Unless this is a ghost town or everyone is overgrown with the same mysterious fungus, you will need some descriptions, at least a name and a single defining trait for each.

# The Locals

The deeper, too-often-neglected secret that shifts Yonder from a name on a map to a place people call home: the locals. Who dwells in Yonder, and what do they do for a living? Are they happy? Rich? Poor? Why? Where do they get their food? Is the place a simmering cauldron of feuds, or does it stand on the howling edge of open bloodshed (just waiting for PCs to come along and tip things into open warfare)? Does a faith or faiths dominate town life? (And if the clichéd secret cult operates behind all those blandly smiling faces, why is it still secret until the PCs blunder along?) Why are the local crazies considered crazy? Is the place growing or dying? (Which leads again to why: why are people dying off or leaving, or aching to come here?)

Back to the folk who are here right now, standing with hands on hips watching the PCs ride in. Are they smiling (pleasantly or otherwise)? Scowling in dislike? Or looking wary or fearful? Again (to quote little Cindy Lou Who) "Why, Santy Claus, why?"

Every local inhabitant is either drifting along through life or working too hard to look up and think—or they have aims and dreams and goals, things they want to achieve, and opinions about what should happen in future (and what probably will happen, instead). In other words, if PCs are openly serving or on the side of the king or the local lord or temple, they may be hated, feared, or welcomed, depending on recent past events and the resulting attitudes of the locals to authority.

## Answering the Questions

Truly, Yonder is a place of many questions; let's have a stab at some answers. Not that there are necessarily any right answers, but for every town you are detailing, some answers go well with other answers to make it seem believable. Some answers make Yonder seem appealing as a home or at least a base from which adventurers sally forth to adventures elsewhere (but want to return to); and others make Yonder come alive and generate ongoing player interest in local events.

Let us step back for a moment from Yonder, sprawled in its green, leafy, vaguely medieval fantasy-campaign valley, and consider it as the setting of a long-running television show.

Yes, a TV program. Done shuddering? Right. Onward.

A sitcom, to be precise: character-based, rather than having Yonder be the blurry, plastic-to-plot-needs backdrop for the antics of just one violent or crazy family or group of bitchily competing neighbors, or the setting for endless murders that have to be solved through intrepid forensics interspersed with car chases.

## The Trick of Subplots

Yonder needs subplots. Feuds between neighbors, disputes about who will host the fall harvest festival or be named the next mayor or May Queen, and the little mysteries of who's stealing garters or horses or prize turnips, who's setting outhouses afire in the dead of night, and who is leaving beheaded crows on certain doorsteps.

What makes books memorable is the big scenes of battle or confrontation or heroism—and the characters. What makes television series memorable tends to be, yes, the characters. From soaps to hospital shows to countryside comedies of manners, it's the characters.

## A Cornerstone Character

So Yonder needs characters. Not just "that old innkeeper at the Broken Wheel" but Gustable Arondur, owner and master of The Broken Wheel Inn and Fine Table, who limps and aches in damp weather and stares longingly at every red-haired woman he sees, because . . . Well, yes, the DM needs to know what in his past aroused this longing. It might feature in play, or might not, but the DM must know. Arondur, who is in awe of elves. Arondur, who despises warriors in the army of the local king but a score-and-more years back was a hero in that same uniform, winning battles hereabouts for the king who was father to the present king.

Why does he never talk of those days, and treat today's soldiery so curtly? Arondur owns all three rooming houses in town and the brothel, too, yet dresses simply and never spends a coin he doesn't have to. Where is all the money going? And who are the masked women who ride into town in the dead of winter and the middle of the night, once a year, to meet privately with Arondur, leaving him gray in the face and shaking when they depart?

Arondur, who can read books peddlers offer him, from lands beyond the sea whose names even they can't pronounce.

Arondur, who is unmarried but keeps an outland girl in his bedchamber who has been blinded and had her tongue cut out. Those who get a glimpse say she is covered in strange tattoos or writing of some sort.

Arondur seems more than a bit over the top, staggering through game sessions with such a load of secrets on his broad, bowed shoulders. Yet Yonder could have a dozen Arondur-types in it, characters who have secrets and pasts and varied interests, both personal and business. Who in town is Arondur's enemy, or at least rival?

For that matter, who in town quietly or openly stands in league with who else? Not every cabal is sinister. From gossips who meet over tea in farm kitchens to the men who drift down to the stables to smoke pipes and grumble about taxes, citizens anywhere will form groups of friends or allies-of-necessity. They may prevent the new mayor from building his own tavern hard by the bridge. Locals will work together until the inevitable disagreements arise. That is when "accidents" sometimes happen that cost a Yonderman or Yonderwoman a barn, a horse, a wagonload of goods, or even their life.

Which brings us to another question: who will investigate such a crime? Not just the town watch, with certain stats and weapons and numbers, but are we talking bullies? Easygoing, thickheaded buffoons? Eager-for-promotion zealots suspicious of everyone? Rulebook-followers? Can they think their way out of a one-seater outhouse, unaided? Are they competent or merely cruel?

## The Law and the Lively

The nature of the law changes a place. If Lawcudgel Uldroon is a buffoon or lazy drunkard, is there an Arondur in town who will quietly enact real justice? Is this vigilante feared and a man of unknown identity ("That demned elusive Pimpernel")?

The law may or may not have the support of the citizenry. Is Arondur operating alone, or can he call on a band of like-minded supporters? If he has a mob or a network of whispering opinionmakers, they may cause "every man's hand to be raised against" a criminal, or even against a notable local who has escaped formal justice.

## My PCs Fought the Law

Adventurers by their nature tend to run afoul of (or at least end up closely watched by) the local lawkeepers. As a result, most GMs have a vague idea of what the law looks like in town. Yet faceless professionals in uniform are inherently less interesting than a constable with a name, failings, and hobbies.

"Officer 32" may evoke just as much fear as old Uldroon, but only the locals know that old Uldroon makes his own dandelion wine, loves roast boar and sugared rhubarb-pies. If he also secretly wears silken underthings made for ladies of a certain size and high social standing, Uldroon becomes undeniably more interesting.

Moreover, both players and GMs can find ways to exploit the wine or love of pies—that is, for those traits to feature in adventures. Officer 32 is little more than a stern or shouting force to arrest, slay, or keep order, but Uldroon is alive. From his belches to his socks that need darning to his inability to cook any meat without setting fire to something in his kitchen, Uldroon sticks in memory as a real person.

Just like Arondur, and the handful of other Yonderians the DM has really detailed. The best Yonderians—back to the sitcom—keep showing up, episode after episode, or rather session after play session, to stick their noses into whatever's happening. Their involvement generates humor, a sense of place ("Oh, aye, we're in Yonder, all right!"), and eventually player knowledge about who to trust with secrets, advice, or directions.

Player knowledge provides a useful gauge of success. When players around the gaming table start independently suggesting their characters go see Arondur or Uldroon or old Lady Looseskirts at the brothel to ask for rumors, rather than asking the GM out-of-character who in town they should go see, the GM has done it: Yonder has come alive.

## Getting It Right

When players look forward to opportunities to roleplay just sitting down in a Yonderian tavern to talk to locals and visiting peddlers over a tankard or two, Yonder has reached the stage of helping to generate new adventures, and the trick is done.

Now, none of this is new. Veteran GMs have been doing it for decades (in my case, 30 years), and every roleplayer knows or senses it. Yet a reminder is always worthwhile: unless PCs ride away from Yonder, never to return, spending an idle handful of minutes detailing something interesting about the cast of recurring NPCs in Yonder is always worth the time.

Recurring characters provide fertile ground for adventure ideas to spring up and new plots to come to mind: could old Angrath in the corner be sick and tired of these adventurers? Could he be thinking of ways to get them blamed for something and banished from town? Yonder, deep and rich and colorful, becomes a place that matters to players, a place worth fighting for when dragons or marauding armies or raiding orcs come to town.

One last question: what is more valuable in life than something or someone we care enough about to fight for?

GMs, when you create a Yonder, you are crafting a treasure. Make it valuable.

# 18

# City Adventures

Love it or hate it, the standard first adventure in **D&D** is still a traditional crawl, even if it isn't set in a dungeon, caverns, or mines. Adventures in the Demonweb Pits, in a dark lord's castle or palace, or even in a forest are all dungeon crawls: they offer free-fire zones for heroes with massive spells, burst lances, heavy explosive crossbows, and what have you.

I always enjoy the subcategory called "city adventures" because they break the established rules of the **D&D** combat arena. Unlike dungeons and other secluded locations, city adventures are constantly interrupted by the presence of bystanders and busybodies, by the forces of the law, and by villains hiding among the innocent. They can be wildly unpredictable.

The classic fiction example is Lankhmar and the adventures of Fafhrd and the Grey Mouser, but there are plenty of others in the core **D&D** setting: the city of Greyhawk, the city of Sigil in **Planescape**, everything in Waterdeep, Ptolus, and Freeport. In a certain sense, the biggest cities define the settings, and adventuring there is a logical extension of the dungeon.

## City Types and Party Types

To start, you have to decide what kind of adventure you're really dealing with. A city adventure can be all about expectations of behavior. As the designer and DM, you set that standard through what you describe.

If the city adventure is set in a standard human city, that's one thing. If it's a dwarven settlement or even a kobold mining camp, the parameters for expected behavior are different. It is partly the ability to figure out what is and is not allowed behavior that makes such non-human city adventures (well, all city adventures) fun. Dwarves might have a high tolerance for dueling in the streets or halls, as long as the duel is conducted according to the proper forms. Kobolds might not blink at ambushes, but might also have different ideas of proper behavior during daylight hours.

## Weigh the Party

Ideally, a city adventuring party always includes one or more characters who have social skills, Knowledge (Local), enchantment and stealth spells, or psionic powers that allow a party to go around breaking some of the expectations with relative impunity. The party trespasses and commits murder in most city adventures, and it's your job as designer to make sure that this doesn't derail the adventure entirely. If the party is all barbarians, clerics of the war god, warlocks and druids, they may not be the right group for a city adventure. On the other hand, just because there's a bard, rogue, or smooth-talking paladin available in the group doesn't mean that the rest of the party should be ignored.

# Contained Violence

The usual default tool for a party trying to solve problems and defeat villains in a city adventure—combat and mayhem—is not part of the code of accepted behavior in most cities. You either need to hide the combat from the citizens, contain it, allow it, or eliminate it entirely. Here are a few strategies:

## Cheats

Anyone can place a city adventure in the sewers, in the mayor's jail, or in an isolated wizard's tower. Essentially it's a standard dungeon with a more convenient trip back to town. These aren't the adventures I'm talking about, though sometimes it's good to have some locations where you expect big combats to take place. I call those locations "ghettoes," in the older sense of the word: a place where a minority must live by law, whether they are rich or poor, as in the ghettoes of Venice or Prague.

## Ghettoes

Noir crime novels often put their bar brawls, daylight murders, and body-dumpings in the "bad part of town." There's no reason not to use this same dodge in fantasy cities. If your players pretty much expect combat every session and their PCs prefer to beat answers out of prisoners, they may not be the ideal party for city adventures anyway. But make sure that the informers, witnesses, crime lords, monsters, and vile cultists all live in an identifiable part of town. For good examples, I recommend reading the *Thieves' World* books by Lynn Abbey and Robert Aspirin, or any of Fritz Lieber's *Lankhmar* stories.

In the Free City of Zobeck, the kobold ghetto is a place that no respectable human or dwarf visits often, and it is a crowded, dangerous place, full of various kobold mine gangs, silver syndicates, followers of the Red Mask and related cults, and perfectly respectable clockworker kobolds who serve as the protectors and stewards of the city's many gearwork doors, bridges, gates, lifts, and scullions, and devices. All kobolds, though, hold themselves as a breed apart, and are instantly suspicious of anyone who comes to visit them. While they can pass unnoticed among the rest of town as servants beneath anyone's dignity, no human or dwarf can visit the ghetto without becoming an object of curiosity. This makes it all the more interesting to force PCs to visit, because it means that the kobold rulers instantly take an interest in whatever the party is up to. Any combat in the ghetto is quickly hushed up by the kobolds; people disappear there all the time, and when kobolds die at the hands of outsiders, well, no one wants to talk about that either. It's the perfect place to stage a huge fight that everyone denies after the fact, because it is out of sight of respectable society.

## Stealth and Limited Combat

Other city adventures are conducted quietly, by night, in disguise or under false pretenses. The party gets to fight incredible monsters because they do it out of sight, and then slip away before anyone asks any really awkward questions such as "Why is there a zombie on my doorstep?" A party actually caught or even just recognized doing stealthy thefts, break-ins, kidnappings, or sewer expeditions at midnight will have a much tougher time explaining themselves to the watch than a group caught in daylight working with a disguise or fast-talking their way in.

Players often overlook the recognition part, but it's the equivalent of robbing a bank and leaving in your own car. Famous heroes who aren't wearing full helmets or hoods will be recognized at some point. Then the awkward questions come up again. No high priest of the Sun God wants to hear "Why, exactly, were you in the City Morgue at the witching hour, your Holiness?" first thing the next morning.

Sometimes the fights are unavoidable: the wererats come up out of the sewers, the steam golem starts rampaging through the Arcane Collegium, the angels of death fly down from the Death Goddess temple. Stuff happens. Heroes get an opportunity to save everyone very publicly. These fights are good city combat scenes because the party has a free pass to kill monsters, as long as they're saving more of the public than they might harm accidentally. I've always found that paladins, rangers, and certain LG clerics respond really well to these super-hero type scenes. Make it clear that there are bystanders to save.

## Pure Investigation

These adventures are not about combat at all: murder mysteries might feature an arrest, but that's about it. Solving a theft or a kidnapping might likewise be done without requiring the party to participate in more than a single combat. These adventures are more properly mysteries than purely city adventures, but the two genres play well with each other.

# City Law and Order

The big difference in many city adventures is the ever-present town guard breaking up fights, preventing spellcasting, curing villains, arresting people before the PCs can question them, and so on. City adventures benefit when it's not just the PCs who are trying to solve the city's problems. Ideally, the city watch and the PCs work at cross-purposes a bit, to make the adventure tougher to solve.

## Permission for Mayhem

Sometimes, the threat to a city is clear, grave, and immediate, so the prince, mayor, or council gives the PCs free rein to kill the city's enemies. There might be questions about this later if they abuse the privilege, but basically, they have a warrant from the law to do what needs to be done. It's the simplest solution to allow parties to cast Meteor Swarm in the town square.

A careless party may start fires, kill innocent citizens, or just drag in the wrong suspect for torture at the hands of a LE ruler. Just because they have permission doesn't mean acting like they're still in a dungeon is smart. Even this fairly relaxed approach to PC limits can feel constrained. It works best for high-level characters. They have a lot more power, so even being slightly constrained feels like a bigger imposition.

## Shorten Combat

There's a second category of limited combat: the fight that ends when the Town Watch breaks it up. If a villain cannot be defeated in four or five rounds (or however many you decide), he doesn't need to get away with magic or a chase scene. Instead, the watch comes and arrests him or arrests the party.

# Use the Innocent

People in a city will do things that bring them to the party's attention. That you can use to speed up the plot, slow it down, or derail it altogether. Urchins will spy on the party and report back to the villain. Busybodies will tell the party about the illegal dwarven still in the basement. Someone will try to steal the paladin's warhorse.

People in the city have Big Plans, and most of them aren't related to the party's goals at all. I looooove derailing city parties this way, with events described at the start of a session. For example:

- Beggars and bards looking for a handout (or do they know something?)
- Heralds carrying invitations to poetry readings by important nobles
- Bells ringing for temples or funerals (who died?)

- Processions by the victorious King's Own Hussars
- Muggings unrelated to the plot (but PCs will often want revenge!)
- Explosive market fairs (the Alchemist's Gathering!)
- Civic and religious holidays (the Anointing of the Mayor, the Blessing of the Fleet)
- Arrival of dignitaries (the elven ambassador and his new wife)

Cities are active places with their own agendas. To avoid derailing a campaign completely you might want to allow the party a Knowledge (Local) check to realize that some of these are normal events and unrelated to the adventure at hand.

# City Characters

In a dungeon, it's easy to assume that the majority of monsters are evil or at least dangerous. In a city, the majority of characters nearby are totally unrelated to the adventure. How the heck is the party supposed to find the villains, much less defeat them in combat? That's often one of the main challenges. Here are a few of the tricks I like to use in city adventures to keep the party guessing.

## Paladins and Watch Captains

One of my favorite "bits" for city guards, especially guard captains, is the party nemesis. This honorable sergeant has his eyes on the PCs as no-good, unemployed vandals and mercenaries. He is always tailing them, questioning people who talk to them, warning others about their shifty ways, and generally making things difficult for the party. Ideally, he's tough, street-smart, and has a high Sense Motive and a strong Will save, to see through Bluff and Diplomacy and to avoid Enchantment spells. A ring of see invisibility is a plus.

## Nobles, Rogues, and Witnesses

You can also make class and status work for you in city adventures, to divide the party. Cities are full of feudal lords and knights who expect a certain amount of special consideration, and who don't expect to answer to lower-class adventurers at all. Likewise, a city's poor or struggling rogues, smugglers, and whores may not feel comfortable talking to lordly paladins, holy clerics, or even to hyper-lawful monks. A bard might be either low-class or high-class, but either way, some ultralawful character might object to the trashy entertainer and prefer to talk to the honest dwarven sorcerer-scholar. Use NPC prejudices to offer a ready excuse for every PC in the party to take point in talking to important NPCs.

Make sure that some of the witnesses or suspects in a city adventure are not the sorts of people who will talk to everyone in the party as equals. Making a smelly, scraggly druid sit in the palace kitchen seems like punishing the player for his character type, but if you spend a couple minutes of the party's palace visit giving the druid a chance to talk to the palace rats, everything usually works out. Because

**123**

city life is partly a matter of status and hierarchy, you can make this a chance for high-status characters to strut a little, and lower-status characters to subvert the social order.

Player characters invariably ask witnesses to provide information. This seems like a great well of free information, but it's mixed. People forget things, people are greedy, and people are unreliable witnesses at the best of times. Never mind when they are charmed by vampires, extorted by wererats, fading from an illness, or just plain terrified of the local Red Wizards. Roleplaying is built in to many of these encounters. Design your witnesses so that half of them want a side quest or other matter taken care of before they talk. The other half will talk freely, but some of them will lie, cheat, or settle old scores of their own. Sense Motive is helpful in these situations, but it shouldn't be a cure-all. Most practiced deceivers should have high Bluff ranks.

## XP for City Adventures

City adventures tend to have lots of roleplaying encounters, skill encounters, witness side quests and the like, and few straight up combats. For this reason, you must design in story awards or encounter-based awards for acquiring information to keep the pace of level advancement reasonable.

I go further than that. Before the game begins, make it clear that you will award XP during city adventures for avoiding unnecessary combats (unless the party is all evil or chaotic PCs). Fighting the town watch should always count as a defeat for the party in an encounter; no XP. This goes a long way to getting the heroes to act heroically in city settings—because the players know that the rewards are there for them, even if they don't fight more than once per game session. It also means that fleeing the Town Watch can become a frequent story element—after any fight or after finding a major clue that offers big XP, the party will be quick to leave the scene, so as not to lose that XP award due to a confrontation with the watch.

## Conclusion

A city adventure is different because (unlike other adventure types) it isn't about combat, but about information and precision actions. It demands different skills from both players and designers and a greater emphasis on NPC interaction and legal niceties. You need to manage combat spaces to make the core D&D problem-solving tool part of the fun. Maintaining that state of tension between civilization and carnage is what makes a great city adventure.

# 19

# The Underdark

The word "underdark" has existed since about 1978, when Gary Gygax first mentioned it in "D1–Descent into the Depths of the Earth." Since then, it has been expanded, most notably by Kim Mohan in the **Dungeoneer's Survival Guide**, by Carl Sargent with the **Night Below** boxed set, and by Gygax himself with the rest of the amazing D series. Bob Salvatore, Thomas Reid and others expanded it in the *Forgotten Realms* novels. (And not to show false modesty, I've done my share in both **Kingdom of the Ghouls** and **Empire of the Ghouls**).

What keeps us coming back to it? The underdark succeeds as a setting for adventure because it pulls on three threads that gamers love: deep-seated myth, the easy grind, and the outsider heroes.

## The Mythic Underdark

The classic underworld caves and caverns are the parlor to the afterlife, one step away from hell, the River Styx, or the Cerberus-guarded gates. It's not just Western myths that go this direction: Egyptian and Chinese hells are underground, and the Aztec entrances to Mictlan, the land of the dead, are within the cenotes and caves beneath our feet.

Freud could explain this as some sort of primal urge to return to the womb at death, but really, we're talking adventure gaming. Humans have a deep-seated image of land underground as an abode of the gods and the dead. That's worth playing with as a flavor element, just as mountaintops and deep forests have their own resonances. So work those resonances: river crossings are creepier if the boatman is a bit reminiscent of Charon (and passage back is dicey in any case). Advance that hell hound as far as it will go, and give it the chimerical or two-headed Template, or whatever strikes your fancy.

Players expect a little bit of eeriness in the underdark: choose your favorite flavor, such as dark fey, decayed undeath, fishy aboleth or kuo-toans, or even the classic drow fane. Push it a little harder: tie the ghouls to Orcus or the Death God, or give the dark fey a black queen who drives them to steal children and leave changelings behind. Give the aboleth secrets of the gods that existed before man, and magic that leads directly to massive power and complete madness. Then send them on the classic Joseph Campbell hero's journey: leave the civilized world behind, enter darkness, and return triumphant from beyond death and darkness. That's the mythic value of the deep dark. Everyone knows it will be a rough trip, and they half-expect the worst of monsters. Give them ghoul dragons and variant daemons and lich drow and suzerain quickling plague otyughs. The players will complain about the nastiness. But they will brag about the adventure for years afterwards, if their character survives.

---

### Death at the Gates

The other part of mythic feel that I like for the underdark is not to everyone's tastes. Characters who die too close to the gates of Hades? They stay dead, though they linger briefly as ghosts until they can pay Charon off. Underdark deaths are permanent. Raising the stakes this way makes a difference, but it's only fair if the players know about it. Make sure some NPC tips them off early in any adventure in which you plan to follow this direction.

---

## Underdark as Wilderness

Darkness, wet, food, and eternal night—it's possible to run the underdark as a form of survival campaign, slowly losing equipment, food, and health to disease, rust, and decay. Ropes rot. Food spoils, and straps and supplies run out. What mushrooms are safe to eat? Ask the druid, and hope he has the ranks in Knowledge (Nature) or Survival to avoid the poisonous and hallucinogenic varieties.

This campaign depends less on the underworld as a portal to the afterlife or on big monsters than on logistics and wilderness fights over long stretches. Each encounter is more or less a stand-alone affair, with hours or days between them, just like a wilderness campaign. To create worthy challenges, you need to design groups of monsters who work as a sequence of fights near one another. Single monsters always need to have a CR above the party level, because the group will be at or near full strength for each encounter.

There are exceptions, of course, the same ones as on the surface: cities and other settlements. Wherever a group of monsters lives together, encounters can pile on top of each other. While the typical underdark city may have evil drow, demons, and ghouls in it, it still needs some form of dictatorial law and order to make it a livable city. Without rules (no matter how vile), the resources needed to sustain a large population do not flow into the city, and the whole place falls apart. A party is safer in a city of monsters than they are out in the tunnels and empty caverns between those monstrous cities. Even in the cities, murder is only a crime if you kill members of the elite.

> *"That's the wilderness reaction you always want: the sound of pants-wetting fear when the party realizes they're trapped, they're out of resources, and they're many, many miles from home."*

This makes the underdark an easier wilderness to grind through than the surface. Tunnels mean you never get lost or miss important sites. The monsters are all evil, and there are no consequences for slaughter, most of the time. There's no civilization to hold people back from bloodlust. Unlike most wildernesses, you never need to worry about getting caught in bad weather, floods, or forest fires. At the same time, it can be wilderness unlike any other. Some players expect a sort of mega-dungeon. That's the wrong way to look at it, in my opinion. It's a wilderness without rest, without rules, without margin for a lot of error.

What works best for me is to provide natural hazards to remind people that they are out in the black depths, but to keep it hyper-real. To make non-mythic elements resonate with your players depends on what you know of their fears and phobias. Do they hate darkness? Drowning? Tight, enclosed spaces? Force them to swim in the dark through a narrow tunnel. Do they hate heights and fear falling? Put them up on the ceiling in a cloaker city above an Abyss that makes Krubera (the real world's deepest cave) look tame (http://www7. nationalgeographic.com/ngm/0505/feature4/multimedia.html).

Acidic waters, noxious gasses, cave-ins, and constant monster encounters can all channel the party in certain directions. You can literally seal a passage behind them, and force a march for miles seeking another exit. Most players think the underdark is a great place to visit for XP and big adventure, but they all get a little nervous when the mountain collapses and they are shut in with all those miles of monsters. "Dropped into the deep end" takes on a new meaning. Suddenly, the trek is a lot less appealing. That's the wilderness reaction you always want: the sound of pants-wetting fear when the party realizes they're trapped, they're out of resources, and they're many, many miles from home.

In the underdark, that is a lot easier to achieve.

# Heroes as Permanent Outsiders

The third thing to remember about an underdark campaign is that pasty-skinned, half-blind surface dwellers are not really welcome. They aren't drow, or kuo-toans, or illithids, or ghouls. They're the normal ones, but every race around them is profoundly weird in their own way—and none of them trust surface types.

Even if they don't fight the PCs, no one does the party any favors. Getting help, supplies, or just a safe place to rest for a few days is a lucky break. There is no backup anywhere.

The prejudices and hatreds of the underdark races against one another is nothing compared to their hatred of those who see the sun. Unless a party spends some resources on Disguise, *alter self*, and so on, they are always immediately recognizable as "not from around here." That matters if they run into a big city or even a small outpost of monsters that they can't fight their way through. Diplomacy and Bluff are useful even in the underdark. When you need to talk your way through the aboleth force gates, it is harder if everyone hates you to begin with.

There's a silver lining to the constant scorn and hatred the PCs attract in the underdark: friends are treated like gold. Svirfneblin are welcome because they are merely wary. A group of deep dwarves or even xorn might be friendly, and can become useful allies for a party with no one they can trust. The pressure of always fighting and skulking means that an honestly kind reception or an act of generosity will stand out a lot more from an NPC in the underdark. Make that work for you; remind the party that not everyone and everything is evil inhuman scum.

Just most things.

## Conclusion

The underdark appeals exactly because it plays into some deep, dark fears and because it is an innately hostile place. That's what defines heroic action. Any DM who makes things easy on the party is making a fundamental mistake about the nature of the classic underdark adventure. Yes, there is a sense of wonder at the strange world below, but it should be a wonder laced with fear and respect from the PCs.

The underdark is at its most powerful when it is both consistently strange and hostile, and it rises above an easy place to find monsters.

## Does Empire Fit this Mold?

Empire of the Ghouls violates some of these statements because **"Most races you enco**unter are so terrified by the ghouls, that most will help out the group." I would argue that the treachery of the aboleths, the paranoia of the dark stalkers and dark creepers, and the madness of the derro all make them unreliable allies, at best. Yes, there is a sense of a greater threat uniting enemies to some degree. Perhaps that's what makes it sustainable for a longer campaign, over three or four levels.

# 20

# Maps, Monsters, and Bottom-Up Design

The one lesson that I never seem to learn, but that 4E has hammered into me again, is that maps are not something that can be done after the fact in a skirmish/tactical game design. About half of the encounters in **Wrath of the River King** are combat-oriented, and so there are maps for them. And drawing those maps always, always, always makes me think of some cool new twist for the encounter.

For example, in the case of the ettercap, suddenly it became obvious that the spiderkin could take cover behind the trees. For the black fey, a fallen log creates a solution for protection of the controller/witch whose magic is crucial to the foes. For the quicklings, the hollow tree and the cliff were already there, but it wasn't clear where to start the PCs. Following the tradition of many minis and skirmish games, I've added a "starting zone" for the PCs—and fiendishly counted squares to make sure that the foes get a good crack at the PCs early.

None of this is edition-specific, of course. The **3E Tales of Zobeck** benefited from a playtest where one of the players decided to swim out to the barge where the ogres were reloading their ballista. This was a truly heroic but thoroughly dumb move that I hadn't anticipated. Leaping from the bridge to the barge suddenly seemed like a good option to consider. And so on.

# The Value of Maps

What maps do, of course, is force a designer to make some tradeoffs. You only get one map for a **4E** encounter. You only get one map for a **Tale of Zobeck**. The limitations of page size and budget really do bump up against what you want the encounter to do. It doesn't matter whether you're writing for Delve format or a more free-form approach that leaves more design options on the table: you've still got only so many maps and illustrations to work with.

So, you pick your favorites, or the ones that really need the maps to work. In the WotC 4E adventures in particular, there's an assumption that every encounter needs to have a map. I've bucked the trend in **Wrath** because there're so many roleplaying and skill encounters, but it's still 15 maps, some of them very simple, and others very complex indeed.

There's a method to good maps. The person whose map turnovers always impressed me most when I was editing **Dungeon** were the ones from Chris Perkins. They were crisp and complete, with a legend you could read, all areas neatly labeled, lines that met at corners, solid black for the earthen sections of the dungeon, and so one. About a million times better than my typical map turnover. But being clear and legible and having a full explanation of what the various symbols on your map mean is only half the battle. The other half is that the map should encourage a variety of tactics and playstyles. The Madman at the Bridge encounter in **Tales of Zobeck** takes the Paizo/4E approach of piling encounters on top of one another in rapid succession, with no down-time between them. The whole point of that combat sequence is to build up tension and to wear down party resources so that the finale is, well, explosive. Things can go horribly wrong, of course—that swimming PC I mentioned earlier should have been out of the adventure due to the player's own stupidity, but it was a GenCon game and his party tried to pull him to shore—exposing themselves to additional ballista fire—so it all worked out in the end. The point is, each encounter is just a few feet from the next, turning an empty city street into (effectively) a dungeon fight.

The goal for other maps is quite different. You may want to channel the party onto a narrow cliff side path, or have them leaping along tree branches, or climbing up and down crates and barrels in a warehouse. But as long as you have considered the map ahead of time and tested it out, you're serving the needs of the tactical-gamer audience. They love hazards, difficult terrain, cover, and options for flanking or charges. Empty terrain is dull, dull, dull.

Which isn't to say that you can't please storytelling and exploring-oriented players with a good map as well. Planting a chandelier to swing on or a set of scrolls to protect from fiery immolation gives more cinematic and knowledge-oriented players something to work on as well, and many a villain may decide to give a nasty little monologue before using the terrain to effect an escape. Build

**131**

that into your design right from the start, and your BBEG's escape from the battlements will flow more smoothly both as a story element and as a tactical one. For instance, a creature in a castle may leap off the highest tower, land in the moat, and swim to safety. This happens more smoothly at the table if the designer has already determined the falling damage into the moat ahead of time, the swim speed of the escaping foe, and the creatures that his splash riles up and that then attack pursuers on the following round. Piranhas or crocodiles are traditional, but there's no reason not to try enormous killer frogs, electric eels, or even a water troll. A little preparation can make this a seamless getaway—and standing by the side of the moat giving a little monologue while the party fights to keep their heads above water and somehow burn the troll(s) should be a scene worth remembering as well.

In other words: Stats are nice, but tactics are priceless.

## Bottom-Up Design: *Know Three Things About Your Monsters*

All this discussion of terrain leads me to a larger point. My adventure designs start with an outline, but they don't end there. Things change mid-stream, and some monsters become more important, some less so. In particular, you may find that your group will want to occasionally talk to the monsters they meet. It's true that for every encounter, your setup helps determine whether initiative rolls and a fight happen immediately. But it's often more satisfying for experienced players to talk to the monsters first.

> *"Faceless hordes are easier to kill than creatures with even the thinnest personality."*

For that, you need to have at least considered a sentence's worth of material. Think a bit about how each creature fits into the larger picture. A design need not have a full family history, quirks, and lore about every monster. But you would do well to include three things about every speaking monster.

The three things are a name, a relationship, and a purpose.

### Name

The name is obvious in some ways, though you'd be surprised by how often you'll find monsters, even major foes, without a name. This is a huge design mistake, because that tiny little element makes a huge difference.

The presence of a name is an invitation to the DM. It says, "Other monsters can talk about this one by name, in tones of fear, or respect, or contempt." It says, "This monster can introduce himself and banter with the party during combat, or urge on his minions." Having a name means that you are promoting that monster to higher billing in the adventure/movie; it's not an extra or a walk-on. I mean, can you imagine a dragon without a name? What a horrible waste of potential!

The reason to give a name is actually broader. The players control when and how they encounter monsters. That is, they decide whether to press on to the next room or retreat. As a result, they might meet a mid-level baddie when they are exhausted and trying to find an escape route or a bolt-hole to heal up for an extended rest. In those cases, they might be willing to haggle or intimidate the monster that they would otherwise crush.

In the end, giving monsters a name saves the DM from coming up with one on the spot that he might regret later. "Bloodlips" might sound okay at first, but . . . Surely something better is likely to come up if you give it some thought.

## Relationship

Monsters also have relationships, and I don't mean they have girlfriends. I'm speaking of intelligent monsters, who are accountable to the bosses in an adventure. The monsters may have rivals, lovers, or minions of their own. This matters, because a monster with friends or enemies has something to say if a parley breaks out. You don't need a flow-chart to realize that a minion knows less and is easier to intimidate than a mid-level boss. A major devil may just be a mercenary to the main villains, but he's got an agenda of his own. Giving each monster a position in the hierarchy can help you later if the PCs question him. It's not something you need to make a big deal out of in the design, but you should have a slot for him in the rankings.

## Purpose

Finally, monsters have a purpose beyond fighting adventurers. They serve themselves (seeking food and treasure), they serve others (as slaves, minions, henchgoblins, trusted advisors, hired assassins, what have you), and they serve powerful causes (a nation, a cult, a church, a genocide, a vision of power, a coup). Some monsters will just attack to kill the heroes. That's fine for the majority, but eventually the game grows pretty stale if every encounter is a fight.

This is easy to fix if you've thought through the facts of everyday life for those monsters. Those monsters who are less devoted to a cause might break and run sooner, and those who are purely mercenaries might be willing to change sides. The lowest kitchen servant might be tired of the constant beatings. He might even make the offer to betray his masters or their cause . . . And suddenly the story-oriented "talky" players will really want to run with that scene, while even the most tactical powergamer will appreciate the value of inside information from a turncoat. Suddenly that lowly goblin is a lot more interesting than his AC and hp might indicate. Make sure to give at least a quarter of your monsters the option to do something with the party other than fight.

So this is design from the bottom up. Yes, you must have a big, powerful, interesting villain (a topic for another time). But it also pays to consider the rank and file, the middle-ground monsters, and the least powerful servants who hear everything. They are rich in roleplaying and story options; they can provide clues and hints exactly because they are less of a threat than the big combat guns. It's still up to the PCs to decide not to slaughter every foe, but I've found that even relatively bloodthirsty players will stop when it's clear that the foe is frightened or treacherous, has information, and has a name. Faceless hordes are easier to kill than creatures with even the thinnest personality.

## Making Monsters Monstrous

Not many monsters should be cowards willing to sell out their cause. Most should be tough grunts, silent undead, or whatever creature type works for the adventure. This is where the use of minions and large numbers of foes in 4E provides a design opportunity. The vast majority of the foes are suddenly cannon fodder for the skirmishes. But the elite and solo monsters are surprisingly durable against a party, and (unlike in prior editions) they can easily retreat and act as recurring foes. It's just a matter of the math; they have so many hit points that they can retreat without fear of dying on the way to the door.

## What Does This Mean For 4E Design Compared To 3E?

It means that recurring villains and recurring monsters are easy to set up in an adventure, though I haven't seen it done yet outside of **Wrath of the River King**. Elites and solos are more than a tough fight; they can be a fight that PCs don't win unless they have planned a way to keep a foe from escaping. Again, terrain and options for escape are crucial. If the party knows that the River King's servants can easily escape by reaching water, it changes their approach to combat. If the party hasn't figured that out, well, tough luck.

> *"You'd be surprised by how often you'll find monsters, even major foes, without a name. This is a huge design mistake."*

It affects story elements as well. Though the Delve format isn't really set up for recurring villains, it is easy to see how a monster can recur throughout an adventure, each time with a new set of minions, each time escaping. This drives players nuts, of course, especially if you've set up some taunting quips as parting shots from the villain as he escapes. Again. And when they finally run him to ground, they may well find it a lot more satisfying.

This is also where 4E's emphasis on movement powers and spells comes into its own. A cooperative party with decent abilities can usually keep one foe from running at will. The fey—with their teleportation powers—can actually escape these nets rather easily, which makes them perfect recurring foils for the party. The talking bear, the green knight: these are characters the party may meet repeatedly and yet never defeat. Should they be worth more XP when they finally are defeated? I'd argue that a recurring villain is worth a minor quest if he reappears once or twice, and a major quest if he reappears more than twice.

## Conclusion

I consider this entire approach to be design based on the encounter and the monster, the smallest discrete units of adventure design. Those small units can connect through the relationships of the monsters, their reappearance and their mutual betrayals, to be a more complex and satisfying set of enemies for the party. This approach is frustrating to the players in the short run, and much more satisfying in the long run, than a simple top-down villain and his faceless swarms.

# 21

# Monster Hordes
## Epic Heroism vs. Smooth Skirmishing

*"No one will remember today except that two stood against many. I ask you, Father Crom, grant me victory, grant me revenge. And if you will not grant them to me; then the hell with you!"* —**Conan the Barbarian** (1982)

You know the classic scene. Conan lift s his broadsword and wades into battle. He slashes down foes by the handful! Hail Crom!

In books and films, the epic stand against overwhelming odds is a fantasy staple. On the tabletop, it's a rarity. While **3E D&D** characters can have Cleave, the **Dungeon Master's Guide** (DMG) says they shouldn't have too many opportunities to use it.

## Page 49 Says "No Way"

**Third Edition** has a chip on its shoulder about using too many monsters to challenge the heroes. It calls out the problem in the **DMG** encounters section, page 49, where it says any encounter that has more than twelve creatures relies on monsters that are not a sufficient challenge. And thus, the table lists no ELs for large groups of foes. This is problematic for heroic fantasy. Feats like Cleave depend on having large numbers of weak foes. The **3E** suggestion to avoid encounters with more than twelve foes eliminates at least three fun encounter types, namely nuisance encounters (a gang of thieves), mooks-as-terrain, and the fun of massive, epic brawls. It eliminates the "defying the odds" brand of heroism.

Mass epic combats are not encounters for every game session, but occasional swarms of brittle or weak foes should be part of any decent campaign. They can play to PC strengths, and they can give a major villain an army of minions that at least look impressive. The rules solution to making large numbers work is to use swarm/mob rules (e.g., the mob scene in **Castle Shadowcrag**) or to streamline the die rolls as needed. The **DMG** is right in one regard: large numbers of foes can slow down combat to a crawl, and they are a challenge to design properly and to DM properly. Here are some suggestions for making epic battles worth the extra effort.

# How to Handle Hordes

The **DMG** prohibition is meant well, because it is meant to maintain a combat challenge. It's limited advice; weak undead in particular are useful in droves because they can burn off Turn attempts. A large number of monsters aren't meant to be a combat encounter at all. Instead, it is a roleplaying encounter in which the numbers are just a threat or scenery, or the numbers are part of the terrain, meant to keep the party from catching up to the fleeing master villain. This is certainly the case in **Six Arabian Nights**, which has at least two adventures where bystanders or crowds of monsters make encounters more challenging. Crowds are useful tools, but how can you make them work in practice?

## One Stands for Many

My favorite trick is to have three or seven kobolds attack a single character and key their attacks off a single die roll. I roll one d20, and then stagger the results up and down. If I roll a 14 and the kobolds have a +1 BAB, the middle roll is 15. Staggering in sets of three might mean a result of 12, 15, 18—meaning that one kobold hits an AC 17 fighter, or two kobolds hit an AC 15 rogue, and all three hit the AC 12 wizard.

For a set of five attackers, I might stagger in sets of two. The same roll of 14 and a +1 BAB would yield a result of 11, 13, 15, 17, and 19. The AC 17 fighter is hit twice, three hit the AC 15 rogue, and four hit and likely kill the AC 12 wizard. This approach has the advantage of being fast, and you can attack three melee characters with minimal die rolls (three for monsters with a single attack form). In the case of monsters with multiple attacks (claw/claw/bite being the classic ghoul example), you can still go through a round of monster attacks with just nine attack rolls against three PCs, rather than 27 or 45.

The downside is that the monsters do have a "good round" or a "bad round" against each PC. If your one roll is high, the PC might be hit by four or five foes in a single round, taking lots of damage and possibly multiple saves. If the roll is low, a single foe or none might hit the PC. It's a crapshoot. I like this effect, as it reflects a horde either overrunning a hero from all sides, or hesitant and fearful, but it is more dangerous for heroes. One attack roll of 20 can lead to multiple confirmed criticals and a dead hero in a hurry.

## The Swarm Subtype for Mobs

Whether it's masses of rats, zombies, or villagers, the Swarm subtype works pretty darn well. Treat the mob or menace as a single creature. When it takes enough damage, it stops acting like a mob and returns to individuals.

This mechanic is especially nice if you have Good-aligned players driven by an urge to protect the innocent. You can twist the knife if the mob contains women, children, and innocent bystanders caught up in the moment. The NPCs might be wracked with guilt (giving clerics or others a chance to console and absolve them), and the PCs might feel bad about having to stop the mob with fire and sword.

## Cleave and Be Damned

Declare a house rule that anyone can cleave a creature of 4 CR lower than a character's class level. They are not getting much XP at this point, and there's precedent in the old 1E rule that creatures below a certain number of HD could always be cleaved.

## Single Point of Failure

Mobs should usually have a single ringleader or officer. If the party can reach him (which should be difficult) and kill him, they may break the morale of the rest. Worst case, if the party inflicts heavy damage, the mob leader may decide to cut his losses and sound an orderly retreat while dragging some unconscious PCs with them as hostages. Give the party a head to chop off, but make sure that it's not a hydra. One leader who may or may not be in line of sight is plenty. Make it clear that there is a single "big" leader (who could be a Small size evil gnome, but you take my point).

As long as that second creature is a single foe, the party can try to knock him out with a spell or focused melee efforts. If that second creature is a group of monsters spread around the battlefield, there's no way to easily contain the big guys' special attacks or firepower. For more experienced players, I'd recommend making the leader hard to Spot, possibly magically hidden, or disguised. Some leaders should be cowards exactly because they know they are prime targets.

## Flee!

The best solution is to describe and show the whole horde but functionally only use 15 or 20 foes. When those enemies are defeated or the single point of failure dies (and the heroes remain undaunted), the 50 or 100 others lose heart and retreat. They might trickle away at first for a round, then mostly disappear, then outright throw down their weapons and surrender, depending on the party's style. Intimidate checks are appropriate for convincing a foe to surrender.

## Crowd Rules

I've written crowd rules a couple of times, in **Al-Qadim**, for the **Book of Roguish Luck** (Malhavoc Press), **Castle Shadowcrag**, and elsewhere. A simple movement penalty is a great start: if the crowd is hostile, the party should always count as flanked, and it should always count as difficult terrain (imposing a movement penalty). Think of a crowd as terrain that separates the heroes from the Big Bad. Using a crowd as a grappling foe works. You may want to permit Intimidate checks for a hero to force the crowd to part for him.

If the mob is truly fast-moving, require Balance checks or a hero suffers trampling damage underfoot. This sounds a little strange, until you remember that death by trampling in a mob happens in the real world all too often.

Beyond mechanics, remember the important flavor element and describe the feel of the bloodthirsty mob. This can unnerve a player; describing "12 orcs with spears" is setting up bowling pins. Describing a tribe of "50 hobgoblins advancing as a phalanx, spears leveled, large shields interlocked," is something else. Crowds can be menacing, dragging people down to be trampled to death. Crowds with weapons are called armies. Make them sound dangerous; the weight of numbers is a heroic challenge.

# How NOT to Handle Hordes

Some approaches to mass combat are sure to fail, and others must be handled with extreme care. Here's some to avoid.

### "Unhomogenousness"

Trying to run a crowd of goblins or ogres with different ACs, weapons, or initiatives is a mess. For all hordes, standardize everything, including hit points. These are faceless evil minions; differentiating them is counterproductive. All flying monkeys of Oz are identical for game purposes. Hordes should be faceless.

### Waves of Foes

A party that meets a few enemies, fights them, and then draws in more and more foes from the surrounding barracks or caves is more likely to end with a TPK than the party that sees all the foes at the Black Gate at the same time. The problem is that once the players commit to the fight, even smart players are reluctant to retreat. The size of the horde must be obvious from the start.

### Strong Mooks

Masses of foes should be pathetically weak. I suggest a CR at least 4 below the party level (and 5 or 6 lower is much better). They should be slow, and have terrible attack rolls, and low damage. Why? Because they will quickly separate PCs and have eight attacks per round against them. A horde encounter lasts more rounds than a normal, one-strong-monster encounter because it takes longer for the party to fight many foes. Their magic can't turn the tide, even if it can burn off masses of enemies.

> *"Think of a crowd as terrain that separates the heroes from the Big Bad."*

If your mooks are too strong, the PCs can't kill a single one quickly. The HP total for a single more-or-less average foe should be in the range that the party's best fighter can dish out in one or two rounds. The fighter should knock down at least one foe per round. With 20 foes, the fighter will knock down half in ten rounds. It's heavy going.

### Nothing But Numbers

It's easy to get lost in the initiative and number-crunching with masses of foes. Roll dice, determine damage, roll again, and keep it moving.

This is a mistake.

Every round choose half the combatants for "flavor duty." Describe how those ghouls work together to drag a paralyzed PC off the field, licking their lips with long forked tongues. Or describe how a half-dozen spears all jab at Sir Abelard the Paladin—and all miss, turned aside by his magical armor. Remind the party every round that they are outnumbered. Sometimes, that weight of numbers will convince a party to withdraw, or to use better tactics than "we fireball and charge." This need not be entirely a DM thing. If you have a player you trust with that sort of description (i.e., someone who won't bend descriptions to favor the players), give them the assignment of providing a 10-second burst combat description for one PC each round. That way, everyone gets some glory, and you can keep crunching numbers.

## Conclusion

There's no reason not to occasionally throw mobs of stuff at the party. Players will soon learn that sometimes that mass of crocodiles should be avoided. Smart parties will find a way around some hordes. Sometimes that mob of foes can be outwitted instead of outfought (illusionists and bards live for this crowd-based stuff and even clerics can use enthrall to good effect against a mob). Sometimes a party just wants to wreak massive havoc with the feats and area spells that do exactly that. If you set it up properly, you can make a great impression without completely bogging down your game.

## *Other Rule Variants for Waves of Combatants*

Waves of foes can be fun when low-powered creatures arrive, are defeated, and (this is crucial) give the party just enough time to recover or get creative before the next wave hits. Mid-to-high level heroes have a lot of spells and firepower available, enough to take out lots of mooks and minions. Waves stagger the attack, so that no particular spell takes out a majority of the foes. Everyone has a chance to shine.

The Green Ronin book Skull and Bones has a twist on this, namely giving the mook monster **all the firepow**er, attack bonus and AC of a normal creature, but hit points equal to their Constitution. A 10th-level town guard can still hit a PC in a town brawl, but he does go down very quickly when hit. This is ideal for minions who brawl in town, and for balancing offensive and defense. (The mooks have a chance to hit, which, say, goblins never would).

One last option Monte Cook suggested: make all rolls in advance to avoid fumbling with dice. This allows for a very large battle, though it falls apart after 15 rounds or so. If you combine this with excel and the staggered dice rolls mentioned above, you could reduce the time spent rolling and emphasize the tone and tempo of the combat itself.

# Hardboiled Adventures
## Make Your Noir Campaigns Work
### *Keith Baker*

*When I was a boy, I heard a voice in my dreams calling me to battle the forces of darkness. When I could lift a sword, I made my way to the Temple of the Sun and trained to fight fiends and monsters. But I was touched by a force more powerful than the sun itself . . . love.*

*Lilith was married to the bishop, and her tales made me question my faith. I never doubted her stories, not even when I drew my blade across the bishop's throat. It was only then that I found out that Lilith was sleeping with another priest, that I was just a tool to be used and discarded. I escaped to Lankar, but I'm still wanted for murder in my homeland.*

*Today, I'm a sword for hire on the streets of Lankar. Love cost me my faith and my honor. But I still have my pride, and any job I take, I'm going to see it through. I've sworn never to enter another Church of the Sun, never to return to Alaria, never to listen to a damned dream, and above all else, never to let love lead me astray again . . .*

*And Lilith just walked through my door.*

In the past, your players have done their share of dungeon crawls. They have slaughtered armies of orcs, defeated dragons and lich kings, and received accolades from king and peasant alike. But you're tired of traditional fantasy. You feel like something harder and darker . . . less *Lord of the Rings* and more

Thieves' World or Sin City. Perhaps you're in the market for some hardboiled fantasy.

"Hardboiled" is a genre of crime fiction, the realm of Sam Spade, Philip Marlowe, and the Continental Op. In a hardboiled world, little is what it seems, and corruption and violence are the norm. First and foremost, this sort of campaign needs close collaboration between player and DM. A hardboiled adventure is a shift from the "kick in the door and take the treasure" model, and if your players don't want to explore a different tone and style of play, you're not going to be able to force it on them. So consider the following subjects, and discuss them with each player.

## Everyone Has A Past

Hardboiled heroes are flawed individuals. They may be remarkable people with exceptional skills, but they are scarred by loss and failure.

The story that opens this essay is the background for Lucas Caine, a 1st-level fighter. Mechanically, he's not actually a fallen paladin; that is simply part of his backstory. He has lost his faith in divinity and love, and all he trusts now is his sword.

Lucas still has the spirit of a hero, but it is wrapped in bitter cynicism; it's in adventuring that he will potentially find comfort and possibly redemption. When you are setting up a hardboiled campaign, work with each player to develop their backstory. This helps both of you. It gives you hooks to use in developing adventures.

For example, Lucas has a strong motivation to take part in any adventure that involves corrupt or evil priests, especially clerics of his old religion. Bounty hunters could come after him for the murder of the bishop. And, of course, his old lover could appear, begging him to help her. Does she have an explanation for the past? And even if she does, can he trust her again?

Just as it helps you create stories, it helps a player get into the mood of the game and sets his expectations. This isn't about creating the perfect shining knight; this is crafting a character who lives in an imperfect world. By challenging the player to think about his flaws, to consider why he's on the mean streets, and whether he spends his evenings drinking alone or in the halfling bordello, you help prepare him for the adventures that lie ahead.

Discuss the following things with each player.

What was your greatest mistake? "None" is not an acceptable answer; in this sort of story, no one is perfect. This could be the murder of an innocent man or an early career as muscle for a criminal gang. It could be something as simple as trusting the wrong person, failing to listen when a friend was in need, or giving in to greed with disastrous consequences.

**143**

Aside from creating story hooks for the DM, the goal is to learn what the character regrets and why. Does he want vengeance or redemption, and is either one actually possible?

Where do your talents come from? If the PC is a wizard, how did he first come to learn magic? If he studied at an academy, why isn't he still there? If he had a mentor, what became of her?

As before, the goal is to add depth to the character and learn his reasons for adventuring. The classic hardboiled detective is a former cop who became a private eye because of insubordination, betrayal by a partner, or another fall from grace. If he's a fighter, was he once a city guardsman? A soldier in the army? A mugger? How did he go from there to become an adventurer?

What's your motivation? While hardboiled heroes are typically flawed individuals, they stand out in a grimy world because some positive force drives them—something beyond mere greed. Professional pride, a sense of honor, a desire to see justice done in a world where the forces of the law won't provide it... something that keeps him from becoming as soiled as the world around him.

### Vices

The classic detective is a hard-drinking man, but the PC might prefer gambling, paid companionship, or brawling to release her tensions. Explore this. If the PC likes to drink, does she prefer hard dwarf whiskey or fine wines? Does she like to carouse with dozens, or drink alone to numb her pain?

### Sex and Love

The gaming table isn't always a place for a serious discussion of sex. Not every group can handle mature issues. However, sex, love, and lust are all powerful forces in hardboiled and noir tales. Even something as simple as knowing that Belgan the dwarf has a weakness for redheads is useful—because when that tiefling walks through the door with trouble in her eyes, you know to make her a redhead.

So see where you can go with this. What does the character find attractive? Does he have casual affairs, or is he only interested in serious relationships? Does he have a love of his life and, if so, what became of her? Some hardboiled characters are after more than money; done right, a character arc about saving a damsel from the mean streets can feed neatly into a character's history.

## Big Risks, Trivial Rewards

In most **D&D** campaigns, PCs typically acquire vast amounts of wealth, digging up treasures from ancient ruins or stealing the hoards of defeated wyrms. In hardboiled tales, money is usually tight; rent, gambling debts, and drinking money are actual concerns. The protagonist has it tough, but because of his professional pride he only works for a fair wage. Unlike the police, he won't take a bribe, and while he may consort with criminals he doesn't stoop to their level; he takes honest pay for honest work.

The hardboiled approach to money means throwing out any preconceived notions of fair reward. A platinum piece is just as impressive to a 10th-level character as it is to a 5th-level character; the PC may be tougher, but experience doesn't magically bring wealth. The world around the PCs also reflects this; NPCs will be more susceptible to bribery, and a wealthy aristocrat may be more dangerous than a fighter of the same level, because his money lets him pull political and legal strings.

Perhaps the adventurers will fight a dragon, but he won't be sitting on a pile of gold. Instead, he will be running a thieves' guild, and all his wealth is spread throughout his operations. He has access to a fortune if he needs it, but an adventurer can't just show up and take it from him. This may mean that the PCs have less magic items, or it may mean that they can't afford to buy magic items but still obtain a few over the course of their adventures.

While the adventurers may not receive vast amounts of gold or ancient magic, there are other rewards to be found. Favors are vitally important; if you help the First Blade of the Assassin's Guild, his friendship may be far more valuable than a +1 shortsword. Reliable sources of information and trustworthy allies are both rare commodities, treasures gold cannot buy.

## The Ugly World

In **The Big Sleep**, Captain Gregory describes himself as "as honest as you can expect a man to be in a world where it's out of style." That is the hard reality of a hardboiled campaign. It is a world where greed and lust are ascendant while honor and integrity are distant rumors. If the City Watch isn't actively corrupt, it often has its hands tied. Characters will spend a lot of time mingling with disreputable characters, and while there may be honor among thieves, it is never a sure thing.

The backdrop of an adventure is just as important as the individual characters the PCs meet. Whether it is set in Los Angeles or Sanctuary, the flavor of the city is important. What is the dominant industry that supports the town? Who are the major moguls? Every critical NPC should have secrets of her own, hidden agendas that will shape any adventure she takes part in.

While a DM should consider all of the questions presented above for PCs, another excellent guide to city themes is Ed Greenwood's essay, "On the Street Where Heroes Live." Before the campaign begins, sketch out the goals of the major players within the city. Are two crime lords competing for control of the brothel industry or distribution of illegal potions? Is the local reeve trying to expose the excesses of the local lords—something that will end in brutal retaliation?

The goals could also include communities or groups in addition to powerful individuals. What are race relations like? Is there an elf underclass, freed from slavery but still considered inferior to humanity? Is the orc street gang as bad as they say, or are the orcs scapegoats imported by a mogul to distract the people from his true agenda? Are there any truly devout clerics in the town, or is religion just an excuse to milk the faithful for tithes?

Moving from the big picture down to the table view, players should see just how grim the world is in the everyday details. Life is cheap, and bad things can happen to good people. The trusted barkeep who provided the PCs with information is killed in a pointless brawl. Adventurers may deal with the rich and powerful, but they should also see the squalid side of things—the parts of the city where people will kill for copper.

In combat itself, things shouldn't be pretty. A hardboiled DM won't just say "You hit him for eight hit points and he falls to the ground." A hardboiled DM will describe how a villain's hands clench around the blade as he tries to pull it from his chest, how the blood spreads across his hands as he spasms. Killing someone with a sword is an ugly business, and people do not usually fall to the ground without a sound.

Make death scenes big. Think up some last pleas and curses ahead of time. Bring out the girlfriend or children of the thug to scream at the PCs. And when players are seriously injured, consider the nature of the injury, and the scars it will leave behind. It's an ugly, dangerous world, and the players should never forget it.

## The Role of Alignment

The alignment system does not always work in a hardboiled scenario. Player characters should ideally be better than those around them . . . but they may still be forced to do terrible things. Likewise, in a scenario where trust is a critical concern, *detect evil* shouldn't result in PCs being unwilling to work with a vital contact.

The simplest answer is to remove alignment from the campaign; however, as it is integrally tied to many magical effects, this isn't always easy to do. A second option is to use alignment as a general guideline of behavior, but to say that "faint" alignment auras have no effect; they cannot be picked up with detect spells and don't make a person a valid target for things like holy weapons.

This means that a *holy word* spell is a powerful tool against undead, outsiders, and evil clerics, but it has little effect on a normal creature with 10 or fewer levels or hit dice. You could also take this a step further and say that normal creatures never produce alignment auras—so a holy sword has no additional power when used on a mugger or a swindler.

## Hit the Books

While these ideas should give you something to work with, the best thing you can do is to read the stories yourself. Raymond Chandler, Mickey Spillane, and Dashiel Hammett are all titans in the genre, but there are more recent alternatives. Frank Miller's **Sin City** brings the hardboiled style to the graphic novel, while Stephen Brust and Glenn Cook make the jump from present day into fantasy. The atmosphere is the most important thing to look for; everything else can be adapted. **The Maltese Falcon** is the story of a group of amoral people fighting for possession of a priceless treasure, but change the black bird into the preserved eye of a mighty archlich, and you have a valid adventure with a big fantasy element at its heart.

So pour yourself another shot of mead, strap on your sword, and head for the streets. There is an arrow with your name on it and a woman you wronged waiting at the tavern. If you survive the day, you may be able to put right that terrible mistake you made. But first, you'll have to survive.

# 23

# What Makes a Night Arabian?

S inbad, Scheherazade, and Saladin. Cinematic action. Deserts, camels, and full-blooded horses. Rocs, cyclops, and a phoenix. Harems, star-crossed lovers, and forbidden romance. Ghuls, genies, bandits, and moustache-twisting viziers.

What really makes an adventure Arabian? How do we define a subgenre? How much is rules, and how much is execution?

## It's Not Mechanical

What makes an Arabian adventure work is not rules; it's the story and the flavor that matter. It's the glory of huge treasures and quick death beneath the sands. It's a change of tone and scenery.

That is hard to design well. Anyone can put a sphinx in the desert and run a combat. But why is the sphinx there? What questions can she answer? Is she an oracle? Does she love an androsphinx, perhaps even pine for him? Now we're getting somewhere. Having focused, controlled backstory that drives player action to the center of the story is the trick to a successful Arabian adventure. Grand, sweeping plots should be distilled down to their essences. Creating new rules or monsters is useful if it supports the scenery and simplifies the action. Creating fun, exotic people and setting them in motion quickly helps a designer capture the storytelling side of the *Arabian Nights*.

Great, you say, how do we weave this carpet of compelling, exotic story? One strand at a time.

## Clear Heroes and Villains

Other campaign worlds stress shades of grey; a fantasy Arabia shouldn't. The appeal of *Sinbad* or the *Thief of Baghdad* is that you know where you stand. Sinbad will sail into terrible danger and escape it through cleverness and bravery. We know that the lover who recovers great treasures to win the hand of the Sultan's daughter is going to make it. It is the journey that matters.

Villains make straightforward attacks on heroes without too much dissembling. They aren't skulking—well, the assassins are—but many are quite clearly big bad evil dudes. No misunderstood villains; they really resonate as the power grabber, the manipulative vizier, or the rapacious bandit who really does want your money. All of it.

### Player Character Attitudes

Antiheroes are out. Rogues and rascals must have hearts of gold, bandits must have honor, and all true heroes must keep their word. To do otherwise is shameful. No one—least of all the Sultan—will trust a shameful oathbreaker. Indeed, the original *Al-Qadim* setting included oathbinding genies as part of the setting, whose task was to magically compel dishonorable characters to keep their word. This sense of personal honor, even for the poorest PC, may drive a party of heroes more than gold.

This is something you need to know about the audience as a designer and know about your players as a DM. Will they go help star-crossed lovers? Will they choose the right thing over greed? Are they idealists or pragmatists? Once you know, you're in great shape. My assumption is that if you want to play in or run an *Arabian Nights* setting, you have at least a bit of a heroic streak, rather than being purely mercenary.

### What About the Rubies?

All this is not to say that player characters can't be greedy. But wealth is a consequence of correct, heroic action. It is not a goal in itself.

This is the hardest thing for players about Arabian adventure: gaining and losing treasures in a hurry. I think a great Arabian campaign hits the heights and the gutter fairly often. Sinbad shipwrecked constantly. Douglass Fairbanks' thief only pretended to be a prince, but he was able to best true princes for love. PC heroes probably aren't fighting for love (it's a tough motive to pin on a party of 4 to 6 characters at once...), but they are able to rise to the Sultan's court and return to the status of peasants in the arc of a campaign.

I think it is entirely in character for a first-level Arabian adventure to hand the party an insanely expensive, pure white warhorse—and then to lose it after just a session or two, to a hungry efreet or a conniving horse thief (who later offers it back to the party in exchange for a quest). This is what Fate can mean on an individual level: quick changes of fortune are part of the atmosphere.

### Strange but Familiar

We understand the desert raider and the caliph as stereotypes, enough that players and DMs are not adrift with the culture. Stereotypes work for us, providing anchors to start from. It is fun to trade warhorses for war camels when the underlying logic of the setting is similar, with a few tweaks around the sacred status of hospitality, the nature of religion, and the role of the elemental forces in the wilderness.

Arabia is the **D&D** world's version of Spring Break: you go there for a change of scenery. For this game, you don't want or need to understand the difference between Shiite and Sunni, or the difference between Persian folklore and Arabian folklore. You just need to know whether the fire mages are on your side or not, and maybe a few simple rules of behavior: the bond of salt, the times of prayer, or the correct way to speed a camel through the desert.

## Nested Stories

For the advanced designer or DM, the nested nature of some Arabian tales, using flashbacks and stories-within-a-story, could yield excellent results. In game play, this is easy to do: when the party visits the oracle or the storyteller in the market, they hear the start of a story. Play out the primary combat or scene within it, and then return to the main story. The same thing can be done with a mirror or dream—you fill in the outer shell as a framing device for the core story.

Or you may decide that it's more literal, and characters are whisked away by genies from the present day to the founding of the Sultanate, or the Age of Giants, or a roiling typhoon around a zaratan. They complete an entire adventure before the genie whisks them back to report to the Sultan.

## Conclusion

Arabian adventure requires mastery of tone and the simple presentation of the exotic. Clothing, sensory details, monster selection, and all other elements of the setting are important to convey a culture that is familiar enough to be playable, but strange enough to appeal to our sense of the exotic and wondrous. Little bits of extra storytelling will win you big points with players interested in an Arabian theme, and the subgenre makes for an excellent break from traditional fantasy.

# 24

# The Mystery of Mysteries
## *Nicolas Logue*

Abody in the alley or floating in the river turns out to be the daughter of Baron Zargaard, and not just another indigent nobody. The Baron wants answers. He wants his precious Becca's killer brought to justice. The task falls to the PCs.

Actually, the task falls to you, Mr. Dungeon Master, and good luck... because a good mystery, while it may be loads of fun for the PCs to unravel, can be a nasty tangle of a knot for you to tie. So let's get to it.

## Step One: *Planning the Crime*

First, let's look at a few cardinal rules to whipping up a conundrum for the party to solve.

### 1. K.I.S.S.: *Keep It Simple, Stupid!*

A lot of DMs overthink the whole endeavor when they sit down to craft a mystery. The basic component of a mystery is nothing crazy; it's just a question that needs answering. Someone is killed, or something is stolen, or something apparently impossible occurs. The PCs don't know how it happened or who is responsible. They need to find out. It's that easy. Start with that. We'll add plenty of spice later.

## 2. Think Like An Investigator

Your PCs will do this, and that will be their experience of playing the adventure, so you should do the same as you design it. Remember, an investigator looks for clues that point to suspects (How was the person killed? When? What traces of evidence were left behind by both victim and murderer? Did anyone see anything?), then investigates the suspects these clues point to (Who had a motive for killing the victim? Who had the opportunity to do so?). Make sure the trail doesn't run cold on the investigators. Leave some clues behind. Provide a list of possible suspects who have motive, opportunity, or both.

## 3. Think Like a Killer

Plot the demise of the victim as if you wanted them dead personally. Be smart. Don't get caught. How do you kill someone and make sure nothing points to you? Do you manipulate someone else into doing your dirty work for you? Do you make it look like an accident? Do you dispose of the body (no body, no crime)? Do you leave clues at the scene that frame another person who also has a good motive for killing the victim? Do you concoct an airtight alibi?

Think like a murderer. If you do your job too well, you'll need to backtrack in order to not break Rule No. 2 (leave a few clues behind), but this is unlikely. There is no such thing as the perfect murder. Just watch a bunch of episodes of **Law and Order** or **CSI** and you'll see just how hard it is to get away with it when a dedicated and competent team of investigators is hunting you.

## 4. There are Exceptions to All These Rules

It's true! Look at **Blood of the Gorgon**. The murders that kick off this adventure are byproducts of the villain's larger plot and not his main goal at all! That's definitely a hard turn away from your standard mystery, but it's a fun turn, and it creates a great mystery. Remember, in a mystery, things are never what they seem.

# Step Two: *Fine-Tuning the Plan*

Great, so we have the basics in hand. Let's look at some nuance. All we've discussed so far applies to mundane mysteries, though these concepts can extend to cover the supernatural. Now let's consider that pesky subject of magic as it concerns mysteries in D&D.

*"Don't be afraid to change the facts as you go."*

## 1. Plan for Divination

If your PCs are high-level enough to cast some interesting divination spells, the mystery might very well be solved before it begins. That's no good. So what do you do about this problem? There are two schools of thought here.

The first is to disallow or otherwise render useless divination. ("The city is in the midst of an omen-storm that blocks the use of divination magic for the duration.") Lame. The second is to give the PCs carte blanche to go divination-crazy and let them solve the mystery in the time it takes them to cast a spell or two. ("Another body . . . no problem. Just let me restudy my spells so we can go kick the snot out of the killer.") Even more lame. I don't like DM fiat, so I never disallow anything, really. Let the PCs use the divination magic they earned or bought. That's part of the game, and part of the fun.

But if the PCs know about divination magic, so do the villains. Don't let divination magic be a problem for your adventure. Instead, make it an opportunity to add new levels to the mystery. A smart villain thinks of what questions a PC might ask a higher power and finds ways to circumvent them.

- **"Who killed so-and-so?"** If the party has access to the ability to ask such potent questions and receive answers, then it's up to the villain to take this into account and make sure someone else strikes the killing blow. If a PC casts *zone of truth*, the villain just needs to get sneaky with his answers or make sure he can answer them truthfully without incriminating himself.

- **"Where were you the night of such-and-such?"** "I was at a party." Smart villains make sure their alibi is true. They show up at a party and get seen while their shadowy hirelings, a slow-acting poison, or a trap dispatches their quarry across town.

- **"Do you know who killed so-and-so?"** "No." A truly devious villain works through many buffers and cat's paws and never meets face-to-face with the actual killers or even learns their names.

## 2. You Get Magic Too!

Magic is friggin' awesome. Use it to the fullest. In **Blood of the Gorgon** we've used fantasy to create murders that are wildly difficult to solve. Look at how we used magic to twist and turn the crime. The gorgon's blood infects the "killers," who then produce blood doppelgangers (or commit the crimes in their sleep), and they don't even know they did it! Now that's awesome. How are the PCs going to figure that out? Great stuff. When designing mysteries for **D&D**, pull out the stops. The PCs get an arsenal of clue-finding spells, so you go ahead and use yours to the best of your ability.

Spells like *nondetection, Mordenkainen's private sanctum, misdirection, false vision,* and *undetectable alignment* are villainous staples, but let's take it a step further. Think outside the box. Want a way to turn the PCs' divinations against them? Let's look at how you can make detect evil blow up in the party's face. A villain casts *magic jar* and trades souls with a key witness or other NPC, maybe even a red herring framed by the clues.

When the PCs cast *detect evil* on this patsy, they'll get a positive result (thanks to your sinister soul mucking up his body). Provoke a fight and abandon this patsy's body when he's nearly dead. Case solved, or so the PCs think, all wrapped up in a nice neat package that you put a ribbon on for them. Justice is served and the streets are safe . . . until you decide to kill again.

### 3. Misdirection is Better than Magic.

Never use magic to cover a crime when old-fashioned legerdemain can do the trick. Pesky spells can pierce illusions. Sure, it might be a great idea to use *disguise self* to sneak up to your victim, but if someone bothers with a *dispel* or a *true seeing*, then the jig is up. Villains who can pull off a great disguise on skill alone, or cover up a crime without resorting to spell-slinging, are the most dangerous. The mere presence of a magical effect or aura is a big red flag to an investigator right away, and suddenly a death that might have been passed off as an accident becomes a definite homicide. If you feel like using magic, make sure you use something that can't be traced or even identified as magic, unless you feel like dropping a pretty potent clue at the PCs' feet.

## Step Three: *The Master's Touch*

Okay, so we have the basics and some thoughts on dealing with magic. Let's move on to the real nitty gritty: techniques for crafting a truly awesome mystery.

### 1. Small Pieces of a Greater Puzzle

Clues! It's all about the clues! PCs love finding 'em. You love hiding them between the cracks. Clues rock! But what makes a good clue?

---

**Let Things Slip**

As the DM, you might think that it's good to "compete" with your players by holding out on clues, throwing lots of red herrings out, keeping the NPCs really tight-lipped, and generally making the mystery part of your game unsolvable. This is a recipe for disaster. Whenever you sense frustration rising, as DM you should be willing to let something slip, or offer a clue, or nudge them in the right direction. Mysteries are meant to be solvable, and as DM, you know your players best. Don't let them get so frustrated that in future they avoid all mystery adventures. Plots are always much easier to understand from the DM side of the table, so be sure to give lots of (small) clues. And small is important here; if the clues give everything away, you've stolen the players' sense of accomplishment. Always make sure that they put together the final pieces of the puzzle themselves, even if you help them a lot with the first few elements of the mystery.

---

First and most importantly, a clue is specific. It should point to inconsistencies with the apparent circumstances. Every clue should tell the PCs something, but a given clue doesn't necessarily need to tell them anything particularly useful by itself. It's when the clues pile up that the real answers come and the fuzzy picture of the murder starts to come into focus.

## 2. Control the Clues

Make sure the first clues you give the PCs offer them a lot of possible suspects, and maybe even mislead them. Read any Sherlock Holmes story and you'll see that our super sleuth gets it wrong more often than right early in his investigations. He barks up a few wrong trees and, after he exhausts these avenues of investigation, he gathers more clues that throw a different light on the ones he discovered earlier. Now he's got the real culprit in his cross-hairs.

You need to control the flow of information in a mystery adventure. You also need to make sure the nuggets you leave hanging out there early on don't give away the real killer or point to your adventure's mastermind in any direct way. Send the PCs fishing for red herrings, lead them on a wild goose chase for a while, and then cough up more clues to get them back on track. Keep the party guessing. Just give them enough info to keep them hungry for more answers, and they, like starving rabid dogs, will devour your mystery and enjoy every damn minute of it.

## 3. Clues Aplenty!

Make sure you have a ton of clues to toss out there. Don't make the PCs' success or failure hinge on one crucial clue that they need to make a DC 30 skill check to discover. This is a sure-fire way to watch your mystery turn into a train wreck. Even with reasonable DC skill checks, a party may miss the obvious or spend too long on a false trail. Have back-up plans in case the PCs miss a bunch of important hints. Maybe a witness, afraid to come forward before, appears later in the game with a crucial piece of information, and then gets killed for helping the party. Bam! Drama and a helpful little hint.

## 4. Don't be Afraid to Improvise

Best-laid plans can explode in your face. Don't panic, don't fret. This is a roleplaying game, not a novel. There is no way to predict what your PCs will get up to. That's the fun of this artistic medium. It's like improv acting—anything can happen. Think on your feet, and find ways to make your PCs' actions part of the adventure even if they are waaaay off the beaten path. Don't be afraid to change the facts as you go.

If the PCs won't drop a red herring, or even invent one all their own, find a way to tie that red herring into your mastermind's plot. Maybe the red herring, terrified she'll be arrested for a crime she didn't commit, does some detecting and churns up some facts on her own. Conversely, if the PCs figure things out too quickly, go ahead and throw some more smokescreen at them. Heck, go ahead and switch masterminds on them if you want. Remember, it's not cheating if it makes the game more fun for the PCs. Don't worry too much about "reality" or adhering too closely to what you prepared. Keep the mystery going.

---

## Resurrection

Long-time Open Design patron and designer Ben McFarland added some pithy comments to this on *resurrection*.

"There's also the option of dominating the killer, the option of modify memory to eliminate his memory of killing the person, and the option of having the mastermind later kill the proxy killer (to eliminate a vital link in the chain of evidence).

"And, in a world where *raise* and *resurrection* are available, I'd have killers who are intent on keeping people dead do things like . . . kidnap people and hold them for a few days while both alive and dead, to make determining the day of demise uncertain without more magics.

Remove a portion of the body when killing the victim, preferably the tongue but the whole head if you want to keep identification slow. Without a whole body investigators can't *raise dead*, they have to *resurrect*—and that's more expensive. They also can't *speak with dead*, which will help foil those who might be hunting for you.

Use an open game license (OGL) material like thinaun, (from **Complete Warrior,** page 136) which captures the soul in the weapon as the person is killed, to prevent that person from coming back or talking.

"You'll want to do all three to both the victim and the proxy killer, which should break most of the chain of association between the victim and your primary killer.

"High-level magic can also use things like *baleful polymorph* followed by an unfortunate drop into a pit of hungry dogs, a butcher or bait shop delivery, or a furrier of some sort. Not only is the killer unaware of his murder, but he has no idea that you gave him the victim. Again, without a body or an idea of time of death, investigators are forced to use *true resurrection* . . . and that's not cheap, or necessarily all that available, depending on the faiths in the area and their attitudes on death. (Take a look at **A Magical Medieval Society** from Expeditious Retreat Press for some ideas on how much coinage a noble's manor might generate.)

"Really high-level magic can do things like *trap the soul*, but that's less killing and more long-term imprisonment."

---

# 25

# "The Anvil in the Dwarf's Soup"

The place of humor in adventure design

*Willie Walsh*

Webster's dictionary defines "humor" as "*that quality of the imagination which gives to ideas an incongruous or fantastic turn, and tends to excite laughter or mirth by ludicrous images or representations . . .*"[1]

"Fun" is defined as "*what provides amusement or enjoyment.*"[2]

In this essay I intend to advocate the inclusion of humor in adventure writing to maximize the fun element of roleplaying games. I will briefly outline some categories of humor that may be adapted for use in adventures and point out the existing *incongruous or fantastic turns* that are sometimes overlooked as already existing in even the most serious of tales.

Some players profess a dislike for humor in RPGs although they can share anecdotes of humorous situations that have arisen in games. It is almost as if humor is an accidental quality so remarkable that it is made memorable simply by arising. I would contend that not only is humor a valuable addition to an adventure, it should actively be designed in. I further contend that there is perhaps more already included in scenarios than people may have noticed.

---

[1] http://www.definitions.net/definition/humor
[2] http://www.merriam-webster.com/dictionary/fun

Humor, where it is used, should be a tool to color and enhance the adventure. It can come in various shades.

Mild humor may be used in the characterizations and reactions of NPCs, and can be used to fix the NPC in the imagination of the players. For example:

*"Ah, deary me!" the stablehand says, stamping the snow off his heavy leather boots. "Cold weather indeed! There are several brass monkeys looking worried out there today, sirs!" He grins and waggles his bushy eyebrows in your direction, head bobbing mischievously.*

Off-stage humor is usually between one or more NPCs perhaps unaware of being under observation. It can be mild or coarser, as the speakers don't know they have an audience.

**[In Trollish]**
*"You don't remember Horsebreath, do yer?"*
*"Naww! Before my time."*
*"He was a good 'un. Once et nearly a whole dwarf from the toes up."*
*"Yeah?"*
*"Yeah. All he left was the beard."*
*"What happened to 'im then?"*
*"Wizard. Went for us, all offended like."*
*"Big 'un?"*
*"Naww! Wizards all do one size only! Had a big magic fire stick, tho. Round here someplace."*
*"How'd you get 'im, wizard I mean?"*
*"Wizard's ain't strong, like. So I sat on 'im. Stuffed the dwarf beard in his gob 'til he stopped wriggling.""*

So-called "silly" humor doesn't appeal to everybody. It does to me, though:

**Entry #35 from Adventure Journal of the Red Knot Company:**

*"In the second chamber of Ulick the Mad's lair, Roghar's temper was sorely tested again, this time by a trap. He was already in bad form over the illusionary monsters in the ante-room and, in his typical barbarian way, he was itching for something to hit. The rogue barely had a chance to give the place a cursory glance when in walked Roghar, looking for trouble. He found it in a hidden pressure pad in the floor that clicked audibly as he trod on it with clumsy feet. A vat of sticky tar poured onto him from somewhere high above. We held our breath, waiting for the inevitable magical flame or other fiery blast to signal Roghar's horrible end. Instead there was a peculiar twang and a whoosh of air as countless white chicken feathers filled the room adhering firmly to Roghar's overcoat of tar. He stood there roaring with impotent rage as we, realising our own mortal peril were he to witness our amusement, ran groping for the exit, blinded by tears of suppressed mirth."*

The appeal of silly humor to me is that it potentially leads up to something deadly serious. Wise players remain cautious in the face of silly humor, because it can be a mask hiding something nasty. The most deadly form of humor is vicious humor. It has to be used with care, however, because if it results in the loss of a player character, it might also result in the loss of a player from your group. A player may accept the loss of a character with regret, but if the loss is accompanied by the laughter or ridicule of other players, he may not feel much like playing any more:

### Entry #40 from Adventure Journal of the Red Knot Company:

*"Alas! The Company is reduced by one with Roghar falling foul of another of Ulick the Mad's traps, this time fatally. Although we counseled him on the wisdom of caution, he seemed to grow more and more maddened as he fell victim to each of the lair's tricks and little japes. No one, Roghar included, seemed to take account of the build up of all of the minor injuries the earlier traps had caused.*

*"We came to a chamber whose door was labelled plainly with the message: 'Caution: Pie Throwing Machine in Operation.' When we'd read out the words to him, Roghar seemed to seethe all the more. Indeed, there was an apparatus at the far side of the next chamber and it began firing out disc-shaped missiles as Roghar charged up. But it seemed that the "pies" in this evil contraption were deadly, for as the first one struck our companion he screamed and fell gurgling to the floor. I poked with my quarterstaff at the remains of the object hurled from the device. The 'pie' was a small, hollowed bowl of granite. It's 'filling' was just enough green slime to fell our valiant barbarian."*

Irony is the close relation of humor that (ironically) can be found in the most serious of adventures. I am a great believer in irony, especially the kind that illustrates the potential of even the most powerful creatures to make a mistake that turns their story in a whole new direction.

Sauron, in J.R.R. Tolkien's *The Lord of the Rings*, makes a master ring to rule over the other magical rings, placing most of his strength into the One Ring. Sounds like a good idea to gain control of Middle Earth. But in battle, Isildur makes a lucky shot and severs the very finger on which the ring is worn. Sauron's spirit flees and he is defeated.

We appreciate the irony of Sauron's situation because it is the kind of dumb luck that is believable in our real world lives. For all his great power, he was undone by someone making a critical hit and his own inability to keep his hand in his pocket.

Isildur's victory forms part of the background story to *The Lord of the Rings*, with his fate too then marking another change of direction. These "left turns," if you like, are what make stories interesting to me.

In a campaign world, it's relatively easy—but dull—to list off kings and queens whose place in history was to beget someone. However, I'm interested in the king who set up the country's first free hospital because, by chance, his coach horse threw a shoe. Stopping outside a poorhouse, the king stepped inside and was moved by what he saw. Ironically, he was eventually reviled as "Bill the Bankrupt" because of his over-generosity to the poor.

I'm also interested in people who learn nothing from history, or worse, take the wrong lesson. A lie, a mistranslation, or a simple misunderstanding can have repercussions. We can even build adventures based on them:

> With stern sincerity, the orcs of Gloomvale teach their children that dwarves eat iron. Although no living orc has ever witnessed the feat, tribal lore passed down the generations says that it is true.
>
> The root of the legend is based on a misinterpretation of the fireside stories of a half-orc traveller named Mut'k. He said that he saw dwarves eating anvil soup.
>
> The recipe for anvil soup did not accompany Mut'k's original telling tale, but the mental image of dwarves crouched over a rust-coloured broth did not overly surprise his audience who tended to meet dwarves on generally bad terms and with little opportunity for in-depth cultural exchange.
>
> Anvil soup was, as it happens, a real dish served in a wayside tavern frequented by one particular dwarf nicknamed Woodentop.
>
> Woodentop was unusual among dwarves in that he was allergic to ferrous-based metals and feared confined places. He was therefore mercilessly jeered by members of neighbouring clans (his own clan simply ignored him as some kind of aberration).
>
> The bullying finally ceased when a plan to humiliate Woodentop backfired, coincidentally making Woodentop moderately wealthy. Apt to dining alone at a particular tavern, his enemies bribed the cook to make and place anvil-shaped crackers in his beef broth, the purpose being to humiliate Woodentop with the symbol of his nemesis rising out of his soup.
>
> But Woodentop quite liked the crackers and he quickly bought the rights to the recipe. Soon a franchised anvil soup was a novel addition to the bill of fare of many roadside taverns in the region. Ironically, the dish proved quite popular among miners and metalworkers and so the legend of iron-eating dwarves eventually came to the orcs of Gloomvale.

The trivial nature of this snippet of history belies its usefulness as a vehicle for developing puzzling and entertaining encounters. For instance, there is probably a clan of dwarves somewhere which claims that orcs work in cahoots with rust monsters. The evidence comes from the habit of certain orcs spreading nuts and bolts in particular areas of their nests. The metal scatterings are commonly near crude traps which the dwarves have interpreted are meant to catch the rust monsters.

Orcs aren't trapping rust monsters. It has never occurred to the dwarves that the nuts and bolts are bait for dwarves.

The theme could be developed into a full scale war precipitated by a rust monster co-incidentally turning a cornered dwarf chieftain into an unwilling nudist. The dwarves will blame the orcs for using the monster as a weapon. And all because of a misunderstanding of the nature of anvil soup.

Player tolerance will determine how much humor can be used in a campaign, and this is something that adventure designers cannot wholly predict. However, it doesn't mean that we should entirely shy away from humor in its many forms. Remember that dictionary definition of fun? Well, it said that fun is what provides amusement or enjoyment. These are obviously going to have different meanings for different players. But I feel that humor has its place, if only a little one, in every scenario. It doesn't have to be as obvious as the barbarian being tarred and feathered. It can be in the meeting with the garrulous stablehand with the quick quip who knows people who know people. Or it can be the overheard chat that gives clues to the location of treasure, or betrays someone's secrets. Whatever the measure, weight, and color of it, I vote for humor as a tonic to jaded GMs and players everywhere. Humor is the extra little something that gives the twist to the fantastic turn of our imaginations.

# 26

# Using and Abusing Misdirection

C astle Shadowcrag makes heavy use of misdirection to keep players guessing, and to send the PCs in the wrong direction. This is part of its formula for success and an ENnie nomination.

## Players Making Bad Choices

There's a reason to lean on misdirection as a tool: forcing a player to go down a single, unpleasant path is much less fun than being offered a choice of paths and the opportunity to avoid the danger. Being forced into a particular action, area, or routine more than once or twice per adventure becomes a burden to players, who grow to resent it. Being offered a choice is suspenseful and entails risks that the player voluntarily assumes. It's a key distinction when considering the player reaction to an area, trap, or NPC.

One of my few worries about the design of the flashback scenes in **Castle Shadowcrag** was that they are initially a one-way ticket. Worse, they are a ticket to something that the PCs don't control, at some random location they didn't choose to travel to, and buried deep in the past of the setting. Fortunately, these scenes make up for this quickly, because the setting is exotic (novelty is worth a lot to players), plus the party has the chance to learn to manipulate Shadow a little bit in the first scene. As soon as their normal powers are restored in the second and flashbacks, the growing sense of "Hey, we know what that black wind is about" outweighs any sense of "Oh no, not again—we're powerless and confused every time we hear that damn wind." It's a fine line.

Misdirection leads the players to make assumptions that lead to entertaining (but wrong) choices for the heroes. Sometimes it's just about a rose garden: when players notice that the roses change color (they will notice, if you mention it often enough), they start trying to figure out what it means. The shadow fey could answer them, and so might Moira, the insane cleric—but the important thing is that they will try to use the roses. They may burn some detection spells, use Knowledge skills, or simply try to figure them out. Nothing comes of it directly, because the rose color is a symptom, not a lever of power. The entire garden is a red herring, the simplest form of misdirection, because it doesn't actually do anything but draw attention.

## Misdirection in Readalouds

The obvious place to design misdirection is in the read-aloud text. That's the first impression players get of a character or location. In Shadowcrag's crypts, there's this description of one room:

> *Skulls sit on shelves next to a small shrine. Small silver sickles, white candles, and an empty oil lamp sit on an offering altar. Behind the altar is a painted screen showing a boatman, a river, and a mass of ghosts and zombies in the water. On the far side of the screen is a golden city glowing on a mountaintop. At the far end is a heap of bones arranged as steps leading up to a chair made entirely of bones. Over the chair hang a tattered black banner and a crossed set of two silvery, untarnished scythes.*

The danger is right there in the open (the scythes are part of a trap), but you will have noticed two things. First, the language leading up to the scythes includes sickles (similar but less dangerous) and is all about the Underworld and the undead. Second, the scythes are "silvery, untarnished" items, which to many players is code for "magic weapon." When I describe the chair of bones in detail, I shift the focus of the description:

> *The chair is made of bones and inlaid with black adamantine runes, showing a carved crown and many names and dates: Kranos Stross, Leander Stross, Adrastus, Haides, Kleitos, Isidoros, Podarge, and a dozen more. The bones themselves include small ones that might be kobold bones, larger human bones, and others that can only be giants, horses, or dragons of some kind.*

This follow-up doesn't mention the scythes at all. Players follow up or base their actions on the highest-priority thing they heard in the readaloud, or the last thing they heard. Highest priority often means a combat threat or a possible treasure. In a case like the throne, which offers a possible treasure in the shining scythes, the idea is to convince a player to inspect the throne with an Appraise or Search check or to just sit in it.

# Fey as a Misdirection-Based Subtype

On a tangent, I have a theory about why adventure design neglects the fey subtype, and why we're unlikely to ever see a "Big Book of Fey" like the **Draconomicon, Libris Mortis,** or **Lords of Madness.** The fey creature type succeeds through misdirection: illusion, trickery, and cheating are their main survival strategy, because their hit points are terrible. Players (especially rogues and bards) enjoy these strategies, except when they are used against the party. Part of this is just the difficulty of the mechanics involved (illusions and disbelief are a pain in the neck, even in **3E**). Part of it is the irksome nature of having tricksters pulling tricks on you; players naturally prefer to be the ones pulling the tricks in the game, rather than being the butt of fey mischief.

When you overuse misdirection and the fey always get the better of the party, it can grow annoying. Annoyance is a great motivator for players, but for some reason, being annoyed by wussy little fey is a little more grating on heroes than, say, being annoyed by brain-sucking aberrations. There's also the matter of fairness.

# Misdirection and Fairness

The ability of the DM to present illusions and hide secret doors means that even when you're describing something to the party, it ain't necessarily so. This can be great fun: Pit traps under woven silk carpets! Illusory chests of gold! A few mirror-image orcs make the raiders look like a mob!). But it quickly becomes self-defeating. Players don't want to memorize the fine points of disbelief rules. Offering choices and encouraging foolish PC actions is the stronger design approach: you are making the player complicit in his or her own undoing.

### *"Predictability is the enemy of GM style."*

To be fair, you can't offer a choice without any context. Even in the most perfect illusion or trickery, there should be a hint that something is not quite right. This is part of the bargain of fairness; players who ask the right questions or have invested in the right skills or spells can make the right decision. In a way, it's similar to the bargain that mystery novels offer to their readers: even if you don't guess whodunit, a proper mystery (or game situation) should contain hints that seem obvious in retrospect.

It is always fair for creatures within the setting to use misdirection based on magic. This is different from the DM deliberately setting out a red herring; it's more tactical, and often an NPC bases it on their skills and powers. An illusory mob is a fine bit of misdirection by an illusionist. Even a simple ghost sound is a good bit of misdirection for a bard who wants to claim that he has allies in the rafters. It's one thing for the DM to point player attention in a particular direction. It's another for NPCs to apply misdirection on their own behalf. You need only be careful with the first form of misdirection.

## Another Tangent: *Treasure Misdirection and Appraise*

At some point, characters want to find the loot. You could use Search checks, but they're pretty dull. I prefer a degrees-of-success list for the interesting treasures. (OK, I prefer degrees of success for lots of checks. I blame Alternity's fantastic success system for this.) For instance, the party finds the stuff on tables and under a flagstone with DC 10 and DC 20 respectively. Finding the gems "hidden" by being incorporated into a chandelier requires that they especially search the chandelier or make a DC 35 Search roll. That way, you reward players who think of looking somewhere interesting, and you reward players who do invest in Search ranks by not having to think.

The same applies to the appearance of treasures once found. The Holy Grail should look like a carpenter's cup, not like a gem-encrusted emperor's chalice. A famous holy sword might look like a mercenary's well-used blade, not an officer's parade sword with an emerald-studded hilt. Things aren't what they seem.

Why does appearance matter if the party is just going to take everything and let detect magic sort it out? It matters for flavor reasons (players want to hear that treasure is really "the good stuff" and description is part of that) and it matters for those times when they can't carry everything or must flee (for instance, a dragon's cave when a dragon returns to find her mate dead and her eggs being carted off). For another example, characters might need to seize loot before a pirate ship sinks, or as a castle is being dragged off into Shadow.... Just like the Search check versus the "description and choice" approach, both approaches reward those who have Appraise ranks and those who just have a good sense of what is truly valuable.

## Conclusion

Misdirection keeps the game interesting for you and for your players, by keeping them guessing about where the threats and rewards really lie. You will need a variety of constantly evolving misdirection strategies, as your players will catch on to some fairly quickly. That's when you move to a rotating strategy: lie, lie, tell the truth. As long as you keep them guessing, your players will enjoy the game more. Predictability is the enemy of GM style.

The DM and players have an eternal catch-up between DM expansion of the play space (with misdirection, emphasis on different skills, and so on) and players narrowing the play space (as they learn all your tricks and optimize against them). This is why I run a 50/50 mix of homebrew and published materials: it keeps the players guessing whether a scenario is based on my own style or someone else's.

# 27

# Stagecraft
## The Play is the Thing

*Nicolas Logue*

A h, roleplaying. What exactly is this wonderful addiction? Why do we do it? How does the fun grab us by the deepest reaches of the soul and never let go? What exactly are we looking for when we sit down with our friends on a Friday night with gallons of our sugary beverage of choice, and enough snacks to slam us right into diabetic shock?

Could it be the dice? Could it be that rare escape from bills, nine-to-five, and all the real-world drudgery? Especially with a jaunt into the liberating days of high adventure where all that matters is the good cold steel in your hand and fire in your heart. Maybe it is the feeling of triumph as you face down a demon overlord in the bowels of the Abyss. Maybe it is the fits of laughter that sneak up on the table when the dice take a dive at the most hilarious of times.

Drama. The play is the thing. For a few hours a week we get together and tell great stories with the help of our best friends and our luckiest dice. We are part audience, part actor, part writer, and all fun.

The number crunching rush ("I just did 245 points of damage!") is part of the fun, but the numbers don't really come alive without a gripping tale to back them up. That natural 20 means so much more when you roll it against the evil Duke who destroyed your village and crushed your character's happiness like an egg shell.

To tell great stories in our games, let's take a look at how the pros do it. Screenwriters and playwrights boiled down the art of story craft to a few essential components. Mastery of these intrinsic storytelling elements comes in handy when we step behind the DM screen. Let's explore some of the basics of conflict and drama though the most elementary pieces of a play or script. We can steal them to inject vibrant drama into our games and to bring our great stories to life.

# Structure of the Story

Before you draw your dungeon or stat up those NPCs, sketch out a rough adventure plot structure. Novelists, playwrights, and screenwriters employ the following structural elements, so let's bring them to our wild world of fantasy gaming. There are three: the inciting incident, the revelation, and the climax.

## The Inciting Incident

An inciting incident is the pebble that brings on the avalanche: that moment in a play or movie without which the rest of the story would never occur. It's not always the first scene in the play, but it can be. It's an important moment that drives the rest of the story into high gear and sets the central conflict into motion. The inciting incident is hard to quantify. It's worth trying. Understanding the nature of the inciting incident can give the DM a powerful sense of how to introduce conflicts and storylines to a regular weekly game.

What's the inciting incident in **Hamlet**? Some people say it's the appearance of Hamlet's father's ghost. Truly though, the central conflict of Hamlet is between young Hamlet and his Uncle Claudius, a tale of revenge that ends in multiple tragic deaths. Therefore the inciting incident is the moment when the ghost of Old Hamlet reveals the story of his betrayal and murder to young Hamlet. Now we're cooking with gas. We've got a conflict; we've got drama. Hamlet's no longer moping around and pontificating on his too too solid flesh. He's plotting against his uncle, planning to find out the truth of his father's death and thirsting for revenge. Now that's a story worth telling (obviously, since we've been telling it on stage for hundreds of years).

What will the inciting incident of your next game be? Nail it down; make it pop with tension and drama. Is it the appearance of a ghost with a story to tell about a PC's past? Is it the discovery of a PC's wife in bed with a guardsman loyal to the evil Duke? Is it when the PCs meet a group of mercenary scum "chastising" a serving boy at the local inn with bone-breaking kicks? Pick a real show starter: thrust them into the conflict in a way that makes them grip the story's reins and hold on tight.

All righty—the first scene has us moving. Now what? We need tension. We need a pot to boil, so that come climax time, steam fills the air and the heat is on. Playwrights use these three things to build up the tension and ratchet up the conflict: exposition, complications, and revelations.

**167**

# Exposition

Exposition is the least sexy tool, but sometimes the payoff for a great backstory is worth the time it takes to tell it. Exposition is what happened before that the audience (in this case the PCs) need to know. Exposition sets up villains and foreshadows events to come. The worst, most common way to do this is have some NPC show up and yap at the party for a long time. It might be cool if your dramatic NPC portrayal rivets them. It could just as easily leave the PCs unengaged, or worse, bored.

Why not take a storytelling convention from the silver screen? Maybe a flashback scene, in which the players take on the roles of characters long dead, and live out an important piece of your adventure's backstory. This great device shift s exposition into present action. Now the players live the drama in your adventure's set-up. When the time comes to interact with villains, places, and situations set up in the flashback, they will have a visceral emotional connection.

If you tell the players, "Duke Joldras is an evil, evil man. He destroyed an entire village when a young priestess from their local shrine refused to marry him." Who cares? But what if you let the players play the young priestess, her secret ranger lover, stern but caring paladin father, and plucky wizard best friend, and they live out the horror of this bombastic evil nobleman of great power showing up? They know firsthand that he tried to force one of them to marry him, and then razed the town and brutally murdered them all when she refuses. Well, when they encounter Duke Joldras later in your adventure as the PCs, they will really hate that son of a bitch.

---

### Flashback Story

DMs love to write backstory and exposition. Players can easily lose interest. (See the essay "Pacing.") Exposition through flashback allows the DM to have their cake and make the party eat it too.

---

# Complications

Make the obstacles on the path to your party's objective interesting. Monsters and traps are great and faithful standbys. What else can get between the party and their goal? Natural terrain? Weather? People who can't just be bought or killed? How about internal conflicts? Consider introducing a small amount of party strife. The goals of the characters may be related, but different enough, that they have to grind some axes among themselves before they decide their best course of action. Bang, now you've got a great roleplaying scene on your hands. So, Duke Joldras who lives in the nearby keep vexes the PCs' community? Great, we go there and kick his ass. 'Nuff said, right? Wrong.

What if the Duke holds one PC's brother hostage? Joldras secretly made it clear to this PC that if an adventuring party shows up at his citadel doorstep, he will turn little Jimarn into a frog and hurl him off the highest parapet. In fact, if this PC doesn't reveal the party's plan of attack in advance, he'll turn little Jimarn into a pint-sized vampire. Did I mention Duke Joldras is a vampire? Let's make him a vampire; vampires are awesome. Little Jimarn's brother better not tell his friends what's up, of course.

Now we have secrets, divided loyalties, and interesting fodder for roleplaying. This PC needs to think fast and persuade his fellows to engage in misdirection when they encroach on the keep, but he can't tell them why. That should be interesting.

Another PC couldn't care less about the Duke. He's after an artifact of power the Duke possesses called the Shadow Stone, because it can retrieve his long-lost wife from exile on the Plane of Shadows. A third PC is dead set on killing the Duke because he murdered her father, animated Daddy's corpse, and forced her to smite it down while he had a good laugh at her tears.

Ah, drama ensues. These complications add variety to the usual mix of monsters, hazards, and traps. They supply fodder for intense roleplaying between the players. If you've laid the ground work right (and that is the tricky bit—I'll explain how in a moment), you can just sit back and watch the action as the party roleplays out these conflicts, as if you were watching a great movie in the theater. No, better, because you wrote this one yourself.

## Revelations

"I'm your father, Luke. Take my hand and together we can rule the galaxy as father and son." Yep, that's powerful stuff. Use it. Make sure there are more than a few secrets up the NPCs' sleeves that will slap the PCs in the face.

Maybe the vampire Duke Joldras is the long lost ancestor of one PC, and the only one who knows how to break a curse that has plagued their family line for centuries. The curse ensures that the bride of every male of their clan dies birthing their first son. The PC just married and his beloved bride is pregnant. In the chamber before the Duke's inner sanctum this PC uncovers an old family tree that reveals his relation to Joldras and mentions that the curse began with the old vampire over three hundred years ago. Bang! Drama! Now the PC's whole take on the situation shifts and they must make a hard choice. Slay the Duke to avenge the destruction of their town and whatever the vampire knows about the family curse is destroyed with him. Is vengeance worth the life of the beloved wife? I don't envy that PC, but what a fun role to play.

### Summation

Exposition, complications, and revelations should present hard choices. These internal conflicts engage players more than the standard ones in adventures (in this case, party vs. vampire). They completely focus on the player's own character, thus making that character the center of the story. They add powerful drama to the standard conflict. If these elements build the drama up during the Rising Action, the conflict with the Duke at the adventure's climax can be a lot more interesting than just the plain, "You must die because you're evil!" There is nothing wrong with "He's evil," but the Big Bad deserves a bigger slice of hate from the PCs.

### The Climax

Pull out all the stops. You built the adventure's tension up. Now it's time for it to explode. Let all the conflicts hit at once.

Boom, the PCs burst into the tower chamber. The evil Duke Joldras has the young brother in one hand, the Shadow Stone in the other, both held over the parapet's edge: "Kill your friends, or I drop your brother to a messy death below! And you there, if you turn and go, I'll give you this bauble, and your wife shall return to our world!" The vampire turns to a third PC and says: "Your son quickens in your lovely bride's womb, but his birth shall be her bloody demise... unless I tell you how to end the family curse."

Conflict! Hard choices! A daring gambit to save a brother and son. Silver-tongued attempts to wrest the secrets of the family curse from the cagey old vampire. Heck, the party might even get to slay him instead of turning on each other in folly.

If you planned ahead, you laid down clues early to defeat the villain and end the curse—perhaps during your flashback exposition scene at the very start. They come to light when the ghost of the young priestess returns to haunt the evil old vampire during this showdown. All the loose ends tie up tightly in a package fraught with action, drama, and intense roleplaying.

Not a bad day's work, Mr. Game Master.

## Conclusion

If you take a nod from the playwright inside us all, you've probably got a blockbuster on your hands. No, you won't see royalties, but what is fame and fortune compared to the satisfied player smiles at the end of a truly epic adventure? Those Hollywood writers don't know what they are missing. We work in the best medium there is. Now go out there and make it happen.

Lights, camera, dice!

# WRITING, PITCHING, PUBLISHING

# 28

# The Three Audiences

A s an adventure writer, you always have three audiences. You need to please all three to be successful. They all want great adventures, but that phrase means different things to different audiences.

The first is the editor. If your pitch or query is too dull, too mechanical, or too long, you'll never get it approved. In this case, the other audiences don't matter because they will never see your work. The editor wants to please his readers. He knows their tastes, he knows what's being talked up on the boards, he knows what products Hasbro's marketing department will want him to push. Yeah, the marketing angle is tacky but true. You can get work playing to the Hasbro release schedule, but you'll hate yourself. I don't recommend it. To please your editor, write a pitch on a topic that you know his audience loves, and do it in a way he hasn't seen before. Easy, right?

> *"The players are the ultimate word-of-mouth authority, who will recommend your adventure or pan it to others, despite never having read a word of it."*

The dungeon master (DM) is the audience you need to please next. The person who edits has to like your work, acquire it, and publish it, but someone reading it needs to respond to it. What do DMs like? What do they need? DMs like enough backstory to understand the setup, without so much detail that they can't import something into their own campaign. They need concrete, short, read-aloud text that sets up an encounter. They need accurate stats, ideally ones that they can't just pull from the **Monster Manual**. And they need a compelling sequence of encounters with some transitions. Most of all, they want exciting fantasy, with creatures and villains that are ideal for fun gameplay.

You will have noticed that the player comes last. The adventure is really for both the DM and the player, yet there is surprisingly little overlap between the two audiences. The DM needs something that gets the players pumped up, that saves a bunch of work, and that makes running the session smoother. The player wants to be the hero at the center of the action: killing bad guys, stealthing around, or whatever fits his hero concept.

Here's the last audience's secret: If the DM loves the scenario, you are 80 percent of the way there. The player sees the game through the DM's descriptions; if the DM doesn't choose to run it, the player doesn't see the adventure at all. At the same time, the adventure needs to be sprinkled with opportunities for all core classes to shine, and it can't be padded with information that the players never see. In other words, the whole thing revolves around the player, though the player never reads the adventure text. Yes, your final audience doesn't necessarily own a copy of your work. But they certainly know it. There is nothing better than hearing from a group that played through your adventure and liked it. You can never be sure whether it's your design or their DM's talents that made it a success. (If they hate it, was it your bad design or their DM's lack of ability?) The players are the ultimate word-of-mouth authority, who will recommend your adventure or pan it to others, despite never having read a word of it.

# 29

# Shorter, Faster, Harder, Less

Freelance game designers are often paid by the word, just like many other types of writer. You might assume that all those RPG supplements that resemble phonebooks are padded, fluffed up, and filled with redundant mechanics and long-winded rules examples—you know, as a way of expanding a starving freelancer's paycheck. It would be logical, right?

You would be wrong, but not for the reason you might think.

## Small Beats Big

Successful game design doesn't depend on wordiness, despite a few notable counterexamples. In fact, many **First Edition (1E)** and **Second Edition (2E) Dungeons & Dragons** adventures that are remembered as exemplars of RPG design are exceedingly brief. "Queen of the Demonweb Pits?" All of 32 pages, and considered large for its day.

"Steading of the Hill Giant Chief?" Exactly eight freaking pages long. That's it. These days, RPG companies determine project length based on sales data and expected profits. Usually, the marketing department or brand manager says, "We need a big book for August" or "We need a short adventure for January." It is not just the companies that tend to prefer big books to little booklets. The Open Design modules have all run long in response to patron requests. People think they are getting more value for their money if the book weighs more. This is the same mistake that readers make when they compare a novel like **The Dying Earth** (156 pages) with one like the craptacular **Sword of Shannara** (726 miserable pages). Length has absolutely nothing to do with quality.

Magazine editors and freelance coordinators both know this. The reader is as likely to enjoy a four-page article proposing a new class for witches (**Dragon #43**) or a simple system for ennobling player characters (PCs) (**Kobold Quarterly #2**) as a much longer work. Short material is accessible and fun. So why isn't there more of it out there?

## Small Writers Starve, Compact Writers Thrive

A freelancer who writes only for short projects will starve to death. Long projects are a requirement to make a living. The same holds true for book publishers, such as Wizards of the Coast (WotC). They print bigger books because they can charge more for them, and usually reap bigger profits. Yes, there is a point of diminishing returns, where a book is so big that no one wants it or the publisher cannot charge what it is really worth. But as a rule of thumb, "lightweight" is pejorative.

Writing tight and short is a critical skill for a freelancer, even though it would seem to make no money. I offer three reasons for every freelancer to value short, tight prose:

1. All your pitches for long work need to be short.
2. Magazine and web editors adore short articles.
3. Even long works must use compression to succeed.

## The Art of the Pitch

You may remember that I cut a prospective writer's pitches for **Six Arabian Nights** down from 4,000 words to around 400. You may have heard that the Paizo Open Call was limited to 800 words or less. You may know that **Kobold Quarterly** wants pitches done in a matter of paragraphs, not pages. Hollywood likes movie pitches in a sentence.

You need to know how to convince someone to choose your proposal from among the hundreds they see every month. The first step is to convince them in a very short amount of time.

### *Periodicals Are All Instant Gratification*

Regarding point No. 1, consider **D&D Insider**'s content goals. Their guidelines ask for adventures under 10,000 words. That's less than half the length that **Dungeon** printed every month; on the web, short is king. Wizards of the Coast does not want to provide competition for its own mega-adventures. So the **D&D Insider** adventures will be fairly scrawny things. Furthermore, since their articles are meant for computer screens, they top out around 4,000 words.

It's not just WotC. **Kobold Quarterly** will happily run shorter articles more often than long ones. They fit neatly into gaps in layout. They make their point and move on.

Give people a thrill with a cool idea. If you can't put three cool ideas down per page, it's time to wrap up the article or project. Yes, gamers are a patient audience and will read longer work complete with charts and tables, but this is no excuse to be dull and expository. Give them sizzle and rules, and keep it reasonably short. No one wants a 30-page treatise on boots. OK, almost no one.

## Long But Short

Even when you write an **Empire of the Ghouls**, a 154-page adventure and sourcebook, there's not enough room to do everything. Every encounter has to pull its weight.

> *"Never write a single encounter that takes more than three pages."*

Each encounter in "Steading of the Hill Giant Chief "is brief: a room, monster name, hit points, and treasure. That's the essence of **D&D**. Don't forget those elements, and give the reader just a little more. I don't mean that **Third Edition** (**3E**) stat blocks are nightmarishly long compared to 2E. I mean, provide the DM with a sensory or tactical hook that makes the encounter memorable without taking a page to describe. Steading did the whole adventure in eight pages. Never write a single encounter that takes more than three pages (or roughly 2,500 words).

## Six Secrets of Text Compression

There are many ways to learn how to write short, and the most important is practice, practice, practice. Write it once, and then rewrite it shorter with each later draft. Here are six other hints.

### 1. It's Not About You

Avoid falling in love with the sound of your own prose. Text communicates with an audience to make that audience care about what you have to say. You should entertain that audience with surprising, wonderful, inventive glee. Which is a good goal throughout: don't be dull just because you are being accurate. The designer's job is entertainment first of all. Developers and editors will tell you when you are inaccurate. Oh boy, will they tell you!

### 2. Don't Bore Yourself

One trick of writing short is to write an outline and drop everything that bores you. Then write the article, and drop everything that bores you about the article.

Do you have a long, awkward setup? Cut it all; go straight to the good stuff. Does the middle drag with lots of historical detail that even you find numbing? Cut it all down to the bloody, murderous, and exciting bits. Are the stats and mechanics overwhelmingly boring? Minimize the stat blocks by using page references to core materials, by standardizing monsters, or by dropping the filler sections.

## 3. The Clunker Readaloud

Read your writing aloud when practical (obviously, this is for pitches and short articles, not for 40,000-word sourcebooks). You may notice lots of "in order to" or "the result of" or "as the army was taken possession of by the spirits of the ancestors" or other long-winded, passive constructions. Flag them as you read, and cut them all. Use active verbs instead. "Ghosts kept the soldiers marching" is concrete and shorter.

Don't try to fix everything right then; keep reading. Every time you trip over your own tongue, mark the passage to smooth it out later.

## 4. Avoid Abstractions

I call this the barbarian test. If Conan doesn't care about it, neither should you. Unless you are writing a treatise on worldbuilding, no one wants to hear your military philosophy or the economic implications of a bit of fluff. Stick with material that drives the game, that is directly relevant to the DM or player. In **D&D**, that means active magic, violent mayhem, and golden plunder, plus a smattering of sex and power.

Political theory, merchant manifests, ancient history, military strategy, magical theory, art history, characters' childhoods, and a dragon's ten favorite lost treasures are all amusing, but probably have little to do with the action of an adventure game. Use them sparingly.

## 5. Sensory Appeal

Concrete language is a ticket to compression. Taste, smell, sight, sound, feel, and temperature should be elements of any scene—but not all at once!

Pick two and go with those: "The derro grunts as he lifts a corpse onto a meat hook. His back is turned to you, and the air carries the iron tang of blood." That's all you need to set a scene. Describing the walls, the clothes, and so on distracts the players from what's going on. Sometimes you want distraction, but do it deliberately (see "Using and Abusing Misdirection").

## 6. Know What Matters

The most powerful trick to compression is to throw away detailed explanatory material, such as backstory. Instead, focus on the one key element of your piece. In an encounter, mention the monster or non-player character (NPC) before the last sentence of a readaloud. In background or in the rules, focus on goals, motives, and tactics. Roleplaying encounters should feature NPCs with concrete plans or intentions. Trust the DM to figure out how to present those intentions to the players. That last bit is crucial. Over-explaining mechanics or an encounter kills them. Present the intended core material, and then get out of the way. As the designer, your strongest ally is the DM. Feed a DM good ideas, solid flavor, and rich mechanics, and you win them over forever. Weak flavor, tired ideas, and derivative mechanics will lose your gamer audience every time.

Compression helps you inject extra flavor into your manuscript. It makes your text stronger, richer, meatier. Word for word, paragraph for paragraph, tight prose wins over editors and readers.

So cut line by line, tighten language, and avoid flabby topics. Don't think about it as cutting word count. Think of it as improving your game.

## What You Gain

If you do tighten and compress language, not only will editors fall all over themselves to green light your proposals, but your text will crush the competition. Even as your range of projects grows larger and larger, your design and your prose will retain their power because they are concentrated.

Armies use the same principle to win battles: von Clausewitz called it the *schwerpunkt*, the focal point of a battle where forces meet . If you concentrate your effort on using the most powerful language where it will do the most good, you will win over your reader. If you spread your efforts around, then, like a weak line of battle, your design will collapse.

Watery game design is a waste of everyone's time, including yours. Brew yours rich, distill it down, and watch the world beat a path to your door.

# 30

# Buckets in the Sandbox
## Non-Linear and Event-Driven Design

B lame it on **Grand Theft Auto**'s wide-open playspace, or blame it on the advent of mega-dungeons and meandering plots, but the buzzword for adventure design the last few years has been "sandbox design." This seems like a straightforward concept: The action is determined almost entirely by the players, because the setting is just a sandbox full of toys, enemies, and interesting locations. There's no need to create a plot arc. It's the opposite of running an adventure on the rails—telling the story in a linear fashion—because it's all up to the players to decide what needs doing. Let them figure out how to approach the end boss, or for that matter, let them figure out who the end boss is.

Well, not so fast.

Just because an adventure has an open structure doesn't mean it has no structure. All too often, a game designer will plop down a bunch of locations, throw some missions or quests on top, and call it a sandbox design.

I can say with some confidence that's nonsense. That's just lazy design. A more successful approach to sandbox design offers hidden structure that is never imposed on the players, but that does provide crucial tools and information to the DM. Don't let "sandbox" be a synonym for "lazy."

# Structure in a Sandbox

A good sandbox design may appear haphazard and freeform to the player, but if it is designed well, it still has structure and design intent behind it. Though there's no plot arc or linear encounter sequence to plan out, the work still needs to hang together to make a satisfying game experience, whether you are talking about **Grand Theft Auto** or the most recent underdark campaign.

In my experience, designers use at least three forms of structure in a sandbox, each of which can be used to varying degrees by a clever designer: non-linear structure, bucket structures, and event triggers.

## *Non-linear Structure*

Non-linear structure is the traditional approach to sandbox design: You work to make a whole experience for the players, but that whole is not dependent on sequencing. The NPCs do what they do while the players wander around, acquiring clues, treasures, and information about where to go next. This form of design is ideal for embedded mysteries, dungeon adventures, and lost cities, all of which are wide open areas that should at the very least provide an illusion of elastic, flexible story—and more often, should actually provide that elastic story element somewhere under the surface.

In a non-linear structure, the adventure can be completed in any sequence, as the PCs find elements scattered around the area (or even elements found in several loosely linked geographic areas), and then decide how to proceed based

---

### *Branching Structure*

Once a path is chosen, it becomes harder to go to another path. The ultimate example of such adventures are pick-a-path books, but the idea applies to any situation where some player choices are irreversible. If you save the orphan, she's grateful for the rest of the adventure; if you let the slavers carry her off and there are witnesses, your character's reputation is stained and your character is not trusted by street urchins for the rest of the adventure. The players have choices at every stage, but ultimately may reach wildly different conclusions regarding what the adventure is about. This is a variant of the triggered structure, but can be built as a set of linked choices that each affect the state of the sandbox until a final choice sets up the finale.

The more general case of triggered or event-driven structure isn't as tightly linked; it can be a set of completely independent events or triggers that only affect subsections of your adventure area. The tightly-knit branching structure is really just a railroad adventure with two or three tracks that tend to weave back on themselves, rather than a true set of tree-like branches, which would rapidly become unwieldy.

---

on the information they have. The key design element is that sequence doesn't matter; if there are four clues, the PCs need all four to get the solution right (or three and a lucky guess!). If the adventure requires them to visit a few sites, they can do so in any order and expect that the challenges will still make sense. Another way to think of non-linear adventures is that they are essentially the same as the plot coupon approach discussed in **Kobold Guide to Game Design, Volume 1**.

In a certain sense, what this means is that you need to design each encounter as an independent mini-adventure, each not depending too heavily on anything outside itself. Each encounter needs to have a clear beginning, conflict, and hooks for further action. In a true sandbox, some encounters might be repeated, so you may want to design for that possibility explicitly, with first and second visits offering elements that change over time. Another option (if your sandbox is more about exploring time than geography) might be to set a schedule for the inhabitants of a place—as was done with "Gryphon's Legacy," an introductory adventure I wrote that describes the inhabitants of a border castle and where they might be found day, evening, and night.

If you design the non-linear structure with a heavy emphasis on character reactions, I'd argue you are creating an event-triggered design (see page 38). Some might say event-driven adventures aren't sandboxes at all, but they clearly share the element of wide-open player options; those options are merely constrained from time to time when player actions trigger some event. Thus, many of the same principles apply, even though an event-driven adventure might be more plot-heavy and less player-driven than other approaches.

## Bucket Structure

The bucket is a style of limited sandbox, if you like. Rather than a single large play environment, the adventure is designed with two or more such environments. At certain points, the action shift s from one such environment to another: the bucket, in other words, is poured out into another bucket. Thought of another way, the sandbox is scooped up into two or three buckets, or two or three smaller sandboxes.

This is tipping-point design, which I used in my design for **Courts of the Shadow Fey**. The idea here is that the environment exists in one form until the players, an NPC, or a timed event changes everything. It's similar to triggered structures discussed above, though I think of bucket structure as the extreme case of triggered structure. That is, a triggered structure is a character-level design approach: In a sandbox this might mean that you've made an enemy, or foiled an assassin, or learned the location of a crucial clue, triggering a chase sequence.

But in a bucket structure, it's not the relationship between characters or the understanding of the players that flips. It's the whole nature of the sandbox. The whole adventure suddenly changes when a zombie invasion hits the sandbox, or when all gang members are wiped out overnight and the PCs are hunted, or when the dragon in the dungeon finally wakes up and every creature for miles around panics. It's a change of state for the entire environment; the sandbox has flipped out of the frying pan and into the smelter.

This structure addresses two problems with a simpler sandbox: the paradox of choice and the lack of closure. I'll get to the closure element in the "Sandbox Pitfalls" sidebar, but let's discuss the paradox of choice for a moment. The problem that some groups and DMs have when given a sandbox adventure is that, while there are plenty of monsters to kill and strange realms to explore, there are actually too many NPCs and too many areas to choose from. If given a choice, they don't know where to start or what to rate as most promising. It all starts to feel either completely arbitrary ("Let's roll a d8 to choose which tunnel to explore!") or overwhelming ("How big is this city anyway? Where the heck are those efreeti lords we were warned about?").

If the party is expected to explore every element of a sandbox, things can drag. One way to limit this is through these forced transitions I call buckets, but there's an older name for them as well: levels. Dungeons with one-way doors and sliding passages essentially do the same thing as a bucket design. You can't go back to the old state once you've slide down the slimy tunnel, and you can't go back to the pre-zombie-invasion state without first completing the adventure either.

### The Classic Sandbox Pitfall

Though some gamers might consider railroad or linear adventure designs less desirable than sandbox or open-frame designs, the sandbox style is not without its own problem. From the design perspective, the greatest trap is concentrating too much on a locale's or NPC's backstory and history, rather than on elements visible or discoverable to the players. This is a natural tendency; if you can't really talk about plot elements in a concise way, some designers will talk about how a place or character came to be.

Resist this urge.

The elements of a sandbox that matter are those that players see and interact with. The backstory or history may be important, but rarely is it important enough to rate more than a paragraph of description. NPC action and motivation with respect to the heroes are valuable; their inner life, their past, and their relationship with their minions should be considered skeptically. Focus on the here-and-now of the adventure and the action, and your design will provide more and stronger tools for the DM to use in actual play.

## Triggered Structure

The PCs are free to wander the sandbox as they will, poking at creatures and characters. This approach is ideal for city and castle political and intrigue adventures, in which NPC reactions are the main driver of the action. Who knows what and when is the crucial design element that you need to prepare for the DM. Lists of rumors, gossip, and information as well as red herrings need to be tracked in some fashion—and the easier you make the drop-in pieces or triggers for the DM to use, the more successful your design will be.

In most cases, a triggered design can be more-or-less linear or at least can lead up to a climax—these are not sandboxes at all, but rather triggered event-driven plots.

However, triggers can be "sandboxy" just as easily as they can be linked to plot elements. The decision is yours as a designer. If the results of triggering a certain event are that the plot advances, and the only way to succeed in the adventure is to advance the plot in a particular sequence, well, you've designed a linear adventure (not always a bad thing; many excellent games are built this way). If each event or trigger affects only a particular character or location instead of the meta-plot, then the triggers can be part of a sandbox. The party may have made an enemy, they may have rescued a grateful henchman, they may have destroyed a tool they might need later. None of these need to advance the plot. Some triggers—the bucket ones discussed below—do move the character from one location to another, or from one social class to another, or otherwise change the setting and conditions of the adventure.

So, the linear element of triggers is not absolute; various event triggers can release mayhem for a short time but not affect the adventure's ultimate goals. As a designer you should weigh carefully how big each event is and how much it changes the setting. Big changes are fun ("I'll flood the whole dungeon!"), but they can start to feel arbitrary or unfair if the players don't see the trigger as a consequence of their action. For this reason, timers and chronologically-driven adventures are (rightly) derided as linear and railroad-ish. Some scenarios make this work wonderfully, with a sense of impending doom and a clear message to players about what they need to do to avert catastrophe. But these sorts of timed triggers have little place in a pure sandbox, where events should unfold at a pace of the players' choosing.

Ultimately, the sandbox triggers will feel more "natural" if the party's actions always trigger a collapse or setback or plot advance. From a design perspective, you must decide how many NPCs or bits of information they need to find the boss or move to the finale. And this leads to one of the paradoxes of the sandbox approach: though driven by player choices, your finales are often predetermined, even if nothing else about the adventure is.

# The Set Pieces of a Sandbox

Although a sandbox is all about providing maximum player options, it doesn't get a designer off the hook for preparing both excellent set pieces to get the ball rolling, as well as a satisfying finale. Sandbox design often stumbles in providing adventures with closure, because with so many plot threads, characters, and hooks dangling all over the place, inevitably the players will not pick up every element. Inevitably some elements are left lying around at the end of the story.

Let's examine these problems in sequence.

To start a sandbox adventure off, you need either a big bang that lures the party to the locale ("Look, an invasion/murder/gold rush/revolution!") or you need a place that is simply boiling over with issues, dangers, resentments, and impending mayhem. Either approach works, and ideally you don't just pick one or three hooks and develop them, but actually brainstorm dozens of possible hooks and bake them in throughout the descriptions of a city, or the NPC descriptions of a court, or the monster descriptions for a mega-dungeon. The more hooks you have into side plots that are apparently unrelated, but that form a larger pattern, the more chances the DM will have to see that his party picks up those clues over time-arrows and indicators that all point roughly in one direction or another.

The sandbox hooks should slowly lead the PCs to realize that, yes, they could slaughter everything in sight, but there's something bigger going on as well. These hooks may be repeated and obvious (better for some play styles) or hidden and quite obscure (for more advanced groups or longer arcs). Frankly, I've had good success designing these very much as a list (events, gossips, clues) and letting the DM sort out when and where to reveal them. The pace at the table and the group's play style should have some influence on the speed at which the adventure progresses from raw exploration to a more focused set of efforts at a player-chosen goal (but likely one of a set of choices baked into the design).

That is, you offer adventure hooks to get the action underway, and then you provide a huge variety of options that eventually narrow down to one, two, or maybe even three options for a finale. In some adventures, who the PCs align themselves with early on will determine who they face in the finale. For instance, a sandbox adventure in a city riven by dueling factions pretty much requires that the PCs make an alliance with one group and defeat the other in the end. Such a battle becomes the set piece of the finale.

One of the dangers of a sandbox adventure is that it can feel aimless, meandering, and ultimately dull, because there's too little going on below the surface. Experienced players are remarkably quick at picking up clues and hints. Anyone with a sense of narrative knows "how this goes"—but in a sandbox, it's up to them to play along with that expectation, or not. As the designer, you should probably plan for one most likely contingency, for example, a raid on a gang boss's house, as well as a secondary contingency, such as the party aligning itself with that boss to take down a rival. In either case, the details of how that scene play out will be determined by the player and the DM—but a good adventure design provides the key statistics, maps, descriptions, and grace notes that make that finale memorable.

In music, grace notes are accents or flourishes beyond the main melody. In game design it's the same way—throwaway bits of dialogue that sound badass (but establish the villain's character), a nasty bit of necromancy that shows the villain's black heart, or even a dramatic reading of the villain's monologue—while minions move in from every side to flank the heroes. Those are the elements that a DM needs to properly deliver the finale. Provide those keystone elements, and the sandbox adventure will end on a high note.

---

### Assumptions in a Sandbox

Some might say that it's wrong to assume certain actions on the part of the players, that this is somehow linear storytelling. This is nonsense. Good design always presupposes that player actions in a game are at least 80 percent predictable; most groups will try to take the treasure, most groups will try to rescue the princess. Just because some groups don't is no excuse for not supporting the many DMs whose groups do follow the most common sequences of events. Most players do play good characters, and most players do want a D&D game filled with action and adventure. As long as the scenario supports that, you as the designer are supporting the DM in delivering maximum play value for their hard-earned dollar.

Frankly, if a DM's group never takes the bait for a hook and never follows the predicted path for most heroes, the group likely has bigger problems than a badly-designed sandbox scenario.

---

# 31

# Collaboration
# and Design

I've done a lot of design collaborations over the years, some with success, some without. The first I can remember was working with Steven Kurtz on "A Rose for Talakara" for **Dungeon Magazine #25**. It was a big hit and generated a lot of fan mail. About eight years later, the collaboration with Monte Cook on **Dark\*Matter** was quite different, but seems to have generated a lot of positive attention as well. And now I've collaborated in different ways and to differing degrees on the various Open Design projects.

Each of those projects gave me insight into what works and what doesn't. Here are seven hard-won lessons that will help you improve your chances of completing a successful project.

## 1. Pick a Dictator

The design collaboration process is many fine things, but democratic is generally not one of them. In the video game world, the dictator is usually a design lead or senior designer, and the collaborator just a regular designer, junior designer, or level designer. In RPGs, the distinction is often between the in-house designer (who always has final say) and a freelancer (who always draws the short straw).

Ultimately, it doesn't matter how you set up the roles so long as someone has the authority to 1) stop discussion, 2) enforce decisions once they are made, and 3) veto creative dead-ends. I've worked on at least one project with multiple designers all treated as peers, and it was horrible. No one could override anyone else. Everyone felt their approach was best. No matter what was proposed, the others tore it down. The project ended in a creative stalemate and did not produce publishable work.

There's a reason that species develop hierarchies as they evolve more and more social traits. Without hierarchy, too much effort is wasted in infighting and duplicate effort. Having one dictator, benevolent wise elder, or the boss's nephew making decisions is far more efficient. I'm a fan of democracy in politics, but not in the creative world.

## 2. Maintain Forward Momentum

In general, forward momentum is critical in collaborations. Dithering and delay will lead you out of the golden honeymoon period without much getting done (see the chapter on "Creative Mania and Depression"), and one or more of the collaborators into growing dissatisfaction.

My general sense of collaborative design failures is that projects collapse when decisions are allowed to be revisited over and over, when decisions aren't made in a timely way, and when too much time is spent on minutiae or material invisible during play instead of in creating usable design elements. These are all failures of collaboration, when one designer is trying to have it all their way. So when I doubt, I err on the side of pushing ahead. Attempting to nail every decision perfectly is a recipe for creative stalling ("The perfect is the enemy of the good," as Voltaire reminded us). Stalling is what leads collaborations into slow waters. You need to keep surfing the rapids to reach a first draft.

This is why that dictator is vital. Even if the leader's decisions are horribly wrong, good game design includes iterative processes that will find and correct the failure. Development, prototyping, internal playtesting, and user testing all find bad design. The price of fixing it in a later stage is lower than the price of never reaching that later stage at all. Putting an imperfect rules set or story arc out for review in a beta form is always preferable to thrashing around before reaching a beta stage.

Given a choice, always emphasize daily and weekly progress, rather than complete agreement on all points.

## 3. Minimize Creative Differences and Shut Down Attention Hogs

That requirement for progress is, of course, where things can go seriously wrong. Collaborators who disagree don't want to move on, even if they are outvoted and their arguments go nowhere. This is where jealousy, sabotage, and general ill feelings can arise. No one likes to feel ignored. No one likes to see their darlings shot down.

Unfortunately, designers can't afford to have too much ego invested in a particular approach, or they'll never survive a teamwork-based project. It's a paradox. Designers need ego to craft rules and worlds, and need to have immense confidence to put those materials up for the bashing typically inflicted by testers, developers, editors, and managers. Everyone wants to leave their mark and claim credit for the good ideas. Ego is required to propose and defend novel solutions, new genres, and new mechanics that overturn orthodoxy.

At the same time, designers who fight hard for bad ideas are doomed as professionals. If you can't let go of the midnight flight-of-fancy that everyone else hates and that even your boss at the design studio smirks at . . . well, you turn into a crank: "Oh, that Frank, he's always trying to push FTL ships into every space game," or what have you. Designers need to be a lot more flexible than that, and never more so than in collaborations where your charming and lovable quirks run headlong into your collaborator's lovable eccentricities and fancies.

My advice is to fight hard for your ideas with the best data you have, the most stirring rhetoric you can muster, and the most Machiavellian deployment of politics and favors you can pull together. I exaggerate slightly on the last point: Machiavelli would probably not recommend collaboration but, rather, extermination or isolation, and you should not lie to or deceive your fellow collaborators. However, I would urge you to consider the reactions and alliances you can form around a design that is the work of many hands. Simply put, collaborative design does include some of the same stresses and problem as politics in other environments. If your efforts fail to win the day, quit. There's no sense being a damn fool about it.

Remember: There are more game design ideas in the world than there are hours in a lifetime to work on them. If one doesn't pan out, abandon it ruthlessly and commit yourself wholeheartedly (not grudgingly or with silent sabotage!) to the new direction. You'll be hailed a man of reason, you'll win friends, and you'll even be able to say later, "Well, we went with your idea back in the Tutorial, so hear me out for this part. . . ." A little humility among game designers is a virtue that can pay powerful dividends.

## 4. Know When to Fire a Collaborator

While humility and a little careful advocacy can work wonders in collaboration, the more frequent problem is that of designer ego sabotaging the collaboration entirely. Some designers are convinced they should take the design lead position and that their take on issues is the correct one. One session of playtesting or user testing is usually enough to convince the designer in question that this is not the case, but some egos don't even agree when the playtesters all balk.

That's when someone needs to have a heart-to-heart with that massive ego, and either talk them into working collaboratively with others, or fire them from the project. If a collaborator can't or won't take feedback and cannot take "no" for an answer, then they don't have the right temperament for collaboration and would be better served working on their own. Maybe the resulting game will be heralded as genius. Maybe it will fade into obscurity. In either case, it will stand or fall without impeding the progress of large, collaborative, team-based work.

If you find you can't work with someone, ask the dictator to shrink the group. Most lone-wolf designers will be happier to strike out on their own, and your group will move toward a finished design faster if you aren't always wrestling with a "never wrong" team member.

## 5. Know Your Design Strengths and Style

Not everyone has the temperament for collaboration. And even those who do may choose only to collaborate rarely; it requires sharing ideas and accepting that some of your proposals may be rejected. Likewise, it requires you to establish good reasons for rejecting the proposals of others. This creative seesaw (when it works) results in stronger work for everyone. In really powerful, long-term collaborations, you'll find there's a division of labor into types.

In musical collaborations, you'd see this in the division of songwriting into melody and lyrics. In game design for RPG adventures, you might see one collaborator working on the flavor, characters, dialogue, and story/quests, and the other working mostly on tactics, mechanics, and rules-based triggers for action. Or you might see one designer working mostly on level design and maps, while another works on monster design, and a third on treasures and equipment.

This works best if you already know and agree on what your strengths and weaknesses are. Collaboration teaches you at least as much about yourself as it does about your partners in crime. They will certainly point out your flaws, gently or otherwise.

## 6. Build Up Trust: Love Truth, But Forgive Error

The Internet style of flamewar and attack is anathema to collaboration; such attacks in a close collaboration are entirely destructive. Yes, you want to fight hard for your ideas and defend them, but winning the argument by savagely deconstructing a partner's design pitch or rules sketch weakens their confidence in their abilities (and remember—confidence and ego are vital to a successful designer) while reducing their trust in you.

In collaborations, you need to find a communication style that works for both sides. One partner may love rough-and-tumble critique of anything and everything, while the other prefers only to offer constructive suggestions and never cuts loose with a flat-out "that stinks and here's why." That collaboration may find an equilibrium if both partners are looking for one. But you have to be watching for what reactions you get, and this is why collaboration is easier in person or at least by phone—you get more tone, inflection, and body language to work with, so you know when your critique has gone too far. Be kind at first, and as you build up a rapport and sense of trust, see how your collaborators respond. You always want to be kind in your critique, of course, but sometimes the kindest critique is to say, "I think this idea doesn't work." In other words, ramp up your level of honesty over time, as you learn to trust your design partner's instincts and your own ability to understand what arguments and design theories matter to others on the project. If you find yourself unable to accept any of the ideas put forward by others, consider that perhaps you are best off designing on your own rather than in collaboration—or at least, better off with other design partners.

## 7. Critique With Kindness, Revise Ruthlessly

In the end, collaboration depends on your ability to both give and take criticism. There's no way around it, because two or four or ten brains working on a single problem need to align all sorts of elements to forge a better whole. If you can't offer critique in a way that other collaborators can hear and accept, if your style is either too abrasive or too shy and passive, your collaboration will fail.

So there's a fine line. You must be honest in your critique, without throwing flamebait. Compassionate critique is what I'd advocate. Keep the discussion on what the text says, how the rules function, what the math or the playtest data shows. Never, ever descend into personal attacks.

Likewise, when you are hearing critiques or reviewing a marked-up document as you try to unify a design, try not to take it personally. Your work can be improved. Even a fl awed critique will deepen your understanding, as you will have to put together the reasoning for why the critique is fl awed. Try to accept criticism with good grace, and if you can't, step away from the keyboard for an hour or overnight before responding.

## Why Bother to Collaborate?

The golden rule certainly applies in collaboration, and beginning designers may find the prospect of seeing their work shot down often (or being asked to justify their modifications of a collaborator's design) intimidating. Part of the joy of tabletop RPG design is the pure fun of having no limits, of doing whatever one likes with a clean slate and no CGI budget to worry about. So why would anyone ever limit that?

Because when things go right, the end design will be richer, the workload will be reduced, and you'll provide stronger, better material to the audience. A great developer or editor sometimes provides this level of added effort, but that's not their main function. Designers should bring strong ideas and sharper game play; the competitiveness that develops as people try to top one another's best is where collaboration takes flight. Design ego forces you to do your best or else admit that your collaborator is pulling more of the weight. That's powerful incentive to really deliver.

A collaboration that is really ticking is one that allows you to improve on your partner's weak points, while they help you cover your own. When you read the result, you'll see that it is greater than the sum of its creators alone.

# 32

# Myths and Realities of Game Balance

*Monte Cook*

G ame balance is one of those things that game designers, aspiring game designers, and hard-core players talk a lot about. In many ways, it's easy to see it like the Holy Grail, Tanelorn, or some other quest object that heroes strive for but few ever reach. Like such quests, it may be that the value is in the quest itself rather than the end goal. In other words, it's the journey and not the destination that counts.

If we're going to examine game balance in a roleplaying game, however, the first question that needs to be raised must be, is game balance even possible? Is there such a thing? I think if we're going to examine this topic honestly, the answer is, actually, no. (Or rather, yes, but not in the way that most people mean—I'll get to that in a bit.)

That's right. I'll say it: In the sense of roleplaying game rule design, game balance is a myth.

But how can I, a game designer with more than 20 years experience, write such sacrilegious words? Let's really look at what we mean. Say that the most brilliant of all game designers put together a game with the goal of true game balance. He's smart, so he keeps it simple. He carefully designs every class/feat/skill/superpower/whatever in the game so that it is perfectly balanced with every other class/feat/skill/superpower/whatever. He still has the problem of the game being out of his control. Some players are "min-maxers" and will simply take what he's created and find the loopholes that others won't, creating unbalanced options and characters that are better than others.

OK, let's assume the game designer is so talented that he closes up every loophole and plugs every hole, so whether you're a newbie or a talented rules exploiter, there's no combination of options that's better or worse than any others. (In effect, the designer's made it so that all choices result in virtually the same character.) Now the game is truly balanced, right?

Except—it's still a roleplaying game. It's still open-ended, based on the players' imaginations and the GM's prerogatives. What the characters choose to do is not going to be balanced. Some will choose to ignore their combat options and focus on their character backgrounds while others use their abilities to their fullest. Even if everyone around the table had exactly the same character, how the characters are played will be ultimately unbalanced. Worse, a GM might (accidentally or intentionally) allow one player special privileges that unbalance the game. Or even if the PCs are all more or less equal, he might throw challenges against the players that are so insurmountable or so easily overcome that the game isn't fun. It doesn't even hold the players' interest.

There's no amount of game mechanic balancing that can overcome such problems.

## But What is Game Balance?

At this point, some readers may be thinking that I'm being pedantic, just arguing semantics. But since the game is meant to be played, ignoring how players use rules when striving for game balance is an exercise in futility.

When people talk about balance in game design, they are often talking about two fairly different things. The first is balance between characters. The idea is that all of the characters should be "balanced" with each other; every character has equal power. The second is balance between the characters and the rest of the game. A character who gets an ability that allows him to overcome difficult—or impossible—challenges easily makes the game unbalanced. Likewise, the reverse: A game with challenges that are far too difficult for the characters is also unbalanced. The first could be considered a measure of fairness and the second a measure of fun.

The first case—character vs. character balance—can be boiled down to how much one player (not character) can do in comparison to other players. The ultimate currency in a roleplaying game is "time to shine." A character designed to be a terror in melee gets to shine when his character cleaves through a number of foes in battle. A character skilled at locks and other devices shines when he opens a locked door or disables the mechanism that closes walls in on everyone. And so on. One could certainly argue, then, that a game that's balanced gives every player/character a moment to shine and that these moments are about equal in time, importance, and fun.

A common mistake, then, is to balance characters based on a single option—combat prowess, for example. If all characters have to be equally good at the same thing, you end up with characters that are mostly the same.

This is fine, but you risk a certain kind of dynamism with that approach. Since you're only focusing on one aspect, you're not really balancing the game. You're balancing one aspect of the game.

Nevertheless, most games make certain options far more interesting, appealing, or exciting than other options. This could be considered unbalanced. I'll start by pointing the finger directly at myself. The Third Edition of Dungeons & Dragons made combat exciting through a number of different options and mechanical subsystems. A player could devote a lot of time developing characters good at certain aspects and not others, and finding new and intriguing options. A player interested in locks and mechanisms essentially had two skills to focus on, both using the same mechanic. While the melee fighter's moment to shine might last an hour or more with involved round-by-round detail, the lock expert makes a roll or two and is done.

Of course, this was intentional. We knew that most players were interested in combat, and combat makes it easy to produce exciting action sequences that are challenging and engaging for a whole group of people around the table—much more so than picking a lock. If we had decided to make every activity as involved as combat, it would have made the game cumbersome. Still, this all means that as game designers we intentionally "unbalanced" the game in favor of combat. We left it up to the GM and the players to balance combat with non-combat activities as they wished. For some, the game would be nearly 100 percent fighting. For others, interacting with NPCs, with the environment, or with each other would equal or even outshine battles, but that wasn't a matter of balance for the rules.

The second type of balance, dealing with characters and challenges, may seem related, having to do with characters being either too powerful or not powerful enough. At its core, though, such balance is a different issue because it has less to do with the players and more to do with the GM.

After all, it's the GM who is responsible for providing challenges for the characters—and the GM has no boundaries or limitations. When GMs complain about unbalanced characters running roughshod over their campaign and how that's the fault of the game, there is a misunderstanding of the role of the GM. You don't bring a knife to a gunfight. If the PCs wipe the floor with the vrock, give them six vrocks to fight next time. Or a nalfeshnee.

**195**

No, it really is that simple. For every spell, there's a counter. For every monster, there's a tougher monster. If the players raise the ante by creating characters who are too powerful, the GM can simply use the sliding power scale of the game (which has no upper limit) to bring things back into balance.

What's more, the GM is also the arbiter of the rules at the table and can disallow options. Ultimately, it's the GM who truly understands what's going on at the table, not some game designer thousands of miles away. No matter what the designer does or doesn't do to balance the game, it's a moot point. An illusion at best. It's what the GM does that provides the balance.

## The Gamers' Social Contract

So here's the real secret of game balance: There is such a thing, but it has very little to do with rules and game designers. It emerges from the cooperation of the people sitting around the table. It comes from the players and, in particular, the GM. It all has to do with mutual trust.

When people sit down at my game table, I expect two things from them. The first is that everyone is responsible for making the game fun for all involved. The second is to trust the GM to provide a fun and balanced play experience. This is the gamers' social contract: the agreement that everyone makes, consciously or unconsciously, at the beginning of every game session.

With the idea that the two axes upon which the wheel of balance turns are time to shine and reasonable challenges, the GM can provide both in a way that the rules never could. A really good GM can run a balanced game where one player is a 20th level demigod and another is a 1st level farmer. All he has to do is make sure that each player has fun and each character has something interesting and challenging to do. I'm not contending that it's easy—on the contrary, it's very difficult. That's why good game designers try to provide tools for GMs to make running a fair, balanced game easier. Well-designed rules make it easier for the GM to judge what he should and shouldn't do, and maybe even protect him so that when he makes a mistake, the game doesn't go wildly off the rails.

For the GM to provide a fairly stable play environment, however, the players have to trust him and have to agree not to use their own position at the table to undermine or circumvent his actions or otherwise spoil the game for others. So it's not just about the GM. It's about the entire group.

Getting players and GMs to understand the social contract is the key to true game balance. The first rule of every RPG should be, "Don't be a jerk." This rule, if adhered to perfectly, would likely eliminate almost all balance problems of any stripe. The players should trust the GM to ensure that no matter what happens and no matter what choices they make, the game will be fair and fun. The GM should be able to trust that no one's going to intentionally try to break the game.

# *33*

# Pacing

Pacing combines a feel for what's going on at the table with an understanding of what events generate momentum, and which ones tread water, no matter how flashy.

## Pacing

This topic was a bit of a nightmare for me, because pacing is not really a design element at all.

In books and movies, the author or the screenwriter has complete control over the pacing. The audience sees what the writer describes, full stop. In adventure design, the designer has almost zero control over the pacing. Instead, the DM and the players control the speed at which things unfold.

Neither the DM nor the players control pacing absolutely as an adventure plays out though. That's why this topic gives me fits. Design controls or mitigates flaws in mechanics, presentation, and challenge. Pacing in RPGs is a matter of improvisation, intuition, or feel.

## Definition

Let's back up a second. What is pacing? It is that rate at which things happen in a narrative or adventure. It is not a mechanical elemental, but it is crucial to successful narratives, including RPG adventures. If things happen too slowly, players get bored and tend to start wandering off in search of their own entertainment. If things happen too quickly, they get confused and irritated.

Good pacing requires advancing the plot toward a finale quickly enough to keep everyone entertained, without leaving anyone behind—which is fine, as far as it goes. The tricky question is, what are the things that happen to increase or decrease the pace?

## Combat and Pacing

Since RPGs are action-heavy, you might be excused for thinking that "things happening" means combat. When the heroes fight, lots of stuff happens: attacks, spells, and saving throws are all important changes to a hero's strength and resources. This is a misunderstanding of pacing, though.

Combat influences pacing by creating a sense of motion. This can be an illusion. A whole session of fighting might still leave the PCs no closer to the adventure goals, and this will only frustrate them. The elements that really affect pacing are the story results—of combat, of roleplaying, or any other type of scene. Why this distinction between story and combat? Because for pacing purposes, the information that matters about a combat is whether the party defeated a foe that figures in the larger adventure arc. Random encounters are meaningless to the plot, which is why they are usually left out of good designs. They are quick sugar fixes for combat junkies, but they put the adventure on hold. Nothing happens to advance the adventure during a random encounter; this is why good design tends to avoid them entirely. They're filler.

When the party wins a fight, they may learn something from a prisoner, they may follow the tracks of a retreating monster, they may even gain a treasure that tells them something crucial about their mission. The melee/ranged/spells part of the fight, though, is a sideshow to the adventure goals. **Third Edition D&D** combat tends to slow the pace of an adventure rather than speeding it up; combats take longer than they did in **1E** or **2E**, especially against large groups of foes and at higher levels.

Since you know how long a **3E D&D** combat can last, be sure it is worthwhile. If you want quick, violent action, consider an ambush of arrows (such as the one in **Castle Shadowcrag**'s hauntings), or a warning shot spell from a villain followed up by a threat (that's really a bluff—the villain runs if called on it). Just say, "You defeat the kobold miners" if the PCs take on foes that are beneath them rather than breaking out the battle mat.

This is in no way intended as a knock on combat-heavy game sessions or a plea to run adventures without combat. I'm not saying don't run combats. I'm saying choose your combats carefully, and make sure they carry a little dramatic weight: the win or lose of the combat is about more than who's tougher, it's about who deserves the sword of the Kobold King, for instance.

Combat is exciting for its own sake. It gives players a chance to show their power, and it is the single best reusable obstacle to throw at the PCs as they fight to reach their adventure goals. However, it is just an obstacle, not the goal itself, and you need to be sure it doesn't overwhelm your game. More time spent on combat resolution actually means less time spent on maintaining the pace of adventure events. And events drive adventure pacing.

## Events and Pacing

As a DM, you already know that events and scenes move an adventure ahead. You may even have felt that too much combat bogs down the story. There's a good reason for that feeling. You need time at the table for both the adrenaline rush of combat and the steadier thrill of plot-linked events. Those events constitute the "why are we fighting" part of the game.

Standard events that keep the pace quick include initial hooks, a crucial dialogue, item discoveries, clues, betrayals by NPCs, new information, getting lost, and increasing stakes that the party fights for. All these "things happening" keep the players focused on the adventure.

> *"More time spent on combat resolution actually means less time spent on maintaining a pace of adventure events."*

Take, just as a random example, a shadowy castle adventure that features five major flashback scenes, a finale scene, and a dozen "shadow events." The party perceives the adventure happening depending on how quickly those five major scenes happen: the shadow events are, like random encounters, filler to keep the party on their toes. If you run short games, you could use a simple hook and run one flashback per game session, ending with the last flashback and finale in the fifth session. The pace would be steady throughout.

A better alternative might be to run it in four parts:

1. The hook and first flashback in the first session.
2. A flashback, some shadow events, and lots of NPC scenes.
3. Two flashbacks and more shadow events, ending with a cliffhanger.
4. The final flashback, finale combats, and success/failure scenes (no filler).

The first two sessions contain one major scene each; the second two contain two and three major scenes each. There's a sense of more happening in the later games. Better still, if you reveal that the castle is in danger of sliding into shadow in the third session, that raises the stakes.

Players always look for shortcuts and simplifications of the scenario, while you as DM look for complications, misdirections, and expansions to draw out the game. This is normal. If the players knew where the big villain and the treasure hoard were, they would go there and be done with it. But the more you add options (new courtyards, the mines, hunting the werewolf lord, the treacherous dwarves) beyond the original goal, the more you force the players to expend resources, think things through, and act as heroes.

When there are no more clues, rooms, or monsters left, the expansion phase of the adventure is over. Your players are ready for the finale.

## The Secret of *Castle Shadowcrag*'s Pacing Structure

**Shadowcrag** superficially looks like a location-based adventure. To some degree it is. Visiting every room in the castle and every passage in the mines is a waste of time from the player perspective (or a valuable expansion and drawing out of party resources, if you prefer). The real structure is entirely contained in the hook, the first character introductions, the five flashbacks, and the finale sequence. Everything else is padding, to some degree.

Now, padding in a novel or supplement is usually a waste. Padding in an adventure serves a purpose: it gives the party somewhere to spend their resources, goals to meet beyond the main goal, and a sense of exploration and the passage of time. Some of the non-core, padding encounters are a ton of fun, either in combat or roleplaying terms. The groom Zarek is a blast to play, for instance, and likewise the werewolf lord—though neither is part of the core path to the adventure goals.

You can run **Shadowcrag** in as little as 8 major scenes: hook, dwarves/Zarek at the castle, a quick set of flashbacks, and the finale. That's the secret core of the structure. But I would not necessarily recommend it. In good adventures, just playing the important bits may miss the point. Padding serves a mechanical purpose by using up resources. It also creates opportunities for encounter variety and changes in the pacing.

### Variety

Gamers like to perfect their skills, doing the same thing over and over until they have got the perfect combat tactics down, or the perfect stealth combo, or whatever. That feeling of mastery is a good thing. You should definitely encourage it rather than trying to deny it with a petty "Oh yeah – try this!" encounter. However, mastery can quickly turn to boredom. Vary the formula just enough so that players never feel they are grinding through a level, and that each new encounter is a discovery. Lull your players into a false sense of security with the shadow events or friendly ghosts or repetition in **Castle Shadowcrag**, and then spring something completely different on them (such as having Silverwing talk to them, or having Evander change alignment, or what have you—the adventure is full of twists).

### Front-Loading

One way to reduce the combat burden and meet party expectations is to start each adventure session with a short combat. Just saying, "Roll initiative" gets everyone's attention, and means you're not wasting time.

This is related to hooks. I did a whole discussion of hooks and inciting incidents (published on the WotC site). I won't repeat that discussion other than to say, it's best to start each adventure with action, either combat (such as a boarding action by Imperial troops to a capture a princess) or an intense roleplaying episode (such as the deadly aftermath of a raid, when Luke finds his foster parents dead). Grabbing everyone's attention prevents the deadly slow start, which can turn into a slow game overall.

As the DM, you can experiment: For example, you could start your first sessions of **Castle Shadowcrag** with the party already traveling in the forest, and begin with the shadow fey/mastiff ambush sequence at sunset. Novels and films often start in media res because it grabs attention. It sets a quick pace, because the players must scramble to catch up with events, and that immediately draws them into the action and carries them along with it.

Doing it every game session is overkill, but I find an early combat is surprisingly effective. It promotes a quicker pace of play throughout the session.

## Cliffhangers as a Resting Place

Ending a session with a cliffhanger is a good way to encourage attendance at the next game, and to keep players thinking ahead. This is especially true if, for instance, your "problem player" is the one who is caught by Vasilios Stross' exquisite suffering touch ability and dragged down into the dungeons, or if a character is caught by the explosion of the dark stalker's death in the kobold mines. Leaving a character in deadly peril is the best cliffhanger, but sometimes a crucial saving throw can also be a good time. "You hear the last of the shadow fey's arcane speech. Next time, we roll your Will save against her seductive magic. Thanks, that's it for this week."

You can see why players might come back. The early serial movies were totally right about the use of cliffhangers. Be shameless. Leave them hanging after the first or second session of a new adventure.

## Increasing Speed by Raising Stakes

While you can create the illusion of a fast-paced session by just stringing together combat on top of combat, you will set a more compelling pace by combining physical danger to the heroes with an increase in the stakes. For dramatic reasons, your opening hook should never, ever be the main threat of the adventure. If the

PCs hear the main threat in the first scene, there is no way to increase the threat. It is better for the opening menace to be just a part of the threat.

For instance, if they are out to find a lost artifact, they learn from a dying foe that the artifact will soon be destroyed. They may learn that the destruction of the artifact will do far more magical damage than they suspected, or that a PC's mentor has already tried to find the artifact, and been captured.

The typical methods for raising the stakes are to set a timer on the adventure, threaten a wider disaster, or make the danger more personal. Every time you up the stakes, the pressure on the players increases. This makes the adventure both more compelling and makes it seem faster.

## Variable Pacing for Investigative Adventures

Typical fantasy adventures assume a pace in which adventures (and sessions) start with a compelling incident, quickly grow more intense, and end with a bang. I call this "avalanche pacing." It certainly works very well for sword and sorcery.

For mysteries and horror scenarios, I prefer for the players to set the pace, poking into corners or not as their curiosity drives them. This is a very languid, punctuated style: events only happen when the players take action, so I call it "triggered pacing." There's no rush except the pressure that players put on themselves, or the timers they discover as they reveal the plot. Different genre, different pacing needs.

# Setting Up the Finale

The most important pacing sequence leads up to the finale. Meeting the BBEG for the first time need not happen at the end; he could be hinted at earlier, met in disguise, or he could even be considered an ally earlier in the adventure. But by the time they meet him at the finale, they will want to kill him quick.

Don't let them.

Finale pacing ruthlessly denies the PCs the chance that they so desperately want, which is to hack their hated foe into tiny pieces or to recover the person or item they have been chasing this whole time. Tease mercilessly. Throw minions in their path as they see the villain run or teleport away. If they make it into melee, have the foe suddenly levitate to force ranged combat. If they finish off the guards, the minions, and the underlings—have the villain (falsely) offer to surrender.

Beyond that, use description and atmosphere and weird terrain and tactics to stall this combat. To feel satisfying, it needs to run longer than the standard "four rounds and done." I usually hope for seven or eight rounds—and if it's part of a continuing series or campaign, the villain may well have a contingency teleport or contingency displacement or other trick.

Whatever you do, don't let the final fight be just another combat. Make sure that the villain has lines to speak, or surprising tactics, or an alliance in an unexpected place. Pull out all the stops to challenge the players tactically and surprise them in narrative terms (see Nicolas Logue's essay, Stagecraft).

### Denouement

There's a reason that *Lord of the Rings* shows us a lot of the trip to Mount Doom, but hardly any of the trip home. The return trip is boring and anticlimactic.

Unless your campaign is all about rations and simulation, I recommend you skip it, gloss over it, and minimize it to keep your campaign momentum going. If you are a great DM, you will set the hook for the next adventure before the prior session—making sure that the pace of play never falters as players try to figure out what's next.

## Conclusion

Pacing isn't so much design as it is reading the table and noticing when your players are not engaged. To get them back into the swing, use both the quick payoff of combat and the appeal of events that advance the storyline. Combine opening combats, closing cliffhangers, and long finales for maximum appeal.

## Player Pacing

DMs can set a pace or encourage a rhythm of play. But players who want to play out every last detail can slow the game to a crawl. My own personal preference is to move by days, weeks, and months whenever possible. Skip over long overland travel through safe kingdoms, skip over healing periods, skip over periods of research or training. In my game, I like those things to take 5 minutes, unless there's some very good reason to focus on the minutiae. My players sometimes want to prepare something more elaborate.

Players often drag the game out for fear of missing something (such as the XP of random encounters or a vital clue). This is illogical, since a good DM will never cheat the party out of the fun bits of action, narrative, and adventure. There are at least three fixes:

Narrative summaries: Just sum up the events as the DM. "Time passes, and you are all healed" works, as does "The sea voyage is uneventful, and a month later you arrive in Newhaven."

Reassurances: Sometimes players just feel that they need every advantage. Gently push the group to move along if they stall for too long. Set events in motion around them when other characters urge them to act "before it's too late" and when oracles and prophecies point to the current time as propitious. Make it clear that too much waiting and planning is a poor choice that strengthens the enemy as much as the party.

Advance the plot: Give the party some smaller goals before the main event. If the city is under siege, give them tasks to scout and raid the besieger, escort a vital shipment by air, keep the Thieves Guild from gouging panicked buyers of stolen foodstuffs, and so on. This keeps players busy and makes a summary or reassurance work.

The design problem with forcing the pace of RPG play is that it can upset the tone of the game and the DM/player chemistry so it's really hard to predict. Some groups power through stuff in five minutes that other groups handle in three long sessions. At best, design can ameliorate this with good use of readalouds and side treks.

*34*

# Playtesting

G iven that I ran two events at GenCon just to get some feedback on a
few encounters, it's worth talking for a while about playtesting. This
essay covers the basics of setting up, running, and reporting a successful
playtest. How you run the table is entirely up to you. As long as someone is
tracking the results, the playtest can be considered a success. However, detail
always helps.

## The Golden Rule

Here's the Golden Rule of Playtesting: "Note it and move on." It's not uncommon
for playtest groups to get caught up in the testing spirit and discuss the fixes for
an unbalanced encounter or a misjudged CR rating. You're probably correct that
there's a problem, but fixing it during play is usually a time sink that keeps the
group from completing the playtest.

Avoid the temptation to redesign at the table; ask people to note the problem,
scribble down any obvious fix, then continue playing. You can always "debrief"
the problem areas at the end of the session and offer some potential fixes then, or
when you write your report. The goal of playtesters, though, is to break things,
not necessarily to fix them.

## Character Generation and Levels

If you already have a set of balanced characters available at the right level, the ideal
is to use those. If not, use a standard 25-point-buy character, roll 4d6 and drop the

lowest random generation, or take characters from the lists on pages 113–126 of the **3.5 Dungeon Master's Guide**. Note the method you use.

If you do use an existing set of characters, be sure to explain how they were generated.

Regardless of how the PCs are chosen, include all the race/class/level details in your write-up.

## Books and Resources

The approved list of playtest books is the **Player's Handbook** (**PH**), **Player's Handbook II** (**PH2**), **Expanded Psionics Handbook** (**XPH**), **Dungeon Master's Guide** (**DMG**), **Spell Compendium**, and all the *Complete* books for **3rd Edition** playtests, and the **PH**, **DMG**, and **Martial Powers** for **4E** tests. While there's a lot of great stuff beyond that both from d20 publishers and from WotC, no one can cover everything. If you're itching for an exception, discuss it with your freelance coordinator.

Note that the **Magic Item Compendium**, **Book of Nine Swords**, **Tome of Magic**, **Forgotten Realms Campaign Setting**, **Eberron**, **Vile Darkness**, **Exalted Deeds**, **Planar Handbook**, and many others are deliberately left out. If you absolutely must include something from these sources, flag it in the character generation notes.

## Notekeeping

Taking notes is crucial for successful playtesting, though it shouldn't override everything else (playtests are still meant to be fun, after all). Because it's important, you should designate one player as the official notekeeper. This person must track rounds in combat, noting major events (like criticals that knock someone down especially quickly, or every PC failing a save or skill check, etc.). The notekeeper also tracks non-combat events such as plot twists or clues, items, and information that helped or hindered the party's progress.

As DM, you may wish to keep a few notes as well. If you modified encounters or you needed more information (and there are lots of gaps in most playtest manuscripts), please mark it down. Likewise, note the smart or dumb things players do (and that you have NPCs do).

## Combats, Death, and TPK

Most of playtesting is combat testing, both for CR and by encounter. That said, there's no reason you shouldn't enjoy all the flavor, character roleplay, and fun of the game. For the write-ups, though, the combats, traps, and skill checks warrant the most attention, so be sure to watch for the following.

- **Combats Lasting Less Than 4 Rounds:** If it's quick and easy, note that.
- **Combats Running Over 10 Rounds:** If it's a longer fight, what was tough about it?
- **Healing Surges:** Track how many healing surges (total) are used in a given encounter.
- **PC Death and Dying:** Even though all PCs are automatically raised and the game continues, please note each time a PC drops dead. Note whenever a PC has to make a death saving throw.
- **Daily Powers:** Note how many daily powers are used in a given encounter.
- **PC Leveling:** Note how quickly the party levels up.
- **Save Success:** Note when a saving throw is especially critical or impossible.
- **Turning Success:** Track all turning attempts and their success or failure.
- **TPK:** If the whole party is wiped out, note it and (depending on time available) either replay the encounter using what you learned from the first combat, or skip it and simply move on as if the party had survived. DMs should note roughly what percentage of hit points or surviving monsters remained at the end of any TPK encounter.

## Problems in Mechanics or Balance

You know what these are: saves, skills, abilities that just don't work. Encounters that are too easy or too hard for your group's levels. Anything that violates the core rules as generally played.

## Problems in Story, Setting, and Logic

These are tough for a designer to see, because he or she is too close to the text and unconsciously fills in the gaps. And, frankly, a typical playtest manuscript has lots of leaps of logic and missing connections between parts. Many areas are still pretty sketchy in their descriptions, because of the realities of publishing schedules that contain limited time for formal playtests.

Feel free to point these out, or just to solve the issues with DM ingenuity and mention your take in a report.

## Praise Where It Is Due

Playtest reports should not be unrelentingly negative, if only to salve a designer's wounded ego.

Also, if something in a description or encounter really creeps players out or makes the whole table go, "Oh Wow!" I like to note that for the benefit of the creator of the adventure or supplement. Sometimes those elements can be further reinforced in later development and editing.

# How to Playtest Successfully

If you want to playtest again (for Open Design, Paizo, or WotC projects), it's worth making sure that your reports are solid and that you have provided the core information about how the encounters went in a timely way. Play the encounters as written. If they're terrible, let that come up in play rather than adjusting for it ahead of time.

Avoid using slang or emotional descriptions of a playtest session. A devastating presentation of the facts will get a lot more attention (and gather you more respect as a skillful playtester) than a string of "elves are wimps" or "this sucked." If it sucked, say why. If the elves got run over by the PCs, spell it out.

That's really all there is to it.

Though session reports written in character are always appreciated, not everyone has the time, and it's not necessary. Given a choice between a timely report written a day or two after the session was played and a wildly entertaining read written three weeks later, most designers always prefer the timely write-up. I know I do.

# Credits

Most publishers will include your name and your players' names in the credits. Please include them in your report.

---

### Convention Playtesting

If you don't want to playtest with your "usual group" (and there are clear problems with having a set of default assumptions about RPGs built up over years), there's no better way to clear away the gaming detritus than to use conventions for on-the-spot playtesting.

Playtest groups at a convention have two advantages. First, you control the PC stats and thus the overall power level. And second, the players don't have a history with you and are really aiming for maximum fun in minimum time. This forces you to generate typical characters (or swipe some from the DMG section on NPCs) and to make the case for your adventure in a short period. Each encounter (and a convention game may have no more than three to five encounters, depending on the length of the slot) will really need to shine.

There's one other big advantage to convention playtesters. If you hand them a piece of paper and ask for their feedback on the adventure, they'll give you a less-diplomatic opinion on what they liked and disliked than your friends and regular gamers will. Conventions playtesters are candid, and that's a powerful reason to run convention playtests.

---

# *35*

# Promises, Promises
## The Art of the Pitch

A pitch is a writer's promise. It says, "I'm going to entertain you, and here's how." The number one rule is simple: Don't be boring.

When you write a pitch for work at a magazine or website, or when you pitch a novel or short story for that matter, you are making a promise to deliver that entertainment. But the promise is more than word count and deadline, important as those are. The real promise is about the style, the genre, and the approach you take. If you don't nail the audience's expectations about those elements, the editor will (rightly) reject your pitch, no matter how great it might be for another audience or venue.

So rule number 2: Know the audience you are pitching to.

## You and the Audience

Most of being a writer or game designer is your relationship to the audience. For most freelancers, this starts with the pitch. You need to know (and explain clearly):

- What you are going to write
- Who you are writing it for

Then the pain begins, because communication is imperfect and people such as editors may (no, they will) bring their own interpretation to your pitch.

How many ways can you go wrong in a pitch? Well, lots. People who you think are your natural audience may be offended or put out by what you write. They may interpret an adventure as supporting some real-world political or religious view (ask me about Eberron fandom's views on whether religions can be both intolerant and good, or whether the Church of the Silver Flame can, at any time in its history, be described as fanatical and zealous).

Worse than that, people can miss the point entirely. They ignore your (natural and completely obvious) genius. That really hurts, especially as it means you failed to make your point clear. What was in your head did not translate onto the screen, and then back through the eyeballs of your readers to their brains. And that's a writer's main skill (and yes, I do include game designers as a very specialized form of writer: text is your business).

So one of the first lessons you learn as a writer is to develop a thick skin where criticism and rejection are concerned. If you fail to develop this trait, you will fail as a writer. Maybe not right away; you might become a powerful jerk in the design world, whose opinions are feared but who is consumed with self-doubt. You might be a frail ego, easily set into a tailspin when deadlines loom and an editor demands another rewrite. But overall, success comes from having some degree of confidence that you as a person and as a designer have worth, and standing, apart from your creations.

If you seek validation only through your work as a designer, you will live a life of misery, because out there are always going to be people who think it stinks. You literally cannot please everyone with a single work of fiction or design. It isn't possible, because different audiences want different things.

> *"Write for love as often as you can, which means pitch what you love as often as you can."*

So, pitch to the audience you want to write for. Know the venue: read the magazine, study the website, read all of the modules from the campaign setting. Sure, usually you pitch for a setting or world you already know and love, but sometimes you'll pitch to someone new. Know their language and the assumptions of their fandom. If that audience fails to connect with you, pitch something else. The work itself may be fine, but if you pitch paranormal romance to the hard SF editor, it will never work. Likewise, if you pitch exotic anime heroics for the clockpunk setting, your odds are slim.

## Pitches = Persuasion

To craft a successful pitch, you need to be persuasive. You need to convince your readers, whether patrons or editors, of at least three things:

- First, you have a smoking hot idea that people will want to read.

- Second, you are putting a new twist on something that everyone agrees is a classic.

- Third, you can be trusted to carry it off.

Most pitches I see fall into two categories of failure. The first category are the easy ones to discard; these are simply boring. You may want to write "10 New Torches," but it's probably a dull read. You may take a great topic, like "Weapons of Japan" and make it boring by adding too many academic or pedantic footnotes. Likewise, an adventure that's really all about NPCs acting and PCs watching is pretty dull.

The other form of failure is the twist that's just . . . dumb. This is mostly a matter of style and taste. Some people might say that an article on the Elven Industrial Revolution is brilliant (and it might work for some), but for me, it's a dud. Likewise crossing real-world dinosaurs with halfling tribes, or making dragons into arcane machines. Might work for some fans, doesn't work for me. These pitches are trying too hard to be original and different, and wind up being weird and unappealing.

But it's tough to know, sometimes, whether your idea for a submarine in Zobeck is going to fly (er, swim). I actually think that premise could be a great idea, but it might be a niche taste. Such a vehicle has some trivial technical problems (river currents, power sources) and some larger story/world problems (Why build a submarine on a river?). With "high concept" pitches, you give it your best shot. If it works, you are hailed as an original and creative genius. If no one bites, you move on.

## Who Pitched This Thing?

This brings us around to the issue of trust. The more of a track record you have, the easier it is to sell a pitch to an audience that knows your prior work. I trust Nick Logue to deliver a great horror adventure on a pitch that might not fly from an unknown. I trust Ed Greenwood to do archmages and high magic right. And so on.

> *"A large part of [a successful pitch] . . . is explaining what the PCs do in the adventure."*

This is why your first publication in any new venue is the most important; it's your ticket to recognition and return visits, and establishes your competence in a particular genre.

Tangentially, then, the most difficult pitches for an editor to discard are the ones that promise the world but the editor isn't convinced you can deliver.

"Reinventing the Cthulhu Mythos" might be a great theme for an entire adventure arc, but it's probably a terrible pitch for a 2,000 word article.

Likewise, a dancing-bears-and-bandits adventure may be mildly interesting, but... Well, to carry that off, you better have some chops. I pitched just such a project to the patrons anonymously for **Tales of Zobeck** and was soundly rejected. The voting might have gone differently if the pitch hadn't been anonymous, as some voters would have trusted me to carry through on a slightly odd premise.

So while your first pitch gets you recognized for a particular thing, your longterm track record gives you more rope to play with. In other words, an editor might trust a long-time freelancer to make something odd work, where he or she would not trust a new voice. This is the so-called inside track, which is widely perceived as unfair by new authors.

And to an extent, it is unfair. The exact same pitch sent in by both Joe Public and Monte Cook is going to get two different reactions. The Monte Cook version will get more of a hearing. It will still be shot down if it is a stinker, but for cases where the execution requires a certain level of talent, Monte would get a green light while Joe Public would get a rejection.

But the inside track is not a conspiracy, and authors who get extra credit from editors have earned it by years of delivering good adventures or articles. Going with a known-quality writer is simply the way that editors, publishers, and Hollywood try to improve their odds in the creative arena. If you rage against it, well, rage away. It won't help you make the first sale, but if it makes you feel better to call the editor a hack and the publisher the tool of sycophants, go ahead. The bar is set at a certain level for a reason.

Which is why I was so happy to submit some items anonymously as pitches to the **Tales of Zobeck** anthology, and see them shot down (and yes, to see one accepted). I was messing around with concepts that I like for Zobeck, but that might not have broader appeal. One was shot down hard, the other I rewrote for round two (and it still went nowhere). Humility is good for a writer's soul, as I keep telling myself. And everyone, even published authors, should expect rejection as a normal (though certainly not enjoyable) part of the creative process. If you feel a need to blame people when your pitches are rejected, you might want to consider another line of work. Writers get rejected often, and must learn to cope with it and even learn from it. My dancing bears pitch went nowhere, alas. It is the sort of thing I might have convinced people to try based on my past reputation, but it was too simple a scenario to make most patrons bite without that extra bait on the hook. Maybe next time. "If you seek validation . . . through your work as a freelancer, you will live a life of misery."

# Design = Doing

So what's the secret to a successful pitch? I think a large part of it for adventure design is explaining what the PCs do in the adventure. This is part of a more general rule of game design, which is that game design is about what players do.

This may seem obvious, but many game designers waste a lot of time on what NPCs do and their backstory, the setting's history, and showing us the environment. These are all hangovers from fiction. RPGs are not fiction, some White Wolf supplements notwithstanding. RPGs are about the PCs and their various forms of mayhem, investigation, exploration, and triumph or insanity. Quick—name these games:

- Heroes kill monsters and loot tombs.
- Heroes investigate cults and are driven mad.
- Heroes fight crime with super-powers.

Pretty straightforward, no? An adventure pitch would (ideally) contain a sentence that does the same. Pitches for Open Design projects would include the following:

- Heroes discover an alchemist with a split personality and destroy the cult that plans to destroy the city.
- Heroes visit the Underdark and stop the Ghoul Empire's latest conquest.
- Heroes visit a haunted castle and set right the consequences of its tragic past.

## Sometimes, It's Not You

There are cases where a pitch is perfect and still gets shot down. These are inevitable. It may be that the editor/publisher/site manager just recently accepted something similar to what you are proposing. It may be that they have a project underway using the same central monster, or drawing from the same real-world source as yours (say, Vikings). Or it may be that they like your pitch perfectly well but have no room for it on their schedule, due to length, edition, or timing.

There's nothing you can do about this. Sometimes a "No" is just a "No." The best way to tell is if the editor or publisher offers a personal note or invites you to pitch again. If that invitation is extended, brush yourself off and get back in the game. Pitches are just promises. Keep offering the promise of something great, and sooner or later an editor will agree.

## Deliver

There's one more step, of course. You may find your pitches are being accepted often, but your articles or complete designs are not. This may indicate that your work is mechanically lacking (your great ideas are translating into dull rules and boring tactics) or it may indicate a lack of craft (your great ideas are getting buried in dull prose).

**213**

These are separate problems for another essay. But learning to pitch is step No. 1 for a freelancer. Practice your pitches, hone your lines, and work will come to you.

### Pitching the Editor

Many writers believe that the best way to succeed with a pitch is not to think about the second audience (the readers) but to think about pitching the editor. This is a dangerous path.

The thinking is that if you can just find out what a magazine editor or adventure publisher likes, wants, or needs, you can pitch that thing and you're set. But it's not always true.

First of all, an editor often doesn't know what he or she wants or needs (they always know what they like!). They are looking to a writer to show some originality, or remind them of a great hit with a new twist, or do something exciting with the standard game and story elements. If the editor knew what it was they wanted, they might very well just assign it to a trusted freelancer ("We're doing drow this issue. You're my ace writer; give me drow by the first of the month.").

The other problem with this approach is that you will never become known for the things you love and do well. Instead, you become a hack or at least a hired gun, willing to write anything that pays. I'm not so noble that I've never taken a job for the cash, but if that's all that you are getting out of an assignment, you are doing yourself, your editor, and your readers a disservice. Sure, make enough to pay the rent, but write for love as often as you can. Which means, pitch what you love as often as you can.

# 36

# Failure and Recovery

T he file is corrupted. Your pitch was shot down—hard. Your project was completed, but cancelled and never printed. You designed it and they printed it, but . . . well, it sucks, and everyone tells you so all day long.

Welcome to being a successful game designer.

With any public project produced under deadline to high standards, the odds are you won't always get it right. I certainly haven't. There are several projects I regret because the realities of publishing meant they went to the publisher at a level I wasn't happy with, the publisher didn't deliver the playtesting or map resources I hoped for, the fans just hated what I did with part of the setting, or the editor changed my favorite sentence to suck all the joy out of it.

As the designer, you think you have control over a game design project—and you do have a lot of control over the foundations and the execution. But you don't have complete control. Sometimes a project is judged on elements—like art, a graphics rendering engine, or an index—that you don't control at all.

No matter why the project might be considered a failure, it's still your name on the cover, and you need to defend that work or move past it. It's okay to fail, of course. Everyone does. But you can't do it often and stay a freelancer because no one will hire you again.

Fail early in the process if you can. Fail often if you must, and defend the failures you can't change. But don't accept failure in your work or excuse it. Here's how to reduce the risks of failure and become the designer with the golden touch.

# Fail Early

If at all possible, fail in your game designs when they haven't even gone to an editor yet. Fail at the in-house playtest. Fail in front of patrons in Open Design. Fail with your first readers and a few trusted, sharp minds who review the project before it goes anywhere. Fail before it matters much.

This is by far the easiest failure to fix. Yes, you are perhaps somewhat embarrassed in front of colleagues, friends, or family, but that's nothing compared to being embarrassed by the same failure in the wider public world.

Some designers resist failure. They become so committed to an idea that they can't see it won't work, or they refuse to listen to the first readers, playtesters, developers, editors, or anyone else. You need to have enough perspective to know when you have a good, original, workable idea that other people will appreciate once you've got it polished and all the edges tucked in neatly—or when you have a shiny turd with beautiful components but no replay value, no sizzle, and no spark of originality.

Don't assume that those who criticize you are trying to thwart your dreams. They may be saving you from a horrible, face-planting disaster.

# Defend It

Let's say that the design failure gets past everyone and makes it into a finished game or system. You're going to have to own that failure in mechanics or worldbuilding. This is the part of failure that may make you grit your teeth. I believe that defending a mistake in worldbuilding or setting design is much more painful than it need be for mechanical or rules failures. Here's why.

The skill challenge mechanic in 4E was pretty much a mess when the new edition of D&D shipped; players and DMs didn't understand it, and the math was all wrong. The initial response from Wizards of the Coast (WotC) (as I remember it) was, "Oh, that's the way it's supposed to work." The rules were perhaps comprehensible to someone who had taken part in all the hard work and in-house playtests and discussion at WotC. But the fact that they met with widespread confusion, rejection, and immediate house rules was a pretty clear sign that they didn't work for the wider world. The assumptions behind those rules—and as it later turned out, the math underpinning the mechanics—were flawed.

Declaring, "It's fine, really," is not necessarily the best move when a mechanic is truly broken, but at least it started a conversation that led to wholesale revision and errata, changing all the numbers associated with those rules. In addition, the company launched an online column devoted more or less entirely to showing the WotC assumptions and methods for using skill challenges. The mechanic was fixed in later printings of the core rules and the rules subsystem is stronger now than it was at launch. The initial failure of the mechanics has largely been forgiven and forgotten, and gamers are pleased that new system works for their purposes.

The worse example of defending failure is in cases where something can't be fixed. The most recent **Forgotten Realms** reset upset a lot of long-time fans and got a lot of bad press, but there's just no way that Hasbro could admit fault and say, "We didn't mean it. No Spell Plague; we'll put it back a better way." They took a creative risk by advancing the timeline and killing off popular characters, but once they took the risk they owned it, success or failure. In a shared world setting, failures are painful because you have to live with the failure and take the heat from fans, sometimes for years, before the next reset allows you to fix it.

And in the case of the **Forgotten Realms** and other setting changes, it's arguable that the company's goal of making the setting more accessible was achieved, even if it came at the price of long-term fans. Every shared world has times when it needs to annoy the fans for its own long-term health. What is considered a failure by the audience may still be marked a success by the publisher.

## Setting Failures

When you commit to a setting, it's impossible to fix it. This is why fantasy RPG settings are inherently conservative; any change will be considered a mistake by some member of the fanbase. The safest course for a large corporation to manage its intellectual property is to offer a lot of action and adventure—but like a TV comedy, to make sure none of that changes the default premises of the setting.

So, what do you do?

Move past it and learn from it.

Those are really your two most professional options. Moving past it may mean creating errata, ignoring canon elements or regions of a setting that aren't working, or updating the timeline with further material in a novel or later adventure.

## The School of Hard Knocks

Learning from failure is the obvious lesson here. When designers are burned by mechanical failures, most tend not to repeat their errors. There's not much you can do about art failures, editing, marketing or other elements, other than being sure to provide full support to those groups when asked. Learn to provide the best core design you can, and then learn to let go so that graphic designers, editors, and others can do their work.

If you don't move past it or learn from it, there is a third road: Blame everyone else and accept no responsibility—learn nothing. This is also referred to as "Leaving the RPG field," because it is professional suicide. I don't recommend it.

There's one last option to fix really large, systemic failures of the rules: note the problem in your design records and make sure to fix it in the next edition. That's how you build a career rather than merely designing a single game.

Failure is a discouragement, certainly, and never fun. Remember the happiness of a successful design, a good review, and fan mail. Some setbacks are inevitable in even the most exciting, rewarding forms of work, and most of those setbacks are great opportunities to grow as a designer, to learn where a piece went wrong, and add new tools to your design toolbox. It's a small price to pay for doing what we love.

# 37

# Why Writers Get Paid

This was a locked entry for the supporters of Open Design that I made public because sharing one's pain is good for the soul. It's a bit of a rant, but that always happens to me at a certain stage of the design process. The adrenaline gives me the ruthless edge that takes a manuscript to where I want it.

Here I am again, trying to close down a first draft that keeps slipping away from me. The second draft is going to be fairly ferocious on this beast, and the maps are not all drawn and I am sure some of the monsters suck. Or at least need major surgery.

Welcome to the muddle in the middle. In any large project (or even with smaller projects for newer writers), this is the stage where it all goes wrong. It goes hideously pear-shaped. The project is beyond recovery, it's all trash, ohmigod, it's so much work to make it not suck.

Ah ha. This is why writers get paid.

The early stages of a project are always sunshine and unicorn giggles, laughter and frolic, all the tasty outer frosting of the writing cake. I love the early stages. I don't have to make any hard choices yet. I don't have to yank entire sequences, or worse, rewrite them to fit new continuity. I don't have to revise a crucial encounter to include more minions—and then remap the area to give the minions space to move. No, there's just the Good Parts of writing: making stuff up, setting NPCs in motion, doing up the fun stat blocks and the clever bits of readaloud.

Unfortunately, at some stage the Good Parts dry up. Every writing cake, as it turns out, has a railroad spike hidden in it. You have to eat the whole thing. Once the frosting is gone, you stare down at dull dry bits of iron left, and even those don't fit together. Allow me to count them for you:

1. The minion stat block with the template that doesn't quite work.
2. The spell selection that needs tweaking. Because it's boring.
3. The backstory that isn't going to untangle itself.
4. The backstory that needs to be cut in half.
5. The shiny intro that . . . is a mass of rust under a chrome veneer.
6. The missing encounters. Where are they?
7. The sections of city detail that are all in your head, but still not on paper.
8. The flavor text that has no flavor, but only clichés that need to be terminated and completely replaced.
9. The big finale that you've put off writing because you know exactly how it's going to work. Except that you haven't written any of it.
10. The mechanics that playtesters flagged, and they are right.
11. The map that is functional but not exciting.
12. The monster write up you kept meaning to fix.
13. NPCs who seemed engaging but are, in fact, completely lame.

And, oh, so many more. Drawn completely at random. Completely. At. Random, I swear. Stop looking at me like that, readers.

This is when most people give up. Only stubborn pigheaded bastards continue to bull through the grind of fixing things, smoothing out all the inconsistencies, adding the connecting bits, checking that the logic mostly works (mostly), and ensuring that the worst holes are spackled over thoroughly.

**Writerly Tip:** If the spackle isn't quite heavy enough, I recommend mortaring recalcitrant text in place with chains near a cask of amontillado, then bricking them into the wall with courses of stone. That'll learn 'em.

Anyway. Toward the end of a project, there tends to be less fine craftsmanship and a lot more covering things up with paint and glitter. The point is that there's always a stage where writing is absolutely no fun. No kittens, no frosting, no unicorns. Certainly no oversexed half-fiendish sorceresses. And just because it's no fun, that is not the point where you stop and send it in.

On the contrary, this is the point where you dig in twice as hard.

Because if you are a good writer or hope to become one, you know the manuscript's every weakness, every hard choice you dodged, every shortcut you took, saying. "I'll fix it in the rewrite." (O fateful words!) The mojo is weak and you know it needs work. Now, this self-loathing is perfectly normal and it can be overdone. It is possible to print a manuscript and go through with a red pen and fix it. That seems hard, and the fixes can take long hours where no word count is added and many of your favorite bits are cut.

Sometimes you do this revision once or twice, if your first draft was sound. Sometimes you do it eight or nine times, if you are perhaps a perfectionist with lots of spare time. Writers who don't revise or even read back through their work do not fool anyone. (See the Erik Mona interview in **Kobold Quarterly** #1 if you don't believe me; he's seen both sides of this fence.)

Most would-be game designers want the process to be fun all the way through, and that is a recipe for failure. A big part of success in the field is sitting down and working over rules, math, and text for core rules design. For adventure design, that means writing, weighing playtest results, and rewrites. The important element is that you try to improve your text enough that someone else can read it and enjoy it. You are manufacturing joy for other people. That doesn't mean joy for you, necessarily. It's joy for them because you have honed that joy out of a bitter slab of granite.

Most people don't ever get through this stage. For me, I have music that helps, up-tempo stuff, cheeseball '80s tunes, Britpop, and worse. No, I'm not proud that Mike Oldfield's "Moonlight Shadow" helps me get in a writing groove, but there it is. For other people it's booze (not recommended), massive caffeine, or staying up late surrounded by heaps of pens and notebooks. Recite the immortal words of that hack Dr. Ben Jonson: "No man but a fool ever wrote but for money." Whatever gets you hitting the keys.

Everyone finds their own way to a writerly discipline. Until you do, you will fail to design to the standards you set for yourself, and you will not meet deadlines consistently. You may get queries accepted, but you will fail to follow up on those queries in a timely way. You will not publish.

### *"No one loves rewrites. Tough it out."*

(That last point, by the way, was a source of much consternation to me as a young editorial assistant. At TSR, we sent out twice as many acceptances for queries as we could use each month, because we knew half of them would never result in an article. This drove me crazy, especially because some of the queries that went missing were for really cool stuff. I learned that I should never reject myself, which is what those writers were doing. If you are fortunate enough to get a query accepted, write it and send it in. It's the editor's job to accept it or reject it. Don't do the editor's job, especially in the rejection department.)

Game designers, artists, and writers are all creative people. Doing our best work is demanding because there is a level of craft to learn, and a level of self control needed to be reliably productive even on off days. And it requires a level of willpower to face the problems with your manuscript and be absolutely ruthless about fixing them. Everyone will have advice for you about how you should proceed and what you should fix. At the bulldog stage, you need to ignore everyone and just maintain momentum on the things you know are broken and that you can improve. The editor will weigh in with other issues—fine. Plowing through the ugly late stages of a draft is about persistence and self confidence in the face of rising insecurity. Can I make this character work? Can I meet the deadline? Can I keep it remotely near the requested word count? Yes, yes, and yes. Be ruthless. Throw side plots and distracting shiny rules subsystems overboard.

I wish I had some pithy Pollyanna platitudes at this stage. They would say that working hard on the draft will make you feel better about it, your editor will hail you as a genius, and your work will surely be published to great acclaim. That doesn't happen.

You may get a sense that the manuscript is as good as you can make it. That is a fine place to be. You probably won't love the manuscript at that point, and you are way too close to it to know whether anyone else will either.

If you wait until you are 100 percent happy with a manuscript, you will never stop fiddling with it. At some point, you will be sick of it, but somewhat content, I suppose. The damn thing doesn't compel you the way it once did. You've worked all the magic on it that you know, and it's still not exactly what you might wish, but it's okay. The editor will probably like it well enough.

Yeah, I know. This is not a rousing endorsement of second and third drafts. But in your designer brain, at some point you may find that you are just tinkering with the adventure. All the big problems are fixed to your satisfaction. You are probably still not satisfied with it, but if you catch yourself tinkering just to tinker (like messing with fonts, or punctuation, or Craft skill points), then it is definitely time to shove it out the door.

So that's my advice: Finish it and send it in. Hell, I should tape that over my monitor, right next to "Zeal never rests" (motto of HMS Ark Royal).

Now will you look at me? I've just procrastinated for over an hour. Enough talk about grinding through it: Back to the keyboard! I have many design sins yet to atone for, and I fully intend to bury the biggest ones as deep as I can.

Okay, maybe that came across as cranky. No one loves rewrites. Tough it out.

# 38

# Talent Won't Save You...

I f you blow your deadlines. It's true; insanely genius-level epic freelancer chops will not get you a second chance if you blow a deadline.

Here are the ways that this can bite you in the butt as a freelancer, because There are only so many venues that publish game design work. Sometimes it's not your fault. Sometimes it's completely your fault. In either situation, you can handle it either more or less professionally.

## Eyes Bigger Than Your Stomach

Sometimes you start a project with the best of intentions, but you suffer some calamity. This is especially common with freelancers just starting out, who may overestimate their ability to write text to a high standard. Here's how that happens. Ye Happy Freelancer is offered a project on an aggressive deadline for good pay and says yes, because he knows he can write 2,500 words a day, and so a 50,000 word project should take just twenty days, right? A three-week deadline? No problem!

That is freelancer naiveté and optimism, and most publishers know better. Freelancers get sick, their children need medical care, their spouses blow up domestic tranquility, their parents unexpectedly visit for weeks at a time, their dogs die. Sad but true: real life interferes. Even getting a promotion at the day job may mean spending more hours at that job and less time on freelance writing. So, know your limits.

What are those limits? I shoot for something around 1,000 words a day right now, and I give myself weekends off and have a magazine to run, so roughly 20,000 words a month is good (yes, I do make exceptions now and again). A single man with no children might shoot for 2,500 words a day, and might write seven days a week to try to break into the industry in a big way. Yow, that's 75,000 words a month! I sense burnout, but it might be sustainable for a while.

On the other hand, a new freelancer who has trouble with some basic craft issues, and needs more time for rewrites, and has a demanding spouse might manage just 400 words a day, with most weekends off. Call it 10,000 words a month. That's 120,000 words a year, which is two good-sized game books or a fat novel. Not bad.

Everyone is different. Publishers like high-output, but as long as you know what you can realistically deliver, they're usually willing to talk about scaling a project size to fit your available time.

## Things Go Horribly Wrong

But let's assume that you know your limits. You can still get in huge trouble. Sometimes you start a project with the best of intentions, but you realize that the work is beyond your abilities. That is, you can't actually deliver the length, complexity, or deadline required. This is super hard to admit to yourself, but . . . it's better to tell the publisher as soon as you realize it. Because you're only hurting your chances for future work if you fail completely.

---

### *Making Wordcount*

The hardest part of getting to your wordcount goal is often getting started. I know that once I'm typing, I'm usually fine for hours.

But some days I'm too tired, too distracted; the room is too noisy; there are too many "honey-do" items or other jobs competing for my time. This is maddening when a deadline approaches, which is why staying ahead is always a good strategy.

Two other tricks to get you started. The first is to choose a set time of day for your writing. One well-known novelist got his start (and continued for years) writing on his lunch breaks. He had to produce at a given time, so he did. If he stalled or delayed, nothing got done that day. I find a set time works for me as well. The second trick is even easier. If you are unable to get started, pick up your papers and your PC and go somewhere that worked last time. It might be another room in the house. It might be a library. Wherever it was, that place was productive before: give it another shot. Maybe it will become your regular writing spot (combined with a regular writing time).

Design time needs to be a habit. Make it one with repeated times and places.

---

Sometimes you start a project with the best of intentions, and then real life interferes. You move cities, you change jobs, you get divorced or married, or you just find that your interests drift away from the project. Um, if merely moving house upsets your writing schedule, you may want to rethink the idea of freelancing professionally. People with regular jobs manage to fit in major life changes without dropping the ball on their work.

If you aren't taking the work that seriously, you have no business agreeing to a game design contract with anyone. I'd recommend doing your game design work as a sideline, and publishing it on a blog or fan site. Seriously. Publishers pay the rent and feed their children with what they earn from their work. They make payroll for their staff and freelancers. Don't be a dilettante.

## How to Save Yourself From Drowning

But let's say you are serious about the work, and events have spiraled beyond your control. The deadline looms, and the manuscript is a complete trainwreck. Now what?

The real problem is that sometimes your dog did eat your playtest notes, and your hard drive did crash, and your parents or grandparents are hospitalized. The thing to do in these cases is always the same, for artists, for writers, and for editors alike: Fess up immediately, and beg for an extension. Before your deadline comes and goes.

Publishers are not entirely cruel and inhuman. Most of them have families or some distant memories of a childhood, or may even have experienced a technical snafu that made them learn the value of frequent, dependable backups. So they are likely to grant an extension for some projects, and will work hard on their end to find some other way to cover the gap in the schedule.

The sooner you tell them you'll be late, the sooner they can start that process, and the more painless it will be for them. The worst time to report this is after you have missed the deadline, because it's almost impossible for a publisher to recover their schedule at that point. The best time is before you sign the contract, but anywhere in between can be helpful. Sometimes another project can be bumped forward, or another freelancer can take a chunk of work, or an in-house staffer can leap in to save the day. The only time there are no good solutions is long after the deadline. That's when publishers get (justifiably) enraged that you signed up for something, didn't deliver, and kept it to yourself.

## It's Not the Deadline, It's the Cover-up

If you blow a deadline and say nothing about it, your name is mud with that publisher. Probably forever. Begging and pleading is all very nice, but it's beside the point. As a freelancer, your job is to deliver the goods on time. This does not mean turning over junk, and it does not mean turning over nothing.

And if you can't deliver, it's your job to give the bad news. It doesn't have to be much, just a "I'm sorry, I'm way behind on this project. Can I get an extension?" is usually enough to get the conversation started. After all, you gave your word to deliver. If it's not working, it's not really the publisher's job to hunt you down. Nevertheless, that's usually what winds up happening.

As humans, we hate to admit failure. We prefer to keep our mistakes out of public view. And yet we all make mistakes. The ability to confess to those mistakes is a source of huge strength to a freelancer. It means you take the work seriously, it means you treat the publisher as a partner and value his or her opinion. It means you realize you screwed up, and you act like a grownup.

You will be shocked to learn that there are surprisingly few grownups in the games industry. The ones who do exist, well, you probably know their names. Because it takes that level of responsibility to become a successful freelancer. Either you know your limits and don't try to do too much, or when you do find yourself unable to meet a deadline you make the problem known so that a solution can be found.

This is why honesty and early warnings get you so much respect as a freelancer. You save a publisher from sleepless nights, from paying ludicrous fees for a rush solution, from tearing his hair and abusing his printer. Saying "I can't" is a difficult thing for any freelancer, because the urge is always there to say "Yes! Totally! I'm on it!" and earn that next contract. But smart publishers know that taking "no" for an answer is in their best interests as well; it won't count against you with most publishers.

## Exceptions to the Rule

Not every venue is obsessive about deadlines; most of what I've been saying here applies to standalone projects such as modules, sourcebooks, and the like. There are some places where forgiveness is much more common.

> *"If you aren't taking the work... seriously, you have no business agreeing to a... contract."*

At the head of the list, magazines are more forgiving. This may seem counterintuitive; I mean, aren't magazines totally deadline-driven? Well, yes, and they assume that half of their accepted queries will never turn into submissions, much less an accepted article. Besides, there's always next issue, and in any case they buy stuff on spec. Even so, it makes you look bad if you swore up and down at the convention that you would have an article in time for the Halloween/April Fool's/Big New Edition Spectacular, and you don't deliver. Even websites prefer to work with freelancers they know they can count on.

Now, there are publishers who will take a manuscript months or years late (they are called Chaosium and Pagan Publishing), and their fans are very patient people. Most fans are not so patient, and certainly book and hobby stores aren't sitting around breathlessly waiting for the releases that they know are unlikely to ship this year.

And finally, there are fan sites and Web publishers and PDF publishers who pay little or nothing, and so (you might think) have less cause to complain if you flake out on them. That's not exactly the case. If you make a commitment to one of those publishers, your reputation still suffers if you fail to deliver.

## Conclusion

Most freelancers (myself included) hate to own up to lateness, but it's one of those unpleasant realities of the job. It's a bit like going to the dentist; the longer you put it off, the more likely that you're going to suffer for it.

Professional freelancers quickly learn to judge their available time and not to overcommit. That word "professional" is the essence of it. Treat your freelance writing as a real job, because writing and game design are a business. A very weird business, but a business nevertheless.

# 39

# The Magic Bullet for Publication

There's a mode of thinking about publishing that is common among aspiring writers and game designers—namely that the game industry is a small one, and who you know determines who gets published.

This is pernicious nonsense with a single grain of truth.

## The Truth About Breaking Into Print (or Pixels)

The truth is that yes, the tabletop RPG industry is exceedingly tiny, with 80 percent of the people who can make a living at it sitting in Hasbro cubicles of some kind. The number of active freelancers is much larger (surely in the hundreds, as any look at the **Pen & Paper** database will show you). The computer-game field is much larger in terms of number of employees, but it is no easier to break in there, because the number of aspiring designers is likewise much larger.

The pernicious assumption is that you need to know a secret handshake, or some mathemagical formula, or just have impressed the right editor, to see your work published. This is wildly and spectacularly untrue.

Editors and publishers are in the business of finding talent and introducing it to an audience. If you are talented, thick-skinned, and persistent, chances are good that your work can be published in the field. The number of markets available for RPG writing has gone up sharply in the wake of the OGL, even after the glut and die-off, even after the retreat of some major players from the field, and even in the wake of the split in the market created by the 4th edition of **D&D**. The size of those markets is much smaller, but there are a lot of small publishers.

True, the disappearance of **Dragon** and **Dungeon** as magazines hurts, but the **DDI** will eventually need to work with many freelancers. Paizo's **RPG Superstar** contest is a brand-new avenue for talent to be recognized. **Kobold Quarterly** is always looking for art and articles that don't fit into the marketing plans of the big companies. I'd say there are so many venues right now that an ambitious freelancer should be able to publish within a year of starting a serious run at it.

## Three Magic Bullets

How do you start? The real magic bullets are organization and persistence. Start at the top: pitch your ideas to Paizo if they have a contest or an open call. Then work your way down the list: try **Kobold Quarterly**, **No Quarter**, or **White Dwarf**. Depending on your article topic, you might drop some of those venues, but they are all fine places to break into print.

If you don't care about print publication, try Wizards of the Coast's **Dungeons & Dragons Insider** (DDI); the competition is intense, but you might hit the sweet spot. And know your markets: the **DDI**, for instance, is only taking adventures and 4E material at the moment, and it is weighted toward staff articles. There are plenty of other online-only venues such as **The Escapist** and **Massively**, though they do mostly MMO and video game articles. Keep looking for markets that match what you want to write; it may be that not every pitch is about **D&D** or **WoW** or whatever you happen to be keen on at a particular time.

> *"An ambitious freelancer should be able to publish within a year of starting a serious run at it."*

Read the submission guidelines for each venue and follow them. Know how to write a query (it's about the sizzle, not the steak). After each rejection, dust the query off, reformat, and sent it to the next market.

And here's the final magic bullet: After you send your query out, forget it and move on to the next one. Never, ever wait for an answer before you send the next one out. I know some writers who keep a spreadsheet of all the magazine queries, website queries, short stories, and complete articles they have in circulation, which markets they are sent to, and so on. You may not be writing that prolifically, but you should be sending out a lot of queries.

Think of it like setting traps for editors. One perfect trap is all very nice, but you'll have more success if you have 100 really good traps instead. Volume matters, because not every idea is a perfect, unique snowflake.

# What If That Doesn't Work?

Of course, it's possible that you just aren't hitting the button for any of the periodical venues out there. If the periodicals won't have you, you could try pitching projects to some of the print or PDF markets. The goal, oddly enough, isn't necessarily to get that project published but to introduce yourself to the publisher as a credible, capable, professional freelancer.

The bigger houses like Paizo, Green Ronin, White Wolf, and Mongoose almost certainly won't take an out-of-house project, but if your pitch is good enough (and you have some credits elsewhere) they might take you on for something else. As with the magazines and sites, be relentless. Start with the bigger houses or with your favorite publisher and work your way down the list.

In all of these cases, it pays to know who you're addressing—meaning you should put a real person's name on your cover email if at all possible, rather than "To Whom It May Concern." It also pays to subscribe or at least pick up a few issues of the venue you are trying to break into, and it pays to keep sending queries on a regular basis. Make it a habit weekly, monthly. Eventually, you'll catch someone's attention with the right hook on a good day.

When you get that first acceptance of a query, you're onto a whole new problem: delivering an exciting manuscript that gets accepted and published. But that's another essay.

## Q&A

Q: What aspects of good play and good DMing translate to good writing and design?

A: The aspects of good play that translate are a powerful imagination and creativity, as well as core understanding of the rules. The good DMing that translates is an appreciation for your audience and narrative power, the ability to spin a story with words, and the ability to extend mechanics from the core to subsystems and variants.

Q: Design doesn't get my blood fired up; development does. Any tips?

A: Development is usually done in-house and is often combined with editorial functions. In my opinion, it's not all that relevant to most freelancers. That said, it is worthwhile to both read your work aloud (to hear the clunkers and fix them) and to give it to a first reader, someone whose game and language skills you trust.

Q: At some point, RPG writers need to be sat down, and their work needs to be vivisected in front of them. There's no game-design analog to comics artists asking professionals about a portfolio, or writers going to writers' workshops. Will Open Design do something like the RPG Superstar and "Flight of the Red Raven" contest? I want to see real editors' reactions to real proposals.

A: You are absolutely right about RPG Superstar, and you raise an interesting possibility for down the road. Open Design does offer this sort of critique in the anthology projects like **Tales of Zobeck** (and soon in another venue that I'm not quite ready to talk about yet). But you're right, a professional critique is very valuable to someone starting out in the field. That's one of the elements of Open Design I enjoy most: seeing the workshop approach to material that senior patrons contribute. We should probably do more of that.

# 40

# Creative Mania and Design Despair

M ost of the time, design is about rather concrete elements of mathematics, level geometry, narrative arcs, area descriptions, and player character rewards. In this essay I'm addressing a part of the work that's a bit squishier than usual, but I think it's an important topic. Namely, how does a designer deal with the ups and downs of working on a manuscript for an extended period, especially when the work doesn't go well?

## The First Phases of Design

Perhaps it's different for other designers, but I know my own pattern really well. The initial idea for a project gets me all charged up and on fire—that's a time of pure mania. I want to work on the manuscript all the time, one idea seems to lead naturally to another, and progress is easy.

This is partly because there are no hard choices to make yet, and partly because everything is fresh. Every designer loves new terrain; relatively few grognards survive long as professional designers, because . . . Well, grognards are filled with a shining love for what has already been, for revisiting the old terrain, and for the rosy glow of the past. I'm fond of past designs, the games of my youth, and certainly for the highlights of the field by other designers. But the job of design is about creating new game-play experiences, new settings, new rules and character archetypes, and new spins on old ideas, as discussed in the "What is Design?"

essay. As a designer, you need to understand the past so you can build on top of it. Give me something new to play with, and I'll be delighted.

My advice to all designers is to ride that early high as long and as hard as possible. Work late, get up earlier, burn lunch hours, unplug your cable, and stop wasting time on Xbox and Facebook. Seriously, this is a window of opportunity when you are itchy to create wonderful new things. Do that. You'll lose that honeymoon glow soon enough, trust me, so take advantage of the enthusiasm that makes it easy to get ahead, to build outlines and crunch numbers, and makes the work seem effortless. Wasting this period while waiting for a response from an editor, from a patron poll, or from anyone, really, is just a waste. You won't recapture the sense of lightning in a bottle later in the project, no matter how cool the twists and modifications make it.

The second phase is what I call the grind—the period when contradictions start to show up in the adventure flow, or the math of the new subsystem falls apart during playtesting. Novelists call this the "muddle in the middle," and it is the part of creating a text or system that just sucks. You have gone past the section that was pure fun, you've done all the bits that bring you joy, and now it's at the level of craft, iteration, refinement, and expansion of all the cool, sexy ideas of the first stage.

At this point, odd as it may sound, you realize that you have a relationship with the manuscript, and sometimes that relationship is going to be difficult. You're going to have to make trade-off s. It's a bit like dating: new love is wonderful, but at some point you either get serious or you drift apart. Getting serious means limiting other dating opportunities; making design choices restricts future options. Your manuscript is an extension of your creativity, and that means it demands attention, honesty, and devotion. You might say it's a one-sided sort of relationship: What does it give back, after all? That's missing the next step, though—the turn-over to development and editing. And that's where my overextended metaphor breaks down.

## Beyond Ideas to the Work

In any case, once the design gets balky the hard choices phase is upon you. This is where the best designers earn their reputations. Some designers never get this: It's not enough to have great ideas, you also need to have great execution, refining those ideas into something more than, "Wouldn't it be cool if ?" brainstorming.

That isn't to denigrate brainstorming. It's just that this stage culls the dilettantes and amateurs out of the herd, because the work required here is hard. It's drudgery. If you are in this stage, you're earning your keep and, emotionally, the manuscript seems less a source of joy and more a source of (perfectly natural) loathing. You are writing material that you don't love but that the design needs to function.

The goal in this phase is to maintain enough love for the project that you can keep up momentum until the end is in sight. Maybe you save some juicy sections to write at the very end. Maybe you have a character you reintroduce late in an adventure, or a particularly sharp set of dragon stats and templates that you set aside to reward yourself with when you see the end approaching. Different writers use different tricks.

The problem here is that the joy of phase one has met reality—and for writing and design, reality is sitting at a keyboard trying to pour your brain onto the page in a way that will reach your audience.

Why is this hard? Two reasons: 1) A premise is always easier to create than all the manifold logical consequences of that premise, and 2) you need to think through the impact of your design decisions on your audience. For most designers, that means evaluating the worth of playtest reports, first readers, editors, or developers. For collaborative design approaches like Open Design projects, it means having even more people offering their opinions and critiques before a project is gelled, outlined, or written. (I'll talk more about the challenges of collaboration in another essay.)

You need to have a strong enough sense of the design goal to ignore the junk or snark, a strong enough design sense to maintain cohesion in the mechanics and logic of the game, and a strong enough set of writing chops to convey both the flavor and the mechanics in a pleasing and accessible way.

## New Demands

You must respond to new demands from the clay of the design itself. The project fits into some molds that you could foresee and some that you couldn't. Because your understanding of the game design deepens over the course of the work, at one point or another you must abandon some of the things you love about the project. In Open Design, this happens sooner and meets the needs of the audience better because criticism starts immediately, like it or not. I think that makes Open Design projects a bit of a shock to designers used to working in isolation, but also makes it perfectly natural to younger designers who collaborate as a matter of course. That is, reaction to massive feedback super-early is partly generational. But this transition to abandoning some elements of a game design happens in all forms of design, not just RPGs.

For instance, I started **Halls of the Mountain King** with the sense that it would be a very traditional dwarven delving with big monsters and combat sections; the brief I used to pitch it to patrons was "a new Moria." But the brainstorm for the project made it clear that the theme of greed (which I pitched as a secondary theme) was popular enough to become the main theme. The idea of a traditional set of monsters fell away when the number of factions grew to include factions within the dwarves, a cult, and some derro. The adventure became event-driven pretty quickly. I had to throw away some of the original assumptions. The feedback on the pitches made us throw away even more.

In the end, we had a much stronger idea of what **Halls** was about, but it was also a less traditional dwarven adventure. That's good; there's no point in rehashing old approaches and stale, "beginner" material for an advanced audience like Open Design patrons. The resulting premise means that the enemies were still deadly and combat was still a primary factor, but my understanding of what the audience wanted changed. And the dream of a Moria-style adventure had to be abandoned pretty quickly to accommodate other cool ideas, like a Masonic-style secret brotherhood, a corrupt gold dragon, and cursed gold that served Mammon's ends.

## Closing It Down With Ease or Rage

Finally, if you are persistent and don't let anything stop you, the muddle in the middle does come to an end. The end phase of a project is either a time of hope or rage for me. When I leave a manuscript hopeful, I've had plenty of time with it, I feel all the elements are in place, and I think it really is ready for another set of hands. I may be a bit wistful, tinkering with strands of it but, frankly, I've grown a little tired of having the manuscript around. Sometimes this convinces me to make a turnover early, because I'm just done with it. These are the times it is easier to close out a project. Things float gently to a conclusion. The deadline seems generous. All is well with the project.

That happens less often than I'd like, but it does happen.

More often, the end stage is more about rage. I wish I had more time! The project deserves another month, at least! Yes, usually the deadline is killing me, and I'm fighting very hard to keep everything together, to fill in all the "XX" place markers and all the "TBD" or "NAME HERE" stopgaps that I used earlier as shortcuts. Sometimes it's not the deadline but the word count. There's either too much or too little space to do what I want to do. And so I slash and burn sections away to make room for something vital, or I fill out a section that I know the editor will want more of. It's a stage of everything coming home to roost, which is especially the case for really large designs (say, over 40,000 words or so, and certainly anything over 60,000).

It's impossible for me to keep everything in my head for a 60,000-word manuscript (this is why I love outlines), so at the end there's some shuffling and struggle to get it all together in a form I like, much less one I love. This is when I recall that someone said that manuscripts aren't finished but abandoned. Large projects are harder to bring to the stage where everything interlocks smoothly with everything else. And very large projects always involve a certain amount of frustration because it is so very hard to achieve the level of quality I want through an entire design beyond a certain size. That upper limit has grown for me over the years (20,000 words used to intimidate me, but no longer), but there's still a realistic limit as to how big a design can be before it becomes utterly unwieldy.

I suspect that the sheer difficulty of marshalling all elements is what delays all larger creative works. They're not just a linear string of text; if the work is any good at all, it has emergent properties, resonances, themes, and layers. In other words, the design has become a set of interconnected systems, references, and dependencies.

## Turnover and Acceptance

The end stage is letting go, committing to saying, "Here's the manuscript. I've worked hard and given it everything I know. Someone else needs to carry it the rest of the way to publication." It's a tough stage for some writers because you're turning over something like a child to others. You hope they love it as much as you do, though inevitably you know in your heart of hearts that you have given more of yourself to it, more hours, more devotion, than others ever can or will. But you trust the editor, the graphic designers, the company you're working with. And so you let it go, because time has run out, because there's nothing more you can do, because you have grown to think there's nothing else you can give to make it better.

Oddly enough, turning over a manuscript to others always leaves me with a case of creative depression. My thoughts are generally morose or gloomy at this stage. I could have done it so much better! I had to compromise because of the word count! The rules in that section are way too complicated—I should have streamlined the bookkeeping somehow, or written a new subsystem. The playtesters/editor/DMs just don't understand the vision I was aiming for.

I am a pathetic Gloomy Gus. For about a week or two.

Then, some bright, new, shining, wonderful idea will catch my eye, or I'll go through my big notebook full of ideas. One of those ideas seems to be so full of promise, so glorious, that surely it will be the shining, perfect sourcebook/adventure/article that I have always wanted it to be. And the mania returns...

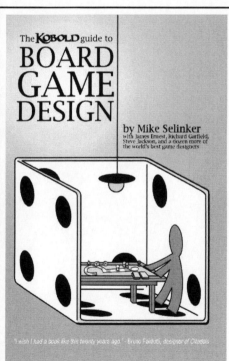

4130221R00136

Printed in Great Britain
by Amazon.co.uk, Ltd.,
Marston Gate.